Curing Corporate SHORT-TERMISM

Future Growth vs. Current Earnings

Gregory V. Milano

Fortuna Advisors LLC

Printed in the United States of America.

ISBN: 978-1-7341551-0-5 (hardcover)
ISBN: 978-1-7341551-1-2 (softcover)
ISBN: 978-1-7341551-2-9 (ebook)

Content Editor: Michael Chew
Cover and Interior Design: Diana Russell, DianaRussellDesign.com
Copyeditor: Mark Woodworth, Mark Woodworth Editorial Services
Author Photo: Lisa Lake
Publishing Strategist: Holly Brady, Brady New Media Publishing

Address permission requests to:
Fortuna Advisors
One Penn Plaza
New York, New York 10119
info@fortuna-advisors.com

To purchase multiple copies of this book at reduced prices:
info@fortuna-advisors.com

To my parents, Vincent and Annabelle Milano,
who always believed in me and
gave me the confidence to aim for success
in this unforgiving world.

CONTENTS

FIGURES

PROLOGUE

A Tale of Leadership in Value Creation

Over the last three decades that I've spent as a management consultant, I have witnessed more than my share of painful, cringe-inducing short-termism. Before getting to a prescription for rooting out this type of behavior in corporate organizations, I offer the following fictional tale that is based on a collection of my experiences advising leaders in various business situations. Its purpose is to illustrate how the principles advocated herein can be used to focus a company and its management team on a better balance of short- and long-term objectives, leading to greater success for shareholders and society alike. All names, characters, and incidents are fictitious; no association with actual persons, companies, places, or products is intended or should be inferred.

A Special Acquisition Meeting of the Board of Directors

The CEO of Blue Dynamics Corp., Betty Manning, and her team had spent three hours presenting the proposed acquisition of Sky Annex Corp. to their board for approval. The deal would add 20% to the company's total revenue, would expand their presence in their most successful business unit (Systems Integration), and would also create a platform for international growth, a dimension that had been severely lacking at Blue Dynamics. Betty had one-on-one calls with several board members over the previous few weeks, but the meeting was the first time that management fully explained the nature of Sky Annex Corp., the benefits to Blue Dynamics' long-term strategic growth, the proposed deal structure, its financing plan, and the strategy for making the acquisition a success. All that was left was for the directors to ask questions before voting to make a decision.

The deal looked attractive from a strategic as well as an operational perspective, but the purchase price seemed high to some board members. One director expressed his concern by pointing out that the price-to-earnings (PE) multiple being paid was considerably higher than Blue Dynamics' current valuation: "How can you expect us to approve paying a price that is higher than what our investors are willing to pay for our stock? What if our multiple gets applied to their earnings? Won't our share price fall?"

Betty acknowledged the seemingly high price but explained to the board that "Sky Annex presents the best opportunity for future profitable growth of any company in and around our Systems Integration business. We have been searching far and wide for investment prospects in order to allocate growth capital and expand our portfolio of high-return businesses, and Sky Annex fulfils this strategic need in several ways. Their product portfolio complements those of our own businesses, so although we plan to operate it separately for now, we can have both sales teams selling *both* product lines to offer our customers more options, with minimum sales cannibalization. Over five years ago, Sky Annex expanded into Europe, South America, and Asia, and it has since built a small but effective presence in each market. This potential acquisition represents a substantial opportunity for us to grow their products while also launching our existing offerings in these new markets. Our reinvestment rate has been below average, and this acquisition will provide us with more-productive ways to deploy capital into value-creating projects after the deal goes through."

Blue Dynamics' CFO, Topher West, added, "And all of this growth that Betty talks about is expected to be very profitable, since Sky Annex operates at a high rate of return on capital—even higher than Systems Integration, our highest-return business."

Another director asked whether that high rate of return would continue to be the case after the acquisition, given the purchase price and all the goodwill that would be added to the capital base.

Topher clarified his outlook: "It's true that with the goodwill, the acquisition will deliver a much lower return. But it's the incremental organic return *without the goodwill* that indicates the rate of return we expect on subsequent investment in the acquired businesses. We need to earn a return on the full investment for this acquisition to create value for our shareholders. The only way to do so is to invest to grow the business at its high organic rate of return, so that over time the overall return of the business, including the 'fixed' goodwill, rises above the cost of capital."

The board seemed satisfied with the explanation on price, and one director even chuckled and remarked, "You get what you pay for." Smiling contentedly, another board member gently wondered aloud why there wouldn't be more cost synergies after the deal. He was accustomed to seeing acquisition integration plans that touted extensive cost savings from combining head offices, using shared services, shuttering duplicate activities, and reducing both the real estate footprint and the total number of employees.

"We do expect some cost synergies," Topher explained, "and we folks in finance will be working hard with the leadership in all departments and functions to identify and achieve them. But as we developed the acquisition plan, our highest priority was to expand this new, high-return platform to enable us to invest more in profitable growth. We do not believe cost savings alone could justify the purchase price, but we *do* believe the growth plan can. In a sense, you can think of the value of the cost savings as a bonus. It's really the icing on the cake!"

After a bit more banter on the synergies, and after the directors felt they understood this aspect of the plan, the chairman asked about their ability to manage and grow the offshore businesses, given the lack of international experience at Blue Dynamics. At her last company, Betty acquired extensive international experience, including three tours living abroad and managing businesses in Seoul, São Paulo, and Zurich. She talked briefly about the differences in business culture that she experienced in each country and described the challenges Blue Dynamics would likely face in making their international expansion successful. But she also spoke about the size of the untapped opportunity as well as the benefits that would accrue from acquiring and building on the established, successful country platforms of Sky Annex.

Betty announced the intention of the Systems Integration management team to retain a majority of the existing Sky Annex country managers to capitalize on their established know-how. Steven Tiles, general manager of Systems Integration, explained that he intended to make each country its own profit center that would be rolled up with the others into a thin, regional group structure. Each country manager would have considerable decision-making authority, coupled with significant accountability. They would be free to adapt their business to fit the local market, yet would be responsible for outcomes, not actions. When the Blue Dynamics leadership team met with country managers while conducting due diligence, it was impressed with their positive reaction to Blue Diamond's combination of decentralized authority and accountability.

This discussion of accountability prompted the vice chairman to consider the bigger picture, so he drew his colleagues' attention to what he deemed a pretty optimistic forecast. Betty acknowledged that the projections were aggressive, but then emphasized that they had all been carefully vetted. Every element of projected growth was tied to a specific investment initiative, and the projecting managers had increased the expenditure on sales and marketing to be sure they were positioned to make the growth a reality. This was their "most likely" case—what they really thought would happen.

Betty then gazed slowly and deliberately at the faces around the long board room table and reminded each and every board member that the annual bonuses of management were based on the year-on-year improvement in BDVA (a performance measure that stood for Blue Dynamics Value Added). To improve BDVA, management had to sufficiently increase EBITDA—or earnings before interest, taxes, depreciation, and amortization—to more than cover a capital charge based on new investment. Their long-term incentives reinforced this target, as well. If managers succeeded in improving BDVA, they would make more money. If not, they would make less—without any opportunity for negotiations, sandbagging, or adjustments. Based on the forecast, then, the acquisition purchase price implied a heavy charge for the corporate use of capital; and this charge, coupled with the expenditures expected in year one to launch the domestic and international growth plans, would reduce the short-term BDVA.

Betty then went on to say, "Our existing businesses are performing well, so without this acquisition my team and I would expect to earn bonuses of about 140 to 150 percent this year; however, with the acquisition this will drop to 40 to 50 percent. None of us are happy to lose the money, but we understand it—and we believe in our forecast. If the BDVA never recovers, this money will be lost forever and some of the value destroyed will come out of our own pockets. *But* if we achieve the forecast, we expect to earn an extra 200 to 300 percent in bonuses over the next few years. We don't have a crystal ball, but we believe the forecast is doable and are willing to put our own money on the line."

The chairman leaned back and remarked pleasantly about how far the company had come since Betty became CEO 18 months earlier. In the past, management would have attempted to sell the board on the long-term merits of an investment, knowing all along that they would likely seek a negotiated adjustment to their current-year incentive plan performance target. Then, every year after that, new incentive performance targets would be set based on budgets, without regard for whether the investment had performed well. The directors never knew how much conviction management really had about their forecast. Under the old incentive plan, if the investment did well, the budgets used to set incentive targets were raised each year, so much of the gain was never rewarded. And if the investment underperformed, the budgets and incentive targets were dropped, too, so that management never paid a high price for their mistakes.

With Betty's no-nonsense management style and the company's emphasis on increasing BDVA each year to earn higher incentives, the board now had greater confidence when considering an acquisition like Sky Annex. The managers now seemed to think and act more like long-term, committed owners who treated the capital of the company as their own. Yes, they were very happy with Betty as their CEO.

Eighteen Months Earlier

"So, tell me again, Topher," Betty inquired, "why does the company use EPS for half of our annual bonus plan? You say my predecessor knew the pitfalls of EPS but felt it was best for shareholders? That's what *they* want? And you say not to worry because our managers always aim to do the right thing… They aren't swayed by the incentive plan? It sounds crazy to me. Why use an incentive that managers have to overcome to do the right thing? Should we really trust that our managers will act in the interests of the company when we're rewarding them for taking a different action? Why force our managers to make a tradeoff between their own financial well-being and that of the company?"

It had only been three weeks since Betty Manning joined Blue Dynamics Corp. as the new CEO, and she was still getting to know the company and her team. She had come from a larger industrial conglomerate where she was the general manager of its second-largest business unit. For years she was recognized as a star performer there, but her path to the top would be tough since her company's CEO and its chief operating officer were both new to their jobs. They were also both younger than she and quite effective as well, so investors and the board of directors were content with them.

She wasn't looking for a new job, but when a headhunter called, her interest was piqued by the thought of becoming the CEO of a public company. She tried not to think about it much, but she knew that's what she always wanted—so she pursued the opportunity. The Nominations Committee of the Blue Dynamics board met a handful of other candidates, but the process ended fairly quickly. Betty was clearly the one for the job, they concluded. The full board of directors was impressed by her immediate understanding of their businesses, competitors, strategies, and financial performance, especially for someone outside the company. Yet the real edge Betty offered was her presence as a natural leader.

Whenever Betty Manning spoke, everyone understood her. She was known for her clear and direct style that made complex matters seem simpler, and she had a way of convincing people of her point of view, seemingly without really trying. She was pragmatic and always appeared to listen more than she spoke. For years she made sure she heard everyone in a room before making a decision. "Why surround yourself with good people," she would ask, "if you're not going to listen to them?"

Her matter-of-fact style was a breath of fresh air, especially given her predecessor's obsession with convoluted strategies that required a never-ending dialogue with the board of directors on what he described as "the nuances" of how the industry functioned. When challenged on the financial merits of his ideas, he often declared, "this isn't financial, it's strategic." Each time he said this, one of the directors always mumbled under his breath, "It may be hard to quantify the benefits, but it had better eventually be financial, or it's not very strategic."

Back in her meeting with Topher, he responded, "As I've told you, Bertrand [the former CEO] was a CPA at heart. Even after he was named CEO, and of course before that as CFO, he was an accountant who was always partial to bottom-line accounting numbers, rather than measures of return on capital, margins, and the like. And he succumbed to all the hoopla over earnings per share on our quarterly earnings calls and in the media. Bertrand often pointed out that, when quarterly earnings were announced, the talking heads on CNBC never said, 'Blue Dynamics missed on ROE'—instead, they always talked EPS (earnings per share). We did manage to get return measures into the incentives for the business-unit bonuses, but for the consolidated company, Bertrand mostly seemed to care about EPS."

Betty had seen this before and asked, "Did you try to help him understand that there are better and more comprehensive ways to view performance?"

"I tried to help by showing him margins and return measures to guide him toward a more rounded perspective of the business." Topher continued, "I emphasized cost efficiency and capital productivity. He especially listened when we were talking about the business units. He liked looking at the business-unit returns when we were allocating the capital budget, though of course he had other strategic motives as well."

That hit a nerve with Betty. The prior week, she had spent hours reviewing the allocation of capital across the business. She recalled being puzzled when she noticed that all the poorer-performing businesses seemed to have been allocated more capital as a percentage of their EBITDA. The best performers got very little. She asked Topher to explain how Blue Dynamics's capital allocation process worked.

"It's pretty straightforward, really," he replied. "First, we decide the total budget, which is usually about five to six percent of sales, depending on how we think investors will react. That's the range we have used for the last few years—although three years ago, when the industry was doing better, investors encouraged us to invest more, and we did. Once we set the overall budget, we ask each of the four businesses to submit a capital budget. Last year, the total came in about 17 percent above what we wanted to spend, so we scaled everyone back 15 to 20 percent until we had the total we wanted."

Betty thought about it in silence for a minute, and then asked, "How do you know five to six percent is the right amount?"

Topher hesitated and then, in a soft tone, replied, "We don't."

"And how come Systems Integration isn't investing more? They seem to have decent growth opportunities...and they have by far the most differentiated products and the highest return on capital. I haven't met with them yet, but it seems to me that investing to grow that business is our best use of capital."

"The funny thing is that Systems Integration hasn't asked for much capital in about four or five years," Topher explained. "Seems they really don't have many good investment ideas. Great business, but they never ask for much growth funding."

"I'm having trouble understanding this," Betty responded. "Their segment is growing. They have a quite low market share, so they could grow even faster than the market. And they haven't even explored expanding overseas. Why in the world don't they ask for more investment dollars? This is a huge strategic error."

"It never troubled Bertrand." Topher paused and then continued. "He always liked telling investors he would balance investing in the business with shareholder distributions. If the capital budget went up, there would be less for distributions. We started paying a dividend a few years ago, but mostly Bertrand liked talking about the EPS accretion from his buyback program. He loved telling investors he was demonstrating his commitment and confidence in the future. He often said he was buying the stock because it was cheap, and investors should buy more, too. I once overheard him tell a board member that half the company's EPS growth was from his buyback program and the other half was from what everyone else did."

Betty stared at Topher in disbelief. Was it Bertrand's arrogance that bothered her? Did the nonsense about buybacks worry her? And did Bertrand really believe that taking a dollar inside the company and giving it to an investor outside the company at fair value somehow created value? Perhaps more important, did Topher believe that, too? She sat quietly and wondered how many good investment opportunities the company had turned down to give money back to shareholders. She suddenly snapped out of her ruminations when Topher said he had to get going. She thanked him for sharing his views and said goodbye.

The following Tuesday, Betty met the Systems Integration management and got a tour of their aging facility, which seemed desperately in need of a new coat of paint and, more critically, some modernized equipment. The Systems Integration team explained the business, and she even tried out some of the robotic simulators. The technology was exciting and she enjoyed seeing it in action. It was the last of the four businesses to meet with her, and she was considerably more impressed with it than with the others.

Steven Tiles of Systems Integration presented her with the business-unit strategy, their business plan projections, and an overview of opportunities and threats. Betty found herself genuinely excited at the prospects, but also a bit confused as to why they weren't trying to invest more to grow this promising business faster. When she asked, Steven deflected her question with talk of being selective and careful. After the second and third time she asked, Steven sat back in his chair and said, "OK, Betty, I'll tell you how it is. We have been blessed in this business with wonderful opportunities. With this and hard work from our team, we have been able to increase our return on operating assets from 20 percent just a few years ago to 45 percent last year. It will be higher this year. It's hard to find investments that earn a higher return than that."

"Oh, I see," she said. "You have built a great business, but you have also been tasked with improving returns; so if you invest at a lower return, it will bring down the average for the business unit."

Steven confirmed her suspicion—"You're a quick study, Betty. Our business-unit management incentive is half-based on the percentage by which we improve the return on operating assets. When they told us about it seven or eight years ago, we thought it made great sense. What could go wrong if we improved our profits and became more productive with capital? But there's no reward for growth. And over time, by trial and error, we realized that investing at returns below the current return cost us money out of our own pockets. As we improved our returns, the hurdle for new investments became higher and higher. It didn't seem right, so we tried explaining to Bertrand that we thought we should invest and grow more. But he said he needed to keep our returns high to woo investors."

After a brief pause, the confession continued. "He also liked having money left over for his buybacks... but I wouldn't know much about that."

When Betty returned to her office, she dug into a stack of quarterly reports going back several years. She stayed late into the night and compared one performance report after another to the capital investment tracking reports. The more data she examined, the more the picture became clear. The focus on improving returns led her best business unit to turn down most investments—even those earning 30% or more. With the business unit earning 45% or greater, the bar had been set too high.

As she worked through the numbers, she felt shocked to realize that the opposite was true in her worst-performing business unit. With a mere 4% return, the Assembly Fabrication unit could improve its returns by investing at 6%. They had planned capital expenditure projects to replace a key manufacturing line with a modest increase in capacity, along with a series of other investments that didn't seem to meaningfully improve efficiency, productivity, or capacity. It hit her that she had one business turning down investments with 30% returns while another was gladly investing at 6%.

It wasn't funny, though Betty couldn't help but laugh. She began to wonder if this was a practical joke. Who would invest virtually all their capital in their worst business and almost nothing in their best business? Who would starve a business earning a 45% return in order to give the money right back to shareholders? Was there a camera in her office to see how she reacted to this madness? Maybe she was being set up on *Punk'd* or *Candid Camera.* As she looked around, she noticed the eye of the duck sparkling in the picture behind her desk, so she stood on a chair to confirm there was no camera. There was no joke…this was her new reality. She wasn't laughing anymore.

She looked further into the capital investment tracking reports. Of course, the low-return investments in Assembly Fabrication were forecast as 12% or 15% returns in the capital requests. The actual performance never seemed to live up to the projections. But as long as it ended up above the existing return—a mere 4%—it brought up the business unit's average return, and as a result the Assembly Fabrication management received a higher bonus. They weren't accountable for hitting their projections or for hitting their cost of capital return.

Betty knew her first hundred days would be important. She needed to set a new course that would not only drive results but let everyone know that she meant business. To this end, she settled on her first major initiative to improve performance at Blue Dynamics. Though she needed to think through the strategies of each business—and there was much room for improvement there—in the short term she realized that her highest priority should be to address the behaviors of her management team. To improve the company's performance, her managers needed to invest more in the good parts of the business, fix its weaker parts, and push harder to deliver results. If she merely realigned the incentives to encourage the right behavior, things would start moving in the proper direction, she concluded.

Assembly Fabrication, she realized, had to hit the brakes and focus on improving what it already had. It was crucial that it cut costs to improve margins. Asset intensity could have been improved by eliminating unproductive capital—for example, by reducing inventory, collecting outstanding overdue accounts receivable, and, most important, by changing how it contracted with customers to get paid earlier. Perhaps it even could have considered a new pricing strategy. But, mostly, Assembly Fabrication needed to stop investing in growth until it "earned the right to grow."

In contrast, Systems Integration needed to step on the gas by investing in every profitable growth opportunity that the business-unit management believed would earn meaningfully more than its cost of capital. It had opportunities to expand its product line and offer high-, medium-, and low-capability alternatives to meet the needs of a wider variety of customers. The software that came with each unit could be enhanced with more-useful features and sold separately as SaaS, or *software as a service.* And maybe Systems Integration could capture an ongoing annuity of revenue, making every sale that much more valuable.

Several Systems Integration assembly plants were old and running over their rated capacity, which increased costs and made it hard to hit client delivery deadlines. Investments in new capacity would be helpful immediately. From a marketing perspective, they could have moved into new domestic end-user markets, and there was clear demand to support expansion into Europe and Asia. Even if their returns dropped from 45% to, say, 35%, while the business doubled or tripled in size, it would be a great outcome since they would still be earning a high return across a much larger base.

To encourage her team to make all this happen, she implemented Blue Dynamics Value Added, or BDVA, as a financial performance measure. It was defined simply as the business's EBITDA less a capital charge based on 12% of their gross invested capital.

Managers were then encouraged to improve volumes, efficiency, pricing, and profit margins, since the resulting increases in EBITDA would increase BDVA. If they could also enhance capacity utilization, drive down unnecessary inventories, and collect on customer invoices in a timelier fashion, they could reduce the gross invested capital required and drive BDVA higher. And, very important, BDVA would increase whenever they invested in growth as long as the incremental EBITDA more than covered the increase in capital charge.

Topher's team completed a historical analysis and found that, though Blue Dynamics had delivered revenue and EBITDA growth in most years, its BDVA had fluctuated and was in fact a bit lower than five years earlier. Betty advocated an incentive framework in which the target BDVA each year would equal the prior year's actual. This seemed fair, given the historically flat and declining BDVA, and, most important, it would set a rigid, target-setting approach that was separated from the budget to eliminate target negotiations and sand-bagging. In the future, if she asked one of her business-unit teams to try to come up with a way to improve performance and plan for it, they may or may not agree—but at least they would know that if they did, their bonuses would be higher and so would Betty's. They were more like partners and less like adversaries.

This novel approach to target-setting provided an incentive to invest in the future even when the immediate effect was a decline in BDVA. As long as they had confidence that the investment would eventually pay off, any bonus they forfeited in year one would be more than earned back if and when the new investment contributed positive BDVA. Betty no longer had to wonder if her business-unit heads believed the forecasts they showed for the recommended investment programs. If the EBITDA didn't grow enough to cover the capital charge, BDVA would decline and some of the value that would be destroyed would come out of management's paycheck. She still had to exercise judgment in deciding what to approve, but at least she knew that the incentives of the managers proposing the investment were aligned with her own. Betty had wanted such a compensation arrangement for years—and she was finally in a position to implement it.

It started to work almost immediately, and even better than she hoped. Right after BDVA was introduced, Steven Tiles and his Systems Integration management team studied their business from every angle imaginable to identify opportunities for BDVA improvement. For example, they allocated costs and capital in order to estimate the BDVA contribution of each customer and customer group, and they tasked the sales team with making improvements both in their pricing models and in negotiating the terms of customer contracts. In the past, such efforts had tended to get bogged down in "analysis-paralysis." This time, there seemed to be more of a sustained drive to achieve results.

The team also analyzed and evaluated each product line to identify those that were contributing the most BDVA and found that such success was associated with how unique and differentiated each product was. So they set about spending more on marketing and sales to drive extra growth in the products contributing the most BDVA, meanwhile also investing in innovation to improve differentiation in those products with lower BDVA contributions. And they even terminated a few products that were contributing negative BDVA, since they didn't think investing to improve them would be worth it.

Most important, the high-performing businesses that Steven managed would no longer be "self-starved" of capital investment. They upgraded and improved the technology being applied in their previously aging facilities, which immediately improved both capacity and product quality. As mentioned, they also increased product development expenditures, and they even began experimenting with new products that might take time to pay off—which had been neglected for years.

Six Months Later
Gradually, Betty's entire management team seemed to get the point of her efforts. She noticed significant improvement in the plans, decisions, and performance in all business units. The focus on BDVA served as a common language across different functions and helped achieve alignment—the good of the whole became more important than who did what. In one notable meeting, a midlevel manager from the Assembly Fabrication unit hinted, confidentially, that corporate should cancel one of his own projects that had been approved the year before and was in line for implementation. Instead, he suggested they give the funding to his colleagues at Systems Integration, noting that "They have potential investments that are better than all but our best ones."

Topher helped Betty revamp the performance measures and incentives to encourage a better balance of returns and growth investment.

The businesses developed new strategic plans, and resources were largely being funneled toward the best opportunities. To make sure there was enough money to go around, they paused the buyback program. Investors balked a bit at first, as did the brokerage analysts. But any concerns faded quickly as stakeholders turned their attention to the growth plan. While some investors decided this was not for them, others whose risk profiles suited growth companies bought in. Though the buyback program was formally still active and they could restart it anytime, Betty viewed it as dead unless their shares took a significant hit.

•••

One Monday morning, Topher entered Betty's office at 8 a.m. for their weekly 30-minute update. Betty immediately began by saying, "Topher, do you realize we spent almost three times as much time discussing and reviewing the Assembly Fabrication plan as we did the Systems Integration plan?"

"Squeaky wheel gets the grease," Topher replied with a smile.

"Yes, maybe, but they spend more time with IT, quality control, legal, and human resources, too. I've spoken to every corporate functional group, and every single manager said that Assembly Fabrication is a drain on their time and people. That business unit has a lot of problems."

"But what's the alternative? They need help."

Betty hesitated for the first time since Topher met her. "Topher, maybe it's time we stop wasting our resources on such a poor performer."

Topher abruptly expressed his view that the company would be better off if they waited until they could turn it around before selling it. If they could improve performance and get some momentum, they might get a higher price.

Betty responded, "Every bit of attention that is siphoned away from Systems Integration and our other more successful businesses costs us money. It's hard to measure, but I believe we're losing more through our lack of attention to our successful businesses than we stand to gain from improving our fixer-upper. Even if we get 50 cents on the dollar by selling it now, it will likely be worth it. And I'm not sure we can ever get the full dollar, anyway."

In days to come, Betty and Topher sat through countless long meetings with bankers and tax advisors and ultimately decided to spin off Assembly Fabrication as its own public company. The business assumed a modest debt burden to maintain discipline, but not so much as to put the new publicly owned company at risk. The spinoff distributed one share in the new Assembly Fabrication public company for every five shares of their company stock. After the transaction, investors could trade the two separately.

The spinoff, they decided, was better than selling the business. In a sale, they would pay tax on the gain over the extremely low tax basis. Both Betty and Topher preferred a tax-free transaction. The bankers advocated selling the business to private equity investors that specialized in turnarounds and using the net proceeds to buy back Blue Dynamics stock. They claimed this would be good for shareholders and made their case with a series of academic studies showing that stock prices typically increased when stock buybacks were announced. They also did the math to show how a business-unit sale and a stock buyback would generate the highest EPS accretion of all the options being considered.

But Betty and Topher didn't think their stock was especially cheap, so they didn't see how the buyback would be helpful to the remaining shareholders. Betty kept asking the bankers, "If we buy back shares at fair value, and the transaction drives up our EPS, isn't our price to earnings multiple likely to fall?" A satisfactory response never came.

After the spinoff, the managers of Assembly Fabrication became much more accountable, since they faced investors directly and had no crutch to lean on. Within two years, returns for the spun-off business were above the cost of capital. Before the spinoff, their plan had assumed it would take four years to achieve this, and everyone thought that was a stretch. And they did it with the same management team that led the business when it was a unit of Blue Dynamics. What's more, management actually started investing and growing the business again, while share price performance appreciated significantly. Betty was one of their biggest fans and maintained a good business friendship with the Assembly Fabrication CEO, who used to work for her.

Back at Blue Dynamics, performance also improved as a result of the spinoff. Betty, Topher, and the corporate staff had more time to help Steven and his people build the Systems Integration business beyond all their expectations. They then made many investments, some of which dragged down the average return. But they still experienced so much growth that they expected to surpass the whole corporation's pre-spinoff revenue and profit fairly quickly—*and* with higher corporate returns and BDVA than ever.

Just Before the Special Acquisition Board Meeting

Before Betty's arrival, a large activist hedge fund had bought into Blue Dynamics' stock. The activist demanded that management stop investing so much in Assembly Fabrication and instead use the funds to accelerate buybacks. The hedge fund even encouraged the company to borrow to fund these buybacks. A rigorous analysis was put forth, suggesting that the company should outsource most of its production to lower-cost regions around the world, which is what their competitors did. And they wanted Bertrand to go.

But the stock popped so much when the activist went public with its demands that the fund decided to dump its holdings; they were in and out in no time. And the share price fell back within months and not much had changed, except that the experience apparently soured some of the board members on Bertrand. He was nearing retirement anyway, but this probably pushed him out a year or two earlier than he had planned.

Although she wasn't there when it happened, Betty decided to revisit this activist episode to better understand the investors' demands and see if there was anything else she should be doing that she had not thought of. Initially, she sat through presentations delivered by her team. Topher gave her the first briefing, but he supplemented this with presentations by folks from investor relations, strategic planning, and the general counsel's office, all of whom had been closely involved when the activist showed up. She then supplemented this with meetings with the bankers and outside law firms that had advised the company.

Indeed, Betty went so far as to visit the hedge fund managers themselves to better understand what they saw that was wrong and why they chose to come after Blue Dynamics rather than another company. The lack of confidence in the prior management led to a depressed stock valuation that seemingly reflected not just poor current performance, but also the expectation of future bad investments that hadn't yet occurred or even been announced. The activist referred to this as a discount for "reinvestment risk," and claimed that merely putting an end to such risk presented a great investment opportunity. It had been a good time for the activist to buy the stock—after all, activist investors tend to be value investors at heart, and the stock seemed cheap. The activist fund manager then sought to unlock value by forcing management to focus all its attention on improving efficiencies, reducing investment in the business, and giving all the money they could back to shareholders—out of the reach of management. Betty remembered one of them claiming that "if management just stopped making bad investments, the stock would pop!"

The activist fund managers congratulated Betty for the company's improved strategy development and tactical execution under her leadership. And the results showed. Where management once had to be careful to avoid investor cynicism—which kept them from trying anything bold—they now were beginning to establish a track record and foster the confidence of their largest investors; and so they felt more at liberty to pursue what appeared to be the best long-run strategy, having the assurance that investors would likely buy in. The activist managers also told Betty that they would not be buying any Blue Dynamics stock, since such a rapidly improving situation just didn't fit their strategy—and they wished her luck. She found the meeting very informative.

For some time thereafter, Betty advocated increasing the amount of investment in the highly successful Systems Integration business. The unit's managers worked closely with her corporate development team to consider all possible ways to augment their already expanded internal investment program with a targeted acquisition. They not only wanted to make a good investment via the acquisition transaction itself, they also wanted to establish an additional platform for new, high-return internal investments after the deal. Betty believed that most acquisitions were justified too heavily by projected cost-cutting and not enough by actual opportunities for revenue growth.

So, Betty and her team identified every public and private company in and around their group of direct competitors. Each potential acquisition target was tracked as an investor might look for buying opportunities, thus ensuring that management's sense of performance and valuation trends would guide the timing of their acquisitions. Strategic criteria were established to assess the fit of the business, including a heavy emphasis on how well the key drivers of the target business matched the core competencies at Blue Dynamics. Betty had experienced poor acquisitions, and she found they almost always occurred when the acquirers didn't fully understand the success factors of the acquired business. By trying to force the wrong strategy, acquisitions often did more harm than good.

In the end, they decided to target Sky Annex Corp., which was attractive on a stand-alone basis, offered a desirable platform for investing in both domestic and international growth after the deal, and would fit in well operationally and culturally under their Systems Integration unit. Betty, Steve, and the corporate development team tracked Sky Annex for some time, met with its management informally at industry and banking conferences, and developed a good sense of the hard and soft factors that they thought would be keys to success for the company if the acquisition went through.

The Sky Annex share price was high, at least in relation to its current performance. It was as if investors were pricing in a premium, knowing that they were a good acquisition target, whether for Blue Dynamics, another strategic acquirer, or a private equity investment fund. But, to Betty, the acquisition appeared to provide so many opportunities for synergy-related growth that it still seemed poised to provide good value.

Once she got the go-ahead from the board to open discussions, the process moved at lightning speed. They completed due diligence, negotiated a tentative deal structure and price, and began seeking approval from the board of directors.

Back to the Board Meeting

After the Q & A period, it was clear that the board of directors was split on the decision. Betty asked the rest of her management team, except the general counsel, to leave the room, and the board continued in executive session. She knew this was the most intense and important moment yet of her 18-month tenure.

The chairman asked the directors to go around the table and share their informal views and remaining questions. They revisited the international strategy, the idea of keeping Sky Annex as a separate business, the need to find some cost synergies, and the board's concerns about the amount of growth in the forecast. One by one, Betty won over most of the less enthusiastic directors, and it seemed more and more likely that the vote would be affirmative.

However, one important director still seemed reluctant. He was a self-made success, rising from underprivileged beginnings to found and build a large, successful private company. He had been one of Betty's strongest advocates both when BDVA was introduced and later when the new incentives were proposed and approved. He had always been a quiet critic of public-company gamesmanship and was not a fan of Bertrand when he was in charge.

He began by expressing his general support for the acquisition strategy and said he too preferred acquisitions in which there were more growth synergies than cost synergies, since this approach had often been more successful in his own company. It was hard for Betty to figure out what his concerns were until he asked what would happen to her base salary the following year. In the past, he had watched CEOs of public companies get almost automatic pay increases when their company grew by acquisition. The larger size and scale of the business stepped up the size of the peer companies that would be benchmarked by the compensation consultants, and bigger companies tended to pay CEOs higher salaries. On top of this, he said his experience was that the enhanced international exposure increased the complexity of the business, and this complexity tended to increase salary as well. Of course, if her salary increased, so would her target annual bonus and her long-term incentive opportunities, since these programs were all set as a percentage of salary.

The director looked Betty in the eye and asked if she would be willing to put a hold on her salary for a few years until they could see how well her team performed in onboarding the new acquisition.

Traditionally, the compensation committee would consider any changes to Betty's salary each year, based on peer benchmarking and other factors, including CEO performance. If she agreed to a fixed salary, she would be giving up a lot, relative to what her peers were getting. But she did understand the perspective and didn't see why she should be rewarded just for making the company bigger. So, she proposed a compromise in which the board would still consider her salary each year, but they wouldn't change the comparison group despite the increase in the size of her company. She further suggested that after a few years, if the BDVA contribution of Sky Annex turned decently positive, perhaps the compensation committee would then consider changing the compensation peer group to include companies that were larger and more complex.

The director agreed to her proposals, and the board swiftly voted to approve the acquisition. Betty knew the real hard work was to come after the deal closed, but she was pleased by the support she had received from the board.

What Changed at Blue Dynamics?

The biggest difference was that Betty was a far better CEO and leader than Bertrand had been; and all the other changes followed from this. She created an owner-like culture in which results mattered more than excuses, the long- and short-term were equally important, and there was a simultaneous focus on investing to grow the business *and improving* rates of return. Those who succeeded were rewarded, without any need to play budget-sandbagging games, and resources were more consistently funneled to the best opportunities for success. Betty's management team members viewed one another more as partners, while viewing her as the managing partner. It's hoped that this story will pique readers' interest in learning more in the following pages.

> *This book is a prescription for curing corporate short-termism in its many manifestations. One of the biggest obstacles to economic growth, employment expansion, financial security, and social well-being is that companies are investing less and less in building their future and instead are devoting more and more capital to activities that provide a quick fix but deliver few, if any, lasting benefits. Many believe companies cannot maintain accountability for period-by-period performance and invest in the future at the same time. Talking about the "long term" is sometimes seen as code for "I'm about to have a bad quarter" or "I need to justify why my budget shows less profit than last year." The chapters that follow will prove this to be a false characterization. With the right measures in place, suitable planning and decision processes, and appropriate incentive programs, companies can encourage managerial behaviors that better balance the long and short term and deliver more success for all stakeholders.*

PART I

UNDERSTANDING SHORT-TERMISM AND THE EVOLUTION OF PERFORMANCE MEASUREMENT

ONE

Corporate Short-Termism and How It Happens

DESPITE THE BEST of intentions, many corporate management teams unwittingly foster a culture of short-termism that saps the financial strength of their companies. In aggregate, this behavior has the collective effect of limiting the overall growth, employment, and prosperity of the entire global economy. This view is often shrugged off as inevitable with statements such as "unfortunately, that's the way it is" and "it's what investors tell me they want, so I have to play the game." Yet nothing could be further from the truth. Most investors don't "want" short-termism, but from a CEO's perspective, investors can appear as a jittery bunch who often seem to overreact to short-term news.

Part of the problem is that some investors don't hold their investments for very long periods. If an investor owns shares of a company for three months and then sells to buy other stock, they rightfully don't care what happens after they sell—they care about share-price performance only while they hold the stock. And these short-term holders can often be extremely vocal, and thereby have an outsized influence on management. Today's highly liquid capital markets may provide immense social benefits, but rapid shareholder turnover does have its drawbacks.

Years ago, I began asking corporate client executives, "Would you be willing to take a strategic action you believe may be misunderstood in the short term, driving down your share price 10% to 15%, if you are convinced you are right and that the share price will be 20% to 30% higher than otherwise after three years when the strategy proves successful?" Most replied, in one way or another, that they would like to think so, but that investor pressures might lead them to pass on the action even if they personally believed in its value. This question, though, poses a tradeoff that gets to the heart of the issue at hand; that was the impetus that led me to pursue an improved framework for developing thoughtful corporate strategies, allocating resources wisely, and measuring performance more effectively.

Short-termism begins with the quarterly earnings cycle. The problem is not that quarterly reporting is bad, but that the process that has been built up around these quarterly reports is fraught with demands and pressures that tend to influence management to over-emphasize the short term at the expense of the long term. Pretty much everyone is aware of the problem, yet few business leaders know how to create an organizational environment with adequate accountability for delivering short-term results *without* sacrificing the long-term potential of the business.

The quarterly earnings call ritual has taken on increasing importance for public company leaders and, in many cases, this triggers decisions that end up limiting success over the longer term. Executives tend to fear that their share prices will be crushed if they don't deliver earnings per share, or EPS, that meets or exceeds analysts' consensus estimates.

And as far as the *immediate* reaction to bad earnings news is concerned, they are right. In 2016, Fortuna Advisors studied the 800 companies in the Russell 1000 that had been public since 2008. Our research showed that, over the quarter in which an earnings announcement is made, meeting or beating consensus EPS affects share price performance more than whether EPS increases.[1] This might help explain why certain managers are far more focused on beating consensus than on whether EPS is increasing.

But when we extended the measurement period from a quarter to a year, which is hardly "long-term," we found the opposite result. Over this slightly longer period, EPS growth mattered much more than whether management beat consensus estimates (defined as the percentage of quarters in which actual EPS either met or beat the consensus). And when we lengthened this time horizon to two or three years, the importance of performance improvements relative to beating consensus became even clearer. Would investors prefer that management exceed consensus and improve results by 3%, or miss consensus but improve results by 10%? If you care about what your share price will be in three years, the actual improvement in results matters far more than whether these results beat an arbitrary short-term benchmark known as consensus earnings.

So, how can beating consensus be that important to managers yet have so little impact on share price performance over time? In many cases, it's because the consensus earnings themselves are derived from a process in which a substantial proportion of the information analysts use to build their financial models and determine their earnings forecasts comes from *management itself.* Since managers typically prefer to be perceived as succeeding rather than failing, they have an incentive to "guide"—consciously or not—the analyst forecasts lower by giving both formal and informal guidance that understates what they believe will happen. They are just being conservative, after all. By tempering the expectations of investors and analysts, management increases the chances that they will "beat consensus" and secure praise from business-TV pundits and reporters—and perhaps from their board of directors as well. In addition, many compensation committees consider consensus estimates when determining targets for incentive compensation, making it easier for management to earn more if they give conservative guidance.

From an internal corporate perspective, this problem of "sandbagging" is, hands down, the very worst managerial behavior problem. Each year, most corporate business units submit a three- or five-year plan in which performance during the first year is projected to go down, but in every year thereafter is strongly up. The appeal of this well-known "hockey-stick" forecast for sandbagging managers is that it provides them with both an easy budget to beat in the annual incentive plan and a strong outlook beyond that, which helps gain top management's approval of the capital requests they need to undertake all their desired investments. Though the internal plan generally promises more performance improvement than does the published guidance, the improvements projected in the plan still tend to significantly understate what management *really* thinks it can do.

This sandbagging problem may well be the most underappreciated problem in the business world. If we asked a group of very smart people with no business experience whether they thought it would be better to encourage managers to develop plans for success or plans for mediocrity, I suspect the vast majority would encourage managers to plan for success. After all, at the start of every sporting event, don't all athletes aim to win, even when the odds are stacked against them? Yet that's not what most people with business experience expect of their team. To be fair, most of them grew up in the system of sandbagging and budget negotiations and never knew anything else. It takes hard work, courage, and consistency to change it.

Hockey-stick forecasts can also result from poor integration of financial and strategic information in projections. Often, because the strategy is presented without any hard financial metrics, forecasts wishfully assume a positive drift in key variables. This is known as spreadsheet extrapolation, a practice that predictably causes the out-year results to be implausibly optimistic.

But short-termism comes from more than just quarterly earnings, sandbagging, and spreadsheet extrapolation. A variety of behavioral problems are also caused by common practices for planning, decision-making, and performance management. The collective effect of these behavioral problems is a drag on corporate performance, shareholder returns, and overall economic growth and employment.

Executives are often surprised by the sources of short-termism they find in their companies. For example, common financial performance measures can result in underinvestment. Consider a general manager of a business unit who is rewarded based on its improving return on invested capital (ROIC), which can be defined simply as the after-tax operating profit of the business divided by the invested capital (which includes working capital and net property, plant, and equipment). The ROIC measure is intended to indicate the efficiency with which a business uses its capital, so rewarding a manager for increasing ROIC would seem to be appropriate.

But let's examine the behavior encouraged by this practice. In 2017, the median ROIC of S&P 500 companies[2] was 12.7%. For this illustration, consider a business earning a much higher ROIC, say

25%. This business would be in the top quartile among S&P 500 companies. Any investment in this business that earns less than 25% will bring down the average return and thus reduce the bonus earned by the general manager. There may be investments that would earn, say, 20%, and yet management would be discouraged from making those investments, since the average ROIC would decline and the managers would accordingly earn less.

Is the incentive to improve ROIC supplying the right motivation? The 20% incremental return on investment would be far higher than the return of the average company, and a *lot* higher than the cost of capital for most if not all companies. The core principle of modern corporate finance is that making an investment that earns a return above the cost of capital creates value. And since the cost of capital in 2017 was under 10% for most companies, investing in a project that earns a 20% return would clearly make the company more valuable—yet management would be paid less for pursuing this value-creating investment. This is a common problem and, unfortunately for shareholders and other stakeholders, it's a prescription for starving the best-performing businesses of growth capital, which leads to less value creation and worse share price performance. It's bad for investors, workers, and the overall GDP growth of the economy.[3] *It's a lose, lose, lose situation.* Even as some politicians claim that "shareholders" are reaping gains off the backs of other stakeholders, the fact is that all but the *most* short-term investors are worse off after such an investment strategy.

In fairness, many managers say they will do the right thing even if it reduces their compensation. But why force managers to have to choose between the good of their families and that of the company's shareholders? The idea that paying people to improve either ROIC or nearly any percentage-based measure of performance could be reducing value is surprising to many, yet numerous other common management processes and quirks wind up encouraging less value-creation.

It's All About Process and Behavior

Ignorance and naiveté can at times be forgiven. But it is surely both inexcusable and indefensible when people know that what they are doing is wrong and still do it. When a chief executive officer and a management team are tasked with leading thousands of employees, overseeing countless customer relationships, producing and improving important products and services, and delivering success for all stakeholders (including shareholders), we would all like to think they will do their damndest to live up to these responsibilities and accomplish these goals.

Nobody can truly say they have seen it all, but with close to three decades as an advisor to well over 200 companies operating in just about every industry and on every continent except Antarctica, I have seen a *lot*. Some of my most surprising, and frustrating, experiences as a consultant have come not from failing to persuade a client of the superiority of a particular strategy or tactic, but rather from watching a client executive first agree that a certain strategy would deliver a better outcome—and then choose not to pursue it and instead continue with the status quo.

Why would executives do this? One answer was provided in 2005 by Duke University's Professor John Graham and his coauthors who published a much-cited study of how corporate reporting was affecting managerial decisions and actions.[4] When surveying over 400 chief financial officers, they found that some 80% of those CFOs expressed their willingness to sacrifice shareholder value simply to meet or beat a quarterly earnings goal.

And given that the short-termism problems found in that survey were identified by fully 80%, and not just a handful, of CFOs, such value-destroying practices are clearly widespread. What's more, we can only surmise that the actual percentage is probably higher, since some respondents may have been disinclined to confess to their willingness to forgo value. For a group that waxes on interminably about "shareholder value," the cognitive dissonance is perhaps understandable.

Bolstering these findings are those of a more recent discussion paper, published by the McKinsey Global Institute. Among other conclusions, it notes that 87% of executives and directors feel pressured to produce strong performance within two years or fewer; and 65% of executives and directors think that short-term pressures have increased over the past five years.[5]

But how *do* companies actually sacrifice shareholder value? In some cases, they cut positive-net present value (NPV) investments that are expensed against earnings, such as research and development

(R&D) and advertising—and in so doing, they reduce the value of both the earnings and the cash flows expected in future years. (Note that Amazon has shown no sign of succumbing to this temptation—and the company's shareholders have been rewarded handsomely for management's inattention to quarterly accounting earnings.) In other cases, earnings-focused executives delay positive-NPV projects that would be expected to grow the value of the company, but that may weigh on short-term results during the early stages of the project.

As bad as this seems, this is only the tip of the iceberg. For every time a senior executive, in finance or otherwise, knowingly makes a decision to achieve a dollar of short-term success by giving up two dollars or more of long-term success, there are dozens, maybe even hundreds, of situations in that same company in which managers at all levels and functions are also making suboptimal decisions. But many don't even know it. They are routinely following misguided business processes, using erroneous decision criteria, or aiming to optimize a flawed or incomplete performance measure or scorecard. This may not even be their fault, since they are doing only what they are being asked and paid to do. Yet that doesn't make it any less of a problem. Senior managements must not only change their own behavior to better balance the short and long term, they also may well have to rethink every management process so they can provide managers throughout the organization with better measures, more reliable decision criteria, and more effective incentives.

It may not seem as outrageous when a manager makes the wrong decision because he or she doesn't know any better and is just doing what they have been told. The problem, though, may well be prevalent enough to create a national drag on productivity. The primary goals of my career have been to create an environment in which these adverse managerial behaviors are less prevalent, and then to implement such principles at as many companies as possible.

Admittedly, most defective processes, decision criteria, and performance measures originate from the best of intentions. For example, when company management chooses to use ROIC improvement as the basis for incentives, they typically do so because they (rightly) believe that if everything else is the same, having a higher ROIC is better. However, they don't think about the adverse behavioral incentives discussed above. As mentioned earlier, ROIC-based incentives can lead to throttling a company's most-promising businesses, and this is made even worse in companies that measure performance using free cash flow (FCF) as a period measure. Rewarding managers for increasing FCF in a single period is an invitation to "milk" a business, since the full amount of an investment is subtracted dollar for dollar from the current-year performance measure.

Moreover, the adverse incentives created by ROIC can end up reducing value in another way. Thus far, we have seen how the approach can starve high-return businesses of valuable growth investments. But tying rewards directly to the improvement in ROIC can also encourage weak businesses to *over*invest. For example, the managers of a business with a 2% ROIC would realize a higher bonus if they made investments earning 3% or 4%, both of which bring up the average ROIC—even though such investments probably lie well below the cost of capital and are likely to destroy value.

Nevertheless, years of experience have taught me an important lesson: If you are going to err, it's still better that your best businesses get the capital they need to grow, even if this means also overinvesting in weak, low-return businesses. That's because the value lost from starving great businesses is typically many times greater than that lost by overinvesting in weak ones. Over the 10 years ending in 2010, the top-quartile companies in the S&P 500 had average total shareholder returns of over 700%—while the bottom quartile delivered a staggering –35%.[6] A simple comparison of these two numbers suggests that preserving a minimum of 1% of the value creation potential in the best businesses is, on average, about *20 times* as important as achieving 1% less downside in the worst businesses. This relationship varies by company, of course.

There is much more that is wrong with the typical management processes than simply the use of poor measures. Often there is confusion about what "strategy" really means. For example, some executives describe their strategy as "double revenue, expand margins, and grow EPS at double digit rates." Though these might be credible goals, they are not "strategies." Strategy involves assessing the competition and environment, evaluating and enhancing competitive advantages, and choosing to allocate resources to grow sales of products and services that are competitively advantaged in attractive markets. Management needs to maintain a firm grip on

the attractiveness of the markets they serve and the strategic position of their businesses within those markets. Attractive markets
offer desirable growth opportunities along with the ability to deliver
advantageous returns on capital. Strategic position comes from the
differentiation achieved by developing distinctive and meaningful
product or service attributes, stronger brands, and better manufacturing or service delivery processes. Many give too little credence
to these important drivers of strategic thinking and care only about
the financial numbers, which is a very bad idea. Goals are generally
meaningless without a strategy to achieve them.

Often executives balk at such observations and boast about their
rigorous strategic planning process. Yet, as with most things in life, we
must not confuse effort with results. At many companies, months of
preparation, thousands of human-hours, and hundreds of pages of
slides often get shelved right after they are presented. The dynamic
and competitive world surrounding the company presents new challenges that were never contemplated in the strategic plan, therefore
management must respond—all the while delivering quarterly earnings. In some companies, things are so bad that the people preparing
the plan *know* it has no meaning; they are just compiling data and
preparing materials as parts of a routine designed to check a box and
take home a paycheck.

The planning process itself has the ability to spur significant value
creation, even as it falls short of this potential at most companies.
Creative thinking, experimentation, and prudent risk-taking are critical to finding ways to both strengthen and capitalize on competitive
advantages and, by so doing, achieve success far beyond the industry
norm. For business units that are struggling, planning offers an opportunity to start fresh, to seek opportunities to consider new strategies,
and to step up execution, thereby "earning the right to grow."

Even when strategic planning is more actively embraced, other
problems can arise. In some cases, managers try to right the wrongs
of the past by developing plans that are essentially just throwing
good money after bad in attempts to avoid admitting failure. Doing
the hard work to recognize poor performance, cut losses, and move
on to greener pastures is almost certain to be more productive than
obsessing over the improvement of recurring losers. Some business
observers have come to refer to this as "long-termism"—essentially,

code for *not* doing a rigorous analysis of existing investments. For obvious (I think) reasons, I find this term to be a misnomer, but it's perhaps worth mentioning all the same.

In other cases, managers ignore evolving market conditions and manage as if everything will stay the same. This often becomes a problem when a new management team is running a company that has been successful for years. They give too little credence to the possibility that competitors will leapfrog them with better products and services, or that consumer needs and desires will change. Even if their offering remains distinctive, success often breeds complacency, leading to bloated operating costs and underinvestment in the future.

Perhaps most important, managers often seem obsessed with extrapolating the present into the future, thinking good times or bad times will endure forever. Some managers are too wedded to the principle of "If it isn't broken, don't fix it." They rest on their laurels, satisfied with the status quo, while competitors innovate new products and marketing strategies—and pass them by. This is one form of "recency bias," a common behavioral bias that is particularly prevalent (and problematic) in cyclical industries. Recency bias also tends to be a more-acute problem in highly successful companies, since managers may not want to mess with a "proven" formula, even as the conditions that made that formula successful change. It may seem like a good problem to have, but this is the cause of many fallen stars—think Kodak and Xerox.

At many companies, a significant process-related problem is the lack of accountability for projections, which in turn creates the need for excessive control. Most companies emphasize profit-and-loss (P&L) measures, such as operating profit and EBITDA, that provide little or no recognition of the cost of capital. Capital is effectively free, and so it has to be tightly controlled.[7] And overly tight controls tend to reinforce a culture of incrementalism, which in turn reduces entrepreneurial thinking, innovation, dynamic course changes, and, worst of all, accountability.

Almost every company says they need a "better" follow-up process to see how well projects deliver on the projections used to justify the investment for approval. At best, these "investment look-back" processes tend to be ad hoc, incomplete, and "for information only," since the data is rarely tracked properly and the findings of these look-backs are fraught with estimates and approximations. The worst part is that everyone understands this lack of follow-through and accountability; at the time of the investments, the managers making the projections to justify them know that their assumptions will most likely be forever forgotten. The entire system has no memory.

Anyone who has ever developed a 5- or 10-year cash flow forecast for a new investment knows how much higher the NPV and internal rate of return (IRR) can be when we step up growth and margins by a few percent, and perhaps assume 30-day receivables, even though the company typically runs 60–90 days. The abundance of great high-return projects seems surreal—which of course it is!—and the only way senior management can put a lid on such capital spending is to erect arbitrary limits for capital budgets and say, "we simply cannot afford any more."

One of my favorite client quotes of all time was uttered by Herb Sklenar, who was chairman and CEO of Vulcan Materials when we worked together in the 1990s. I once had a one-on-one meeting with Herb so that I could gain a thorough understanding of the company and its strengths and flaws from his vantage point. During the meeting, Herb expressed frustration that he regularly approved 15%–20% return investments and, as a company, they kept earning 8%–10% returns. He began by saying that because nobody can really accurately forecast the future, we should expect actual performance to deviate from projections. But, as he went on to say, if the inability to perfectly forecast the future were the only problem, there would be just as many projects that exceed the forecast as those that fall short. The reality, of course, was that *most* projects fell short of projections, as they do in most companies. We then discussed the misalignment between the capital approval process and performance measurement; together with the rest of his management team, we began the process of implementing a performance measure called Economic Value Added, or EVA. Loosely speaking, EVA is net operating profit after taxes minus a capital charge that reflects the cost of equity as well as debt. In the case of Vulcan Materials, management adjusted the measure further after our work together, so they could establish their own customized measure, which they called "EBITDA Economic Profit,"[8] still in use by them today. This measure shares some attributes with Residual Cash Earnings (RCE), a measure we developed at Fortuna Advisors that we will return to later in the book.

Vulcan Materials has been an extremely strong performer, with a cumulative total shareholder return (TSR), including dividends and share price appreciation, of 426% over the 20 years ending in 2017. This far exceeds the performance of the overall market, which delivered TSR of 294% over the same period.[9] That result is downright outstanding for a company that basically crushes rocks and sells construction aggregates, asphalt, and ready-mix concrete.

In any event, the primary problem with corporate processes is that management spends far too much time dillydallying on process efficiency, scalability, and metrics, and not enough on the behavior that it should encourage. It is imperative, therefore, to review every important process with careful consideration of the behavior that is encouraged, and then to make improvements that channel the behaviors of management in the desired direction. And, like any organizational change process, such changes require strong support from senior executives, who must visibly embrace and actively conform to the new behavioral template. After all, this is a *cultural change*.

People Are Not That Rational

We are all human, at least most of us (the jury is still out on Jeff Bezos, Warren Buffett, Bill Gates, and a handful of others). And as humans we are susceptible to human biases. Most people intend to behave rationally and do the right thing but, owing to these innate human biases, they often miss the mark and don't behave as described in the economics textbooks. We humans are not all that rational—at least not consistently.

Consider the stock market, which is generally believed to be fairly efficient. Was the stock market efficient when both the S&P 500 and the NASDAQ Composite peaked in March of 2000? How about on October 9, 2002, when the S&P 500 was down 49% and the NASDAQ had fallen a massive 78%? Just five years later, on October 9, 2007, the S&P 500 again peaked at over twice the previous trough and the NASDAQ was up over 150%. A mere 17 months later, the market was again in the doldrums, with the S&P 500 and the NASDAQ each down over 50% from the 2007 peak. As of July 26, 2019, the S&P 500 was up 347% from the 2009 bottom, and the NASDAQ was up 557%. As Peter Lynch once quipped, "Everyone has the brainpower to make money in stocks. Not everyone has the stomach. If you are susceptible to selling everything in a panic, you ought to avoid stocks and mutual funds altogether."[10]

If markets were truly rational, company valuations would be higher, as a multiple of earnings, at the bottom of the cycle, because investors would be anticipating that at some point there will be an upturn. And, of course, valuation multiples would be lower near the top of the cycle as investors expect a downturn. At both the top and bottom of the cycle, investors would be unsure when these cyclical patterns would occur, but they would be pretty confident that at some point cyclical troughs will turn up and cyclical peaks will turn down.

But what really happens? Of the 500 companies that make up the current S&P 500, 294 were public both at the peak of the Internet bubble and in the trough that followed. These companies had an average PE multiple of 29.0x at the top of the cycle in 2000, when they should have been pricing-in declines, and an average PE of 23.4x when the market bottomed 31 months later. As this example suggests, instead of dampening the effect of cyclical earnings by tempering the extremes of the market, investors exacerbate the problem by forgetting (or ignoring) that these cycles exist.

This is a more telling example of the recency bias discussed above. And along with its effects on investors, recency bias has all sorts of negative consequences for managerial planning and decision-making. Like investors, corporate managers tend to act as if cyclical highs and lows will continue forever. Consider, for example, the near-universal tendency of corporate strategic plans to show more growth at the top of the cycle than they do at the bottom. This tendency leads to more investment in the business in the upper portion of market cycles, when assets are most expensive and capacity is least needed, given the downturn that invariably follows.

And it's not just organic investment—acquisitions tend to peak when companies are at their highest values and grind to a halt when acquisitions are cheap. Managers often say sellers don't want to sell in downturns, but that is because the acquiring companies don't adjust their perception of fair pricing. Bankers show the pricing of comparable acquisitions and say, "It's okay to pay X% premium." But the reality, of course, is that it's the price that matters to the selling companies, and not the percentage premium over their (currently depressed) values.[11]

In addition to recency bias, there is also a behavioral bias toward "herding," or doing what everyone else is. In 1841 Charles Mackay published *Extraordinary Popular Delusions and the Madness of Crowds*,[12] in which he wrote, "Men, it has been well said, think in herds; it will be seen that they go mad in herds, while they only recover their senses slowly, and one by one."

When everyone is doing deals, there is a tendency to want to join in for fear of missing out. This herd-like mentality leads many companies to acquire more at the top of the stock market cycle than at the bottom. And one big problem with herding is that it creates competitive bidding and increases the final price paid, which cuts into, if not eliminates, the deal's value-creation potential for the acquirer's shareholders, effectively transferring that value to the seller's shareholders. Indeed, during the 10 years from 2001 through 2011, total U.S. acquisition volume was nearly 70% higher in the five years when the S&P 500 was above average than in the years when it was below average.

When the stock market is down, the board of a selling company often demands a higher premium to cede control of their company. But the purchase-price premium, as we suggested earlier for sellers, is not the most reliable indicator of value for buyers, either. The median transaction premium in 2009 was 34%, which seems expensive when compared to the 21% premium in 2006. However, if we examine the acquisition prices in relation to book value, we get a better sense of the absolute value paid at each point in the cycle. It turns out that despite the lower premium, the average price paid in 2006, when measured as a multiple of book value, was 25% higher than the average price paid in 2009. When the stock market is low, it can be worthwhile to pay a higher premium over the prevailing market price of the acquisition target, if that's what it takes to make a value-creating deal.

To understand why companies don't pull the trigger on organic investments and acquisitions at the bottom of the cycle also requires understanding another bias, this one known as "loss avoidance." Academics who focus on behavioral finance have shown through empirical testing that people feel losses more than twice as strongly as they feel profits of similar amount. This loss avoidance bias interferes with decisiveness and delays decision-making. Loss avoidance also tends to bias executives against making contrarian investments, which are the essence of "buying low and selling high."

To overcome these natural human biases and deliver higher TSR, companies must implement well-designed processes and objective decision criteria. The management processes in many companies simply don't encourage managers to gather enough information, including historical statistics on their own business, and to use it in a rules-based way to make objective, unemotional decisions.

Sound crazy? One company I worked with filled in the cost, investment, price, and terms data in its pricing evaluation model only *after* it had negotiated a deal with a customer—and this on contracts worth hundreds of millions of dollars! Another client showed the same contempt for analysis by filling in its discounted cash flow (DCF) valuation model only after the CEO had used "gut feel" to agree to the transaction price on an acquisition worth over $1 billion. Why have a process to estimate the present value of free cash flow of a business deal if you are going to do the analysis *after* you sign the deal and the parameters are set in stone?

Undeniably, these management problems are not as sensational as the ones involved in the Enron, Worldcom, and Tyco scandals. But collectively, over decades and across thousands of companies, these common management pitfalls are costing society much more in potential economic output, jobs, and wealth creation. *It has been estimated that short-termism has cost $1 trillion in forgone gross domestic product (GDP) over the last decade, and if the trend continues, this could rise to $3 trillion by 2025.*[13] Every company should carefully consider all management processes to ensure that they don't encourage value-reducing behavior.

Decision-Making Should Hinge on Long-Term Shareholder Value

To improve management processes requires understanding and embracing the goal of delivering long-term improvements in shareholder value. Put simply, if a business decision creates long-term value, it is good—and if it does not, it is bad. Of course, at times management must approve investments that seem to destroy value, and they typically justify these as "strategic." But what this usually means is that it's hard to quantify and communicate the value creation, despite management's conviction that the value is real. For this reason alone, maintaining discipline on strategic investments is tough, yet extremely important.

Nevertheless, a clear and purposeful focus on long-term shareholder value should be the goal of all business planning and decision processes, performance measures, and incentive compensation. Otherwise, management teams and organizations can get lost in the endless number of possible priorities, which then can lead to suboptimal or value-reducing decisions and results.

Regrettably, many executives have become disillusioned with shareholder value. The very term "shareholder value" sounds so politically incorrect to many that the concept may be dismissed even before the discussion begins. Critics of shareholder value often promote "stakeholder value" instead, a concept that is reinforced by the reduced emphasis on capitalism in favor of more-progressive principles. But the pursuit of stakeholder value, however noble, is close to useless as a way to run a business—since it is neither objective nor easily measurable.

Further to this point, Fortuna's own research from 2019 demonstrates that companies that produce more shareholder value (measured as TSR) are far likelier to be recognized for their contributions and commitment to stakeholders at large. What's more, the 50% of S&P 500 companies with above-median TSR for the 10 years through 2018 increased aggregate employment by 61%, compared to just 2% for those companies with below-median TSR. In the process, the high TSR companies created 3.3 million more jobs than their low-TSR counterparts. All this suggests that shareholder and stakeholder value are much more aligned than the current public perception might suggest.[14]

In any case, corporate managers need a way to decide where to invest, and then how to manage those investments and optimize operations. Measuring the improvement in shareholder value is both practical and accurate—it is the right way to evaluate performance.

Where consideration of long-run shareholder value becomes especially important is in the critical task of balancing the two main pillars of corporate value: growth and returns. To achieve the optimal balance in the ever-present growth vs. return tradeoff requires consideration of long-term value.[15] When companies focus exclusively or excessively on either, resources are misallocated. Our research in many industries—including, for example, healthcare[16] and tech[17]—shows that delivering long-term value through a combination of growth and returns produces the highest TSR.

• • •

Different companies must face a surprisingly wide range of problems—and there is no panacea for all of them. Even within a single company, different business lines or regions may face entirely different short-term pressures.

Even so, the benefits of addressing short-termism at an organizational level can be substantial. Yet there are no guarantees of success even for companies that have been successful in recent years. As shown in figure 1, the fact that a given company has been a top-quartile performer for shareholders during one five-year period tells us less than one may think about how the company will do during the next five years. Indeed, during the five years ending in 2017, the companies that were top-quartile performers during the previous five years were slightly more likely to be bottom-quartile than top-quartile.

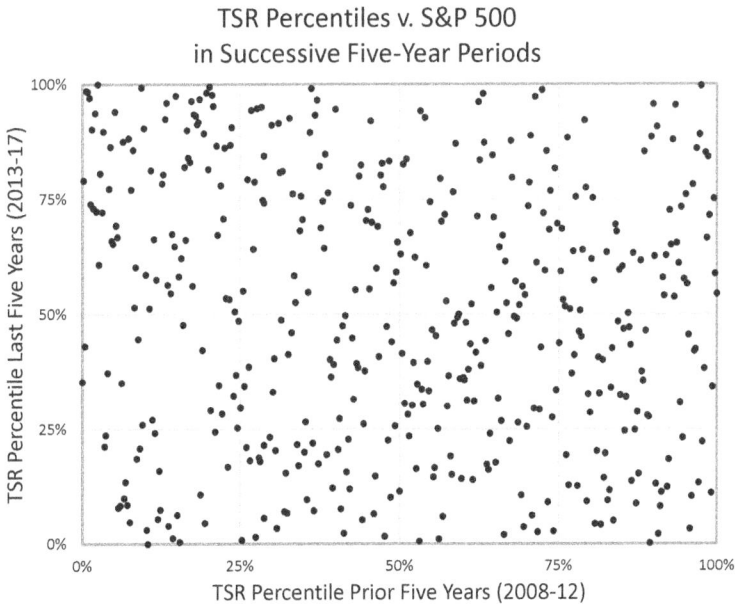

TSR Percentiles v. S&P 500
in Successive Five-Year Periods

Figure 1—Past Performance Is No Guarantee of Future Success

But despite this tendency to give up ground, the good news is that however well or poorly a company performed over the last five years, there is considerable upside for companies that develop objectively informed strategies; allocate capital and other resources more effectively; make all value-creating investments by ensuring accountability for delivering growth *and* returns; and encourage all of the above with better performance measures and incentive compensation designs. That upside is likely to take the form of significant increases in annual cash flow, higher rates of return on capital, more revenue growth, and substantially higher TSR. This is supported by recent research by McKinsey Global Institute showing that, on average, long-term companies had a 50% greater likelihood to be top decile or top quartile in TSR by 2014, while market capitalization of long-term firms grew by $7 billion more than that of other firms between 2001 and 2014.[18]

Getting there, however, requires a concerted plan and sustained corporate-wide efforts to overcome the overwhelming tendency to focus on the short term. Companies must improve processes and behaviors to overcome organizational inertia and ongoing human biases. To reinforce this longer-term focus, management should seek to create an ownership culture in which managers throughout the organization participate in, and assume responsibility for, decisions, results, and consequences. When each manager and each employee accept their business obligations as if they owned them, organizations create more value.

Notes

1 Gregory V. Milano and Allison Cavasino, "Stop the Quarterly Madness!," CFO. com, August 16, 2016, https://fortuna-advisors.com/2016/08/26/stop-the-quarterly-madness/.

2 Note that financial and real estate companies were removed from the sample, because returns are generally defined differently for these sectors. The data source is Capital IQ.

3 Dominic Barton, James Manyika, Timothy Koller, Robert Palter, and Jonathan Godsall, *Measuring the Economic Impact of Short-Termism*, Discussion Paper, McKinsey Global Institute, February 2017.

4 John R. Graham, Campbell R. Harvey, and Shiva Rajgopal, *The Economic Implications of Corporate Financial Reporting,* Working Paper, Duke University, January 11, 2005, https://faculty.fuqua.duke.edu/~charvey/Research/Working_Papers/W73_The_economic_implications.pdf.

5 Barton et al., *Measuring the Economic Impact of Short-Termism.*

6 Gregory V. Milano, "Are You Wasting Time on Poor Performers?," CFO.com, July 8, 2011, https://fortuna-advisors.com/2011/07/08/are-you-wasting-time-on-poor-performers/.

7 Thanks to my former partner Bennett Stewart who probably said this over a hundred times when we were in meetings together.

8 Annex A to the Vulcan Materials Company Schedule 14A (a.k.a. the proxy) filed March 26, 2018.

9 Market performance was measured using the "SPY" ETF, which tracks the S&P 500.

10 Peter Lynch and John Rothchild, *Beating the Street* (Norwalk, CT: Easton Press, 1993), rule #17.

11 Gregory V. Milano, "Do Acquisition Premiums Matter?," CFO.com, July 29, 2011, https://fortuna-advisors.com/2011/07/29/do-acquisition-premiums-matter/.

12 Charles MacKay, *Extraordinary Popular Delusions, And, the Madness of Crowds,* New York: Crown Publishers, 1996.

13 Barton et al., *Measuring the Economic Impact of Short-Termism.*

14 Gregory V. Milano, Michael Chew, and Jinbae Kim, "Companies That Do Well Also Do Good," CFO.com, May 15, 2019, http://fortuna-advisors.com/2019/05/15/companies-that-do-well-also-do-good/.

15 Gregory V. Milano and Jim McTaggart, "Overcoming 3 Roadblocks to Strategic Resource Allocation," FEI Daily, February 28, 2018, http://fortuna-advisors.com/2018/02/28/overcoming-3-roadblocks-to-strategic-resource-allocation/.

16 Gregory V. Milano, Marwaan R. Karame, and Joseph G. Theriault, "Improving the Health of Healthcare Companies," *Journal of Applied Corporate Finance* 29, no. 3 (Summer 2017): 18–29.

17 Gregory V. Milano, Arshia Chatterjee, and David Fedigan, "Drivers of Shareholder Returns in Tech Industries (or How to Make Sense of Amazon's Market Value)," *Journal of Applied Corporate Finance* 28, no. 3 (2016): 48–55.

18 Barton et al., *Measuring the Economic Impact of Short-Termism.*

TWO

What Gets Measured Gets Done

ODDS ARE, WHEN Mick Jagger and Keith Richards wrote the line "you can't always get what you want," they weren't thinking about the relationship between executives and their shareholders. The difference between the expressed demands of investors and what they value, based on their actions in the stock market, probably wasn't top of mind for Mick and Keith when they went on to write: "if you try sometimes, you just might find, you get what you need." But as it turns out, these transgenerational lyrics convey an important message that executives should embrace.

Corporate leaders must determine the performance measures that, when improved, will drive shareholder value higher over time. They must relentlessly pursue improvement in these measures even when the strategies and tactics required to lift the chosen measures appear to conflict with what their investors claim to want. That's right: Like the rest of us, shareholders don't always know what's in their own best interest. So, for corporate management to do the best job possible, they must give their owners what they *need*, which may not always be what they think they *want*.

The anthropologist Margaret Mead once remarked, "What people say, what people do and what they say they do are entirely different things."[1] To recast this phrase for our purposes, "It's better to go by what investors *do* than what they *say*." There is an abundance of rhetoric on how performance influences share prices. Every corporate executive is subject to a continuous barrage of often misguided viewpoints and undue pressures, with their shareholders frequently

expressing their opinions about the strategies and tactics they themselves believe will lead to a higher share price. But many investor
demands are completely, or at least largely, at odds with what extensive
capital market research demonstrates actually drives a share price
higher over time. What are executives to do?

A chief executive scarcely faces a more important managerial
policy decision than establishing the performance measures for rewarding performance throughout the company. It is said that "what gets
measured gets done,"[2] and my experience has shown this to be an
understatement. That motto should actually read: "what gets measured
gets *extremely aggressively* done." Executives must consider the behaviors
that their metrics encourage and must ensure consistency between
what they incentivize and what they want accomplished. If the strategy
involves innovation, market share expansion, and substantial revenue
growth, yet the performance measures motivate only price hikes, cost
efficiency, and capital productivity, then the company won't be innovative—and it won't win market share or deliver substantial revenue
growth. You get what you pay for, to coin a phrase.

Unfortunately, almost all performance measures are imperfect
when used in isolation. Since most individual metrics represent only a
piece of the performance measurement puzzle, at times such measures
will decline, due to positive events, or increase, as a result of poor
performance. These measurement shortcomings often stem from
using metrics that overlook important benefits of corporate investment. Using such incomplete measures to evaluate performance is
akin to squeezing one side of a balloon—the air is simply displaced,
leaving a distorted view.

Such measures pose the risk of motivating decisions that are
liable to undermine both performance and share value. Many
companies maintain tight managerial controls to restrict precisely
the kinds of behaviors these incentives can encourage. It seems
crazy, not to mention incredibly inefficient—instead, why not use
measures that more reliably go up when good things happen and
go down when bad things happen? Defining such measures may
seem easier said than done, but it really can be accomplished.
And when such better measures are implemented, then we can
get rid of the excessive controls—and let the incentives motivate
the right behavior.

For example, revenue growth is in most cases a significant driver of long-run value and, to some observers, more growth may always seem to be an unambiguous indicator of success. But would a narrow-minded focus on revenue growth encourage managers to terminate a business relationship with a very unprofitable customer? Such an action can preserve value even as revenue declines, by halting the destruction of value. Or, in another situation, consider a potential new product or service being sold at such a large discount that the resulting revenue doesn't even cover the variable costs involved in delivering it. An incentive driven purely by revenue growth may encourage the sale, but it would destroy value. Yes, revenue growth is extremely important, as will be extensively discussed later, but companies that emphasize revenue growth above all else are likely encouraging value-reducing behaviors.

Most long-serving executives recognized these shortcomings of revenue growth decades ago. Many began measuring profit, so only profitable growth was pursued. Problem solved? Not exactly…. It turns out that the unfettered pursuit of profit growth can encourage heavy investments that *do* deliver profit but not enough to cover the required return, meaning the cost of capital, of the investments. Managers can gather capital from lenders and equity investors; and as long as the investments they make generate enough cash flow to cover the depreciation and interest expense, profit increases. And if they reinvest retained earnings, there isn't even any interest—they simply have to cover depreciation to improve profit. As would be expected, companies emphasizing profit alone tend to overinvest, particularly in very low-return investments. They wind up carrying a much heavier load of assets and capital, which can end up dragging down their share price—like a runner weighed down by a sack of potatoes.

To be fair, many executives realize that an excessive focus on profits leads to bad motivation. But rather than improving the measure to make it more complete and so eliminate the bad incentives, they put in place tight policies and procedures to constrain capital investment. They push down "required assumptions" and forecasts, they establish unrealistically high hurdle rates, and they impose a general atmosphere of skepticism to make investments proposed by their business units and operations appear less desirable. This way, they can control their organization's insatiable appetite for new investments and can limit total capital spending within what seems to be a reasonable overall capital budget, often set based on an arbitrary percentage of sales. But I digress....

The profit measure that gets the most attention is earnings per share, or EPS. Put simply, EPS is the net income of the company divided by the number of shares outstanding. For over 20 years I've said that, paradoxically, EPS would be a much better performance measure if nobody knew we were measuring it! But instead, it's the measure that is most watched, most discussed, most estimated, most analyzed, and, unfortunately, most managed. Every business or financial television and radio program, and every financial newspaper article, talks about EPS. Brokerage analysts, as is their wont, estimate future EPS, and many investors and commentators wrongly view the analysts' consensus as a prediction of the future. When quarterly earnings are announced, everyone looks to see if actual EPS "beats" the consensus. The headlines read, "XYZ announced earnings today and fell short of consensus EPS by $0.03"—and everybody shudders.

Are there problems with EPS? Let me count the ways. First, the net income used to determine EPS is based on the accrual accounting rules in generally accepted accounting principles, or GAAP. As any corporate manager could tell you, GAAP rules are readily massaged by setting up or releasing reserves for potential liabilities, such as inventory losses, doubtful accounts receivable, or future expected or potential warranty exposures.

Second, net income can be "protected" by managements that occasionally—or not so occasionally—take extraordinary charges to set up restructuring reserves that are later used to shield earnings from costs. And these restructuring charges are often excluded by management and investors who look at "adjusted" EPS. If EPS could somehow be insulated from both arbitrary reserve accounting and this so-called "big bath" accounting, it would be a much more reliable measure.

As Warren Buffett wrote in his 1988 annual report, "Even honest and well-intentioned managements sometimes stretch GAAP a bit in order to present figures they think will more appropriately describe their performance. Both the smoothing of earnings and the 'big bath' quarter are 'white lie' techniques employed by otherwise upright managements." Buffett went on, "Then there are managers who actively use GAAP to deceive and defraud. They know that many investors and creditors accept GAAP results as gospel. So, these charlatans interpret the rules 'imaginatively' and record business transactions in ways that technically comply with GAAP but actually display an economic illusion to the world." Bear in mind that Buffett wrote these words more than 30 years ago, and they are as true today as they were then.

Third, GAAP requires that R&D investments be charged as annual expenses against EPS. Unless all the benefits of R&D are expected during the fiscal year, such expensing would distort EPS and reduce the usefulness of the measure. Companies that invest heavily in R&D tend to show lower EPS, while companies that are rapidly increasing their R&D spending typically show lower EPS growth or, in extreme cases, even a decline. The same logic applies to brand-building advertising, but since the disclosure of such investments is less consistent than for R&D, it is harder to evaluate the effects.

One company with heavy R&D investments that are rapidly increasing is Amazon.com. In 2003, Amazon's spending on technology and content—generally considered R&D[3]—was $257 million, a sizeable investment. It increased to $1.7 billion over the next seven years through 2010, for an astounding annual growth rate of 31% per year. Many companies reduce their rate of investment once they achieve scale, but no siree, not Amazon! Over the following seven years, through 2017, Amazon's R&D jumped every year, reaching a whopping $22.6 billion in 2017, for a 44% annualized growth rate. The company increased R&D at a rate never seen before for such a large company. And in 2017 its R&D investment was fully 7.5 times its net income.

Amazon is a particularly interesting case because of the large gap between its profitability and share price. Because of this, considerable skepticism has been expressed about its high valuation. But as I just pointed out, GAAP earnings provide a distorted picture of a company's true "earnings power" whenever large and increasing investments in R&D are expensed as if the benefits were expected to be entirely realized in the current year. In Amazon's case, the benefits are more likely to be spread out over several years, if not decades. Later on in this book, we will show that Amazon has likely been appropriately valued using a performance measure that more thoughtfully accounts for the company's unconventionally high R&D expenditure. But in the meantime, back to the pitfalls of EPS.

The flip side of this observation that heavy R&D can make earnings an unreliable guide to value is that companies can manage EPS by "managing" R&D. If they think they may have trouble hitting consensus EPS, they can cut a few R&D programs and, ipso facto, they meet the consensus. Never mind that they may have sacrificed their future to meet a quarterly performance target...they hit the target! If R&D and brand-building advertising were treated by GAAP as a capital investment rather than an expense—and thus in the same way as corporate investments in property, plant, and equipment—EPS would be a much more reliable measure.

A fourth problem with EPS relates to the share count, a.k.a. the denominator in determining EPS. It's true that many investors view "per-share" measures as being of great importance, since they can relate them to the per-share price. Any increase in shares dilutes the EPS, while any decrease in shares tends to drive EPS accretion or increases. A strict focus on the share-count impact on EPS would suggest that dilution is bad, and that reducing the share count is good. Unfortunately for those who think this way, research by my colleagues and me shows that this logic is flawed. For example, companies that generate EPS growth by buying back shares to reduce their share count tend to have declining price-to-earnings multiples that reduce the potential share price benefit that accrues from shrinking the share count.

A rising share count, typically resulting from issuing shares to raise funds for acquisitions or other growth investments, tends to be associated with higher share-price performance. The obsession with buybacks that has led the S&P 500 members to deploy $2.9 trillion to buy back their own stock over the five years ending in 2018 was fueled, in many cases, by a misguided emphasis on reducing share count to increase EPS. As with arbitrary reserve and "big-bath" accounting, if we could insulate EPS from financially engineered changes in the share count, EPS would be a much more reliable measure.

After both EPS and operating cash flow, EBITDA (earnings before interest, taxes, depreciation, and amortization) is the third most-cited performance metric in the "management discussion and analysis" section of public companies' annual financial statements.[4] EBITDA was popularized by leveraged buyout (LBO) firms, and later on also by private equity firms, that had a business model of finding under-performing companies that had just finished large capital investment programs. For years the investment banking industry has also valued companies based on multiples of EBITDA. This approach may have been derived from free cash flow, which, when forecasted over time, is the basis for the discounted cash flow valuation model. Free cash flow, or FCF, is simply the cash generated less the cash invested back into the business. It's what's freely available to both equity and debt investors. Despite the insights derived from evaluating free cash flow over time, most financial folk realize that as a period measure of performance, FCF is deeply flawed. To maximize free cash flow in a single period, the majority of companies would be encouraged to simply stop investing in the future!

An interesting example of this is provided by the case of Walmart from 1981 through 1996. Over this 16-year period, Walmart's FCF was *negative in all but one year*—and it was only slightly positive in that single year. The company generated literally tons of cash (how's *that* for a unit of measure?), but invested more than 100% of it in the future, increasing its store count from 330 to over 2,600 and exploding its growing total revenue from $1.7 billion to over $94 billion. Despite its persistently negative FCF, the company's total shareholder return was *more than 4,500%* over the period. (Good thing it wasn't trying to maximize free cash flow each year!)

Investment bankers realize that profit measures are distorted by noncash charges, such as depreciation and amortization, so they use EBITDA in their multiples. Although the noncash charges do distort profit measures, the lack of adequate recognition of the cost of capital is even worse with EBITDA than for profit measures. If a company were to invest $100 million and realized only $1 of cash flow, EBITDA rises by—wait for it— $1. The cash flow doesn't even have to cover depreciation or interest expense; *any* cash flow makes EBITDA increase. So, while EBITDA might provide useful valuation insights, it's terrible as a period performance measure, and it encourages even more overinvestment than profit measures.

The important thread connecting my preceding arguments is that revenue growth, profit growth, and EBITDA growth simply don't recognize the cost of the investments required to produce such growth. And using FCF as a period measure exaggerates the cost of investment by expensing it all in the year of the investment, instead of gradually over time. So, the next evolution in performance measurement was tracking some form of profit or cash flow in relation to the cumulative investment that has been made, in order to realize the profit or cash flow. Thus, rate-of-return measures were conceived to combine the income statement, which reflects profit, and the balance sheet, which reflects investment.

Rates of return are a significant improvement over measures that focus on revenue, profit, or cash flow alone. For the first time in this evolution of performance metrics, we have a means of trading off profit margin and asset intensity—two potential performance drivers that can at times be at odds with each other. Making an asset-intensive investment? That can be fine, as long as it will generate enough of a profit margin to maintain a decent rate of return. Have a low-profit-margin business? That can be fine too, as long as it uses very little capital. But whether asset-intensive or asset-light, businesses deserve the infusion of new investment funds *only* when they can generate an incremental profit margin that is large enough, in relation to the additional capital required, to deliver an adequate rate of return over time. Rates of return have revolutionized the process of managing a portfolio of different businesses by allowing comparisons across varying business models.

Many rate-of-return measures can be used, including return on net assets (RONA), return on invested capital (ROIC), and return on equity (ROE). For a typical industrial company, RONA and ROIC are widely viewed as effective, because they measure the performance of the business without regard to the proportions that are financed by debt or equity. Yet for financial institutions, where all but the longest-term debt is considered funding debt, and the interest on that debt is akin to a cost of goods sold, ROE tends to be favored. Nevertheless, in each of these cases, the return measures allow tradeoffs between the income statement and the balance sheet that are not evident in the revenue, profit, and cash flow measures discussed above.

All is not rosy with rates of return, though, because all rate-of-return measures are percentage measures. As such, they are measures of the *quality* of corporate investment only, but not the *quantity* of such investment. Would you rather invest $100 earning a 50% return or a million dollars earning 40%? This may seem like an academic question, but it's highly practical. When it comes to creating value, size matters.

Consider a management team with an annual incentive entirely based on improving ROIC. They have been very successful, they currently manage about $1 billion of invested capital, and they have increased their ROIC from 20% only five years ago to 40% during the year that just ended. Investors were undoubtedly impressed, and the share price performed well. Management, too, was paid well.

They ponder whether to invest $250 million to acquire a smaller, privately owned competitor with considerable cost overlap. With a reasonable estimate of cost synergies, the acquisition will deliver a 30% return, quite a bit higher than the company's 10% cost of capital. The acquisition seems valuable; but as management prepares to make the acquisition, the head of financial planning and analysis shares the table in figure 2 and points out that, after the acquisition, the returns of the consolidated company will be lower—so they will all be paid *less*.

	Current	+	Acquisition	=	Consolidated
Net Operating Profit After Taxes	400	+	75	=	475
Invested Capital	1,000	+	250	=	1,250
Return on Invested Capital	40%		30%		38%

Figure 2—Rate of Return Dilution

Even though the acquisition is expected to deliver a high-enough return to create value for shareholders, it's not as high as that of the base business. So, when it's added to the mix, the average ROIC will decline. This decline in both ROIC and incentive pay could induce management to pass up this valuable acquisition that is expected to earn three times the cost of capital. If they choose to pursue the deal, either management will be paid less when ROIC declines, or they will negotiate new targets with the compensation committee. How do committee members distinguish when management is suffering a true, undeserved compensation shortfall from when they are simply trying to negotiate their way out of the consequences of poor decision-making? The negotiation process takes time, and while the haggling ensues, the target company is sitting there waiting for closure…or another suitor.

Why not use a measure that better reflects when both good and bad things happen? We will get to that shortly, but before leaving the rate of return topic, it's important to note that this all can happen in reverse, too—with potentially worse consequences.

Consider another company, again with $1 billion in capital, earning merely a 5% ROIC. This may sound low, given the discussion above; but according to the S&P Capital IQ database, almost 50 of the nonfinancial members of the S&P 500 had a ROIC below 5% in 2017—so this example applies broadly.

If the company has a cost of capital of 10%, the management team undoubtedly realizes they are underperforming, so they are likely to focus on improvements, especially if the members' incentives are tied to improving ROIC. Just as in the case above, this can lead to really awkward incentives.

Consider a $500 million acquisition that management projects will deliver a 15% incremental return on invested capital, which is adequately above the 10% cost of capital. After some consideration, the board of directors approves the acquisition, and management closes the deal three months later. The announcement is well received, and management celebrates their anticipated success.

Unfortunately, during the integration of the acquired company, it is discovered that a number of key managerial assumptions used in developing their forecast weren't based on accurate information. Some buildings that had to be exited turned out to have higher than expected lease cancellation costs. Certain of the management information systems weren't compatible with the acquirer's systems. But the big one was the discovery that the main products sold by the acquired company weren't faltering due to an inept sales and marketing program, as previously thought. There were actual product flaws in the eyes of the customers, and new market entrants were stealing market share almost effortlessly. The company still had a loyal base of customers, though the growth forecast prepared before the deal now morphed into, at best, a flat volume profile—despite the growth of the overall product market.

As each unexpected obstacle to success was discovered, management lowered its forecast, and after several months they realized that what they thought would be a 15% return would be lucky to end up at 8%. For the first full fiscal year after the deal closed, that's exactly what the acquired company contributed, and there didn't seem to be much upside thereafter. The board of directors was frustrated and demanded a "look-back" into how such a debacle could happen. The stock price, which rose on the acquisition announcement, now floundered 15% below where it was before the deal—and this, despite a slight upturn in the overall market.

With all this doom and gloom, the management team was disappointed, too. The CEO demanded that someone pay a price for providing misleading information about the upside prospects. He assured investors they would, in those immortal words, "get to the bottom of it" and "never make these mistakes again."

In an almost comic irony, despite the dreadful failure of the acquisition for the company's owners, plus the rage from the board of directors, management actually made money on the deal. That's right— their incentive plan actually rewarded the improvement in ROIC. Never mind that they got there by investing a huge sum in a failed acquisition or that the share price collapsed as the bad news poured forth.

As shown in figure 3, although the deal woefully underperformed management's projected ROIC and meaningfully underperformed the company's cost of capital, the 8% ROIC on the acquisition was higher than the 5% they had before the deal. Even with all the problems encountered after closing the deal, it turns out that the acquisition was less bad than what the company was already doing. As a result, the average ROIC of the company's investments, and thus its overall reported ROIC, both go up.

Yet many observers would counter that the increase in the return on invested capital was in fact "good." In a word—no. If we get money from our shareholders and lenders at a combined expected return of 10%, and we invest at only 8%, we have destroyed value. It's that simple.

	Current	+	Acquisition	=	Consolidated
Net Operating Profit After Taxes	50	+	40	=	90
Invested Capital	1,000	+	500	=	1,500
Return on Invested Capital	5%		8%		6%

Figure 3—Rate of Return Accretion

Let's use a simple example to prove this. Imagine that the $40 million in net operating profit after tax (NOPAT) was sustainable. Many probably don't remember this from their school days, but the way to determine the present value of a sustained, or constant, stream of numbers is to divide the annual amount by the discount rate, which for a company is its cost of capital. Thus, the present value of $40 million repeated over and over is $400 million, or $40 million divided by the cost of capital of 10%. Note that the $40 million provides a 10% annual return on the $400 million.

OK, sorry to drag you through present value calculations, but here's the punch line: The company paid $500 million to acquire a company worth $400 million. Not good—whether the acquirer had a return on capital of 40%, 10%, or even 5% before the deal, it's never a good idea to invest $500 million to buy something worth only $400 million. It destroys $100 million of value, and this is why the company faces a sagging share price. Despite all that, the management team earned higher bonuses!

It's true that management's stock and option-based long-term incentives would decline because of the softness in the share price. But for reasons we will explore later in this book, managements typically focus more on their annual bonus than on their long-term incentives. So, don't count on long-term incentives to overcome the disincentives of short-term bonuses. It's better to align both long- and short-term incentives by using more-thoughtful measures and incentive structures.

True, it's perplexing that the very essence of value creation is the ability to invest at rates of return above the cost of capital, yet measuring improvements in the return on capital can provide such ineffective signals on when to invest. For those still unsold on the fallacy of rate-of-return metrics, here's one more way to see the problem.

Consider what would happen if the two examples above were business units of the same consolidated company. One business unit is earning a 40% ROIC, and the annual incentive plan would penalize its managers for making an investment earning a 30% return. At the very same time, the other business unit managers would be rewarded with higher bonuses for investing at merely 8%—and that's madness! Why would we want to punish one group of managers for an investment earning 30% while rewarding others for investing at 8%?

Does this sound like an archaic technicality that occurs once in a blue moon? I assure you that this seemingly odd quandary isn't as rare as you may think—it's happening right now across corporate America. Often, it's hard to see. But for management teams that think internal processes are none of their investors' business, they should know that curious investors, particularly activist investors, can learn a *lot* from the outside.

For companies that publish segment financial information, it's often possible to see what's happening with publicly available data alone. If the company publishes revenue, profit, and assets by segment, a crude analysis will show which segments earn higher returns by simply dividing profits or cash flow by assets. This can then be compared to an assessment of which segments are showing the most revenue growth—is the company actually growing the higher-return businesses? Or even better, we can look at capital expenditures as well as the change in assets each year, to see if the company is investing a greater percentage of segment profits back into growing the businesses that have delivered higher returns.

To illustrate this, consider United Technologies (NYSE: UTX). For the five years ending in December 2017, the company reported four primary operating segments: (1) Otis, (2) UTC Climate, Controls & Security, (3) Pratt & Whitney, and (4) UTC Aerospace Systems. For each segment, the company reports revenue, gross profit, operating profit before tax, assets, depreciation & amortization, and capital expenditures. They also report some items under "eliminations & other," as well as general corporate expenses. Investors can spend considerable time determining if these items should be allocated to the primary operating segments and, if so, how. For the purposes of this example, these items have been allocated proportional to the amount shown for each of the primary operating segments. In other words, if a segment were 20% of the assets shown for the primary operating segments, they would be assigned 20% of assets listed as eliminations & other. This is not precise, but it's a decent first step and adequate for this illustration.

For each primary operating segment, depreciation & amortization can be added back to operating profit to get a rough estimate of EBITDA. This can then be divided by segment assets to get a ballpark indication of the cash return on assets. Using this simplistic segment cash return measure, we see in figure 4 that over the last five years the Otis segment has averaged a 26% cash rate of return, while Pratt & Whitney has averaged only 9%, or about one-third of the rate of return.

United Technologies Segment	RETURN	REINVESTMENT RATE
	Estimated EBITDA/ Assets	CapEx/Estimated EBITDA
Otis	26%	5%
UTC Climate, Controls & Security	14%	10%
Pratt & Whitney	9%	41%
UTC Aerospace Systems	8%	19%

Figure 4—United Technologies Segments

We can evaluate the amount of investment in each business by examining capital expenditures as a percentage of the rough EBITDA estimate. This reinvestment rate metric (admittedly a bit primitive) has averaged 5% for Otis over the last five years, while Pratt & Whitney averaged 41%, or about eight times the reinvestment rate. This analysis is not precise, but no matter how we allocate the eliminations

& other items, the story will not change. UTX invests a lot more in a lower-return business *both* on an absolute basis *and* as a proportion of the cash generated.

This is not meant to criticize UTX. It could be that Otis has such a high market share and that it has very few adjacent business areas to enter, so there's really nothing to invest in. And the Pratt & Whitney segment may generate benefits that show up in the rates of return in other segments. It's easy to see, though, how such an analysis would help an investor, or especially a manager, know what questions to ask.

This very real example illustrates the problems with rate of return measures. If Pratt & Whitney invested in projects expected to earn a 15% rate of return, its average rate of return would rise. But if *Otis* invested in those very same projects, its rate of return would decline. In other words, its 26% return would be diluted by blending in some 15% return projects. If the business unit managers were paid to improve rates of return, it's easy to see how the reinvestment rate in Otis would be expected to be *lower* than in Pratt & Whitney, since Otis's current higher performance effectively sets a higher hurdle rate for management.

Investors typically have numerous clues available to assess the situation. For example, a review of the executive compensation section of the annual proxy statement will describe the measures that the compensation committee uses to reward management. Are they being rewarded for improving returns? A review of transcripts from earnings calls and investor presentations will offer additional clues on what management finds important. Sometimes they will come right out and say, "We have been searching for ways to invest in [our highest-return business], but thus far we cannot find anything that doesn't dilute its high returns." Bingo.

We need a performance measure that recognizes the importance of rates of return without creating a disincentive to invest in and grow our high-return businesses. The principle of economic profit first appeared in the literature as long ago as the 1800s.[5] The key performance drivers of revenue growth, profit margins, and asset intensity are brought together by economic profit into one tidy measure designed to signal whether a business is generating enough profit to overcome all costs, including the cost of capital. For those readers who have taken economics classes, the notion of *economic rent* means essentially the same thing.

For about a century or so, the notion of "economic profit" mostly languished in academic textbooks and journal articles, with an occasional practical application in the business world. One such early use almost a hundred years ago was by Alfred Sloan, who gave his General Motors executives a share of GM's "economic profit."[6,7]

Then, beginning in the 1980s, my former partners Joel Stern and Bennett Stewart, the lead founders of Stern Stewart & Co., developed, trademarked, and popularized a financial metric known as Economic Value Added,[8,9,10] or EVA®. It is worth noting that Institutional Shareholder Services, the proxy and governance advisory firm that advises investors on how to vote on public company proxy votes, acquired Bennett Stewart's company, EVA Dimensions, in 2018. So, companies should expect investors to exert more pressure to adopt EVA-like measures in the future. And, as my partner Marwaan Karame has explained,[11] it's also important that companies customize the measure to be suitable for their business model and accounting policies.

To calculate EVA, one would start with the net operating profit after tax, or NOPAT, and subtract a capital charge based on the weighted average cost of capital multiplied by the amount of capital invested in order to produce the NOPAT. For example, consider a business with $1,000 in revenue, $700 in operating costs, and a 40% corporate income tax rate. There would be $300 of operating profit before tax ($1,000 – $700), and after subtracting $120 of tax ($300 × 40%), the resulting NOPAT would be $180. If the company deployed $1,500 to fund facilities, production capacity, and working capital, and if its weighted average cost of capital were 10% (isn't it always?), then the company would have a $150 capital charge ($1,500 × 10%). The EVA would then simply be the $180 of NOPAT less the capital charge of $150, or $30.

With EVA, and its generic form of economic profit, huge advances were made over all the measures discussed previously. For the first time, we have a complete measure that captures growth, margin, and investment. And, importantly, EVA measures *both* quality and quantity. Eureka!

To illustrate the power of EVA, we will use the same examples that confounded ROIC and encouraged investments at 8% while discouraging investments at 30%. Consider the high-return business that currently earns a 40% ROIC and is seeking to invest in a $250 million acquisition that it expects to earn a 30% ROIC. The annual bonuses based on ROIC discouraged this, but what if bonuses were tied to improving EVA? As shown in figure 5, EVA would encourage this value-increasing investment.

	Current	+	Acquisition	=	Consolidated
Net Operating Profit After Taxes	400	+	75	=	475
Invested Capital	1,000	+	250	=	1,250
Return on Invested Capital	40%		30%		38%
Capital Charge at 10%	(100)	+	(25)	=	(125)
EVA	300	+	50	=	350

Figure 5—EVA Accretion

Notice that EVA rises by $50 million when this investment is pursued. The EVA of the acquisition (the middle column) is equal to the change in EVA; it's readily calculated with simple math, and much clearer than seeing how combining 30% with 40% yields a 38% ROIC. Regardless of whether the existing business earned 40%, 10%, or 5%, this new acquisition would add $50 million of EVA. Good is good.

And the same works in reverse. The managers of the other business earning 5% that were rewarded by their ROIC-based bonus for making an investment earning 8%, a rate below the 10% cost of capital, wouldn't be so fortunate under EVA. Indeed, they would see their annual bonuses decline whenever they invested at a rate of return below the 10% cost of capital, the minimum threshold for success. This can be seen in figure 6.

	Current	+	Acquisition	=	Consolidated
Net Operating Profit After Taxes	50	+	40	=	90
Invested Capital	1,000	+	500	=	1,500
Return on Invested Capital	5%		8%		6%
Capital Charge at 10%	(100)	+	(50)	=	(150)
EVA	(50)	+	(10)	=	(60)

Figure 6—EVA Dilution

In this case, EVA declines by $10 million and would do so regardless of what the acquirer's business looked like before the acquisition—bad is bad. So, EVA restores a sense of sanity in that good investments increase the measure while bad investments reduce it. Remember that value is created whenever an investment is made that earns a return above the required return on the investment.

Sadly, EVA is not flawless. To improve the measure relative to merely using reported figures in the calculation, Stern Stewart recommended making various adjustments to the accounting numbers. For example, it recommended adding back the bad debt reserve to accounts receivable and adding the change in the bad debt reserve back to NOPAT. Similarly, inventory valuation methods, warranty reserves, goodwill and intangibles, the loss on foreign currency translation, and pension expenses were all adjusted to reflect a more economic view on performance. The firm utilized economic depreciation rather than accounting depreciation in some cases to smooth the total cost of owning assets (depreciation plus a capital charge) over the life of the assets. And cash operating taxes replaced tax provisions, because they believed the cash payment was more important to investors than the tax provision on the accounting books.

At times, EVA became overcomplicated. I can attest that, when I worked at Stern Stewart, we took great pains to make only the most important adjustments to accounting for each client, so that the measure would be more understandable. But in practice, the internal accounting and finance staffers would often insist on a more "pure" measure. Translation: It often became overly complicated. What seemed like performance measurement heaven turned out to be hell for many who were regularly confused about how to calculate and apply it in making decisions.

The cynic in me thinks, at least in some cases, that the complexity was deliberately added by the accounting and finance comrades to help maintain their control and job security. Operating folks would be confused by the complexity and would have to turn to the finance intelligentsia to work out the numbers—what a shame. The idea was to give people transparent measures and a clear sense of how performance related to success. Complexity thwarted this noble goal, and the finance politburo maintained their control.

For companies that were careful in their EVA implementation and comprehensive in their communication and training, the potential complexity problem could be overcome. It took me nearly a decade to notice another much larger problem with EVA, and the better part of another to find a solution to it. The problem: EVA discouraged investment in growth.[12] Still, there *is* a way to fix it.

Notes

1   This phrase has been attributed to the anthropologist Margaret Mead. *Teaching Music Through Performance in Band*, vol. 3 (2000), edited by Richard B. Miles, Larry Blocher, and Eugene Corporon, p. 13.

2   This quote has been attributed to Peter Drucker, Tom Peters, W. Edwards Deming, and Lord Kelvin, among others.

3   Amazon doesn't disclose R&D. Capital IQ puts the full technology and content amount on its R&D line, so this is the treatment I have used when evaluating the company, though I acknowledge this is imperfect.

4   "Look Beyond EBITDA," GBQ, accessed June 22, 2019, https://gbq.com/look-beyond-ebitda/.

5   Alfred Marshall, *Principles of Economics* (London: Macmillan, 1890).

6   J. McDonald, A. P. Sloan, and C. Stevens, *My Years with General Motors* (New York: Doubleday & Company, 1972).

7   Stephen F. O'Byrne, "Three Versions of Perfect Pay for Performance (or, The Rebirth of Partnership Concepts in Executive Pay)," *Journal of Applied Corporate Finance* 26, no. 1 (2014): 29–38.

8   EVA is a registered service mark of Stern Value Management, Ltd. (originally by Stern Stewart & Co. in 1994) for financial management and consulting services in the area of business valuation, and is registered as a trademark by Institutional Shareholder Services Inc. (originally by EVA Dimensions LLC in 2008) for a number of uses.

9   G. Bennett Stewart, *The Quest for Value: The EVA Management Guide* (New York: HarperBusiness, 1998).

10 Joel M. Stern and John S. Shiely, *The EVA Challenge: Implementing Value-added Change in an Organization* (New York: Wiley, 2004). Incidentally, I wrote the book's epilogue, on "EVA and the New Economy."

11 Marwaan Karame, "Prepare for This Pay-for-Performance Measure," CFO.com, accessed December 4, 2018, http://fortuna-advisors.com/2018/12/04/prepare-for-this-pay-for-performance-measure/.

12 Gregory V. Milano, "EVA and Growth," *EVAngelist*, no. IV. *EVAngelist* is a publication produced by Stern Stewart & Co. for its clients. I was a partner at Stern Stewart when I wrote this article.

THREE

EVA Is Good, but Not as Good as It Gets

IN JANUARY 1992 I began working as an associate at Stern Stewart & Co., primarily implementing EVA. Over more than a decade I worked with more than one hundred companies in North America, Europe, Asia, and Africa. With each successive client came a stronger and more complete appreciation of EVA, not as a shiny, new performance metric but rather as a means of motivating managers to act more like long-term, committed owners.

I was—and still am—convinced that EVA is *far* superior to the measures my clients were using before. As discussed previously, EVA combined revenue growth, margin, and investment in a new and practical way that helped companies implement better measures, more effective management processes, and enhanced incentives. Our goal was to change the mindset of managers, and it worked! Nearly all my clients significantly increased their recognition of the cost of capital and began treating their shareholders' and lenders' capital more like their own money. The EVA management framework became popular, and by the late 1990s I was frequently invited to speak at conferences to explain EVA and talk about the cultural transformation I was helping to bring about.

Back then, I often described the benefits of EVA as akin to those provided by a leveraged buyout (LBO), but without putting the company at risk. The mostly successful 1980s wave of LBOs had left an indelible mark on my thinking. Countless public companies were taken private with a sliver of equity and a mountain of debt. If you acquired a $100 million company with 10% equity and 90% debt, the upside was potentially enormous. If you could increase the company value by 10% to $110 million, the shareholders doubled the value of their investment to $20 million because the debt stayed fixed at $90 million. If you doubled the value of the total company, the investors could realize a $100 million gain—10 times their investment!

The ideal target was an undervalued, mature, and cash-generating company in a stable industry with management that somehow demonstrated an inability to control costs and capital spending. It seemed like cash burned a hole in managements' pockets like a $20 bill in a 17-year-old's wallet—they couldn't resist spending it.

Imagine a hypothetical company that could generate $500 million a year in cash flow from producing and selling high-quality products. The stable cash flows insulated management from any sense of urgency. Over time, this destroyed whatever discipline might otherwise have existed, leading to ballooning costs that cut the $500 million down to $400 million and to a penchant for capital spending on unneeded and wasteful property, plant, and equipment that consumed half the rest. The company was being valued in the stock market based on delivering $200 million of sustainable cash flow each year, when its real potential was $500 million. If the stock price was $20, it could have been $50, or more. The squandered potential resulted from management's being too cozy to be concerned with continuous growth and improvement. The real eye-opener of that business best-seller *Barbarians at the Gate*[1] was not the lengths to which KKR and its rivals were willing to go to gain control of RJR Nabisco, but rather the sheer waste of capital and value that was occurring "inside the gates" under CEO Ross Johnson. And RJR Nabisco could be viewed as just the tip of the iceberg in terms of the kinds of corporate largess being dispensed before LBOs helped rein it in. Suffice it to say, corporate airplanes probably shouldn't have been used to transport the beloved family dog.

Nothing lasts forever. Largely unbeknownst to the executives leading these wasteful cash cows, by the early 1980s Michael Milken had convinced a large group of investors that high-yield debt, or junk bonds, had higher yields than warranted by their actual default rates. This stimulated strong demand from investors for junk bonds, which in turn provided the fuel for LBOs.

The demand by fixed-income investors for junk bonds made it easier to borrow outrageous sums with almost no equity at all. So private equity investors, such as KKR and Forstmann Little, borrowed all they could and embarked on a company-buying spree. It is estimated that some 2,000 LBOs valued at over *$250 billion* were completed in the 1980s. And the vast majority were successful for the investors. Often this success came with reduced employee numbers and slashed capital budgets, which in turn reduced employment in every mature U.S. industry with significant excess capacity, including oil and gas, retail, tires, banking, airlines, paper, construction, and financial services.

The heavy debt loads taken on by LBOs not only instilled an urgency to drive cash flow, but had the effect, as Michael Jensen put it, of "making the cost of capital both explicit and contractually binding."[2] And putting this kind of pressure on management proved highly effective in eradicating wasteful spending, purging unnecessary capital investments, and instigating the sale of noncore and underutilized assets. The cash flow generated by these actions was typically enormous, which facilitated debt repayment and distributions to the private equity investors. These actions also tended to increase the eventual exit value after a period of transformation.

As it is said, however, leverage cuts both ways. The substantial potential upside was balanced by the immense financial risk imposed by mountains of debt. If management struggled to turn the LBO around, or if the changes happened too slowly, they would begin missing required interest and principal payments on debt. This often led to more draconian cuts that in many cases reduced the long-term value of the company in order to meet short-term cash flow needs. This ended up being bad for investors as well as for employees, customers, vendors, and other stakeholders.

As the 1980s wore on, these risks became more significant, and a greater percentage of LBO companies faltered. This was largely due to the increase in LBO acquisition prices, which necessitated taking on even more debt. These high prices were driven by the generally rising stock market coupled with the bidding up of acquisition price premiums as a result of the expanding number of LBO investors—more than 600 by the end of the decade. The later

LBO-target companies were also often less suitable, since the most attractive companies had already been acquired in prior transactions.

Toward the end of the decade, the perils of the LBO craze were beginning to surface. Some of the largest buyouts went bankrupt, including Revco and Federated Department Stores. It didn't end well for Drexel Burnham Lambert and Michael Milken, either.[3] Though there were many pains along the way, I believe the net effect of the LBO wave in the 1980s was to the long-term benefit of both the economy and the country. But in the short term, losing your job never seems right, and the magnitude of job loss was attracting enormous public—and political—interest.

I note two ironies here. First, many of the investors in the funds raised by the private equity firms were pension plans. These organizations were charged with protecting the retirement of countless workers by intelligently and safely investing retirement assets. In their pursuit of higher returns, on many occasions they backed investors that significantly reduced job security for employees not greatly different from those whose future they were supposed to protect.

The greater irony was in Washington, D.C., as it often is. Voters, lobbying groups, and political action committees were outraged—so senators and congressional representatives were outraged, too. There was extensive criticism of LBOs, their management teams, and the leaders of the private equity firms that pursued the deals. In 1988, Representative Dan Rostenkowski of Illinois said, "There's no question that the Committee on Ways and Means will be looking at leveraged buyouts and mergers and acquisitions—and do something about it."[4]

What all those individuals and institutions didn't seem to realize was that the government, and its poorly understood tax code, had significantly increased the incentive to pursue LBOs in the first place. Because interest payments are tax-deductible to the company, profits paid out to lenders are only taxed once, as a tax on the lenders. But equity profits are taxed first at the company level and again when investors receive dividends or sell their shares. This relative tax benefit of debt made the cost of borrowing much cheaper for both the LBO firms and the companies they acquired. All the tax that was saved by deducting enormous interest payments on a large pile of debt accrued to the shareholder, which, after a leveraged buyout, was the LBO firm and its fund investors. If this debt tax benefit didn't exist, there would have been far fewer leveraged buyouts. But Congress couldn't— and still can't—agree on a single tax system for shareholders, so the incentive for LBOs persists today. So much for solutions from our congressional representatives.

Most political discussions at the time suggested that the solution was to increase taxes on debt to put them in line with those on equity. But some feared that this would render American companies, and financial institutions, less competitive globally. The better solution, they suggested, would be to adjust taxes on equity so that they would be incurred only once. Many other countries take an approach to level the cost of equity and debt without compromising competitiveness. For example, Australia allows investors to use the tax paid by the corporation as a credit against tax payable by the investor. Such "franking" of the dividend, as the Aussies call it, removes some of the incentive to pursue LBOs—and in a way that helps maintain competitiveness.

To be fair, the tax benefit probably wasn't enough by itself to motivate many LBOs. The private equity (PE) firms and their investors saw tremendous upside in finding companies with bloated spending budgets, and they made piles of money by putting them on a crash diet. So much of the spending was unnecessary that they often could slash without any burn. And they motivated management of the LBO'd companies with lucrative equity stakes, often at least partially purchased by the executives by selling other investments or mortgaging their homes. Almost all the capital was debt, so the cost of capital, as Jensen implied, became a very real cash cost. It provided a huge incentive to be successful—"make the debt payments or the company goes bust, you lose your job, and your equity stake will be worthless." Most adventurers succeeded, and a large number delivered extraordinarily high returns on investment. Unfortunately, some *didn't* succeed. Either the target company was a bad LBO target, or management didn't get it, or they were unlucky. And some good companies disappeared—because LBOs are risky business.

These days, activist investors take a similar approach to identifying target companies, but they avoid paying a control premium by only buying a minority interest. These activists then seek to win over other institutional investors in order to collectively pressure management to embrace their own strategic agenda.

My point in all this is that leveraged buyouts, and even activist investors, on average, actually serve a useful purpose. When a public company is not reaching its true potential, it becomes an LBO or activist target. I believe that aggregate U.S. national wealth is higher today, and pension plans are better funded, because of LBOs along with the cost and capital efficiency they have motivated. And this had a salutary effect even on those many other companies that worked hard to avoid being taken over in an LBO. But, as already noted, in some cases LBOs failed, shareholders lost everything, and many good people were out of work.

EVA Instills LBO-Like Incentives

What if we could create management incentives similar to those in an LBO without taking on debt and putting the company at risk? By basing management incentives on the improvement in economic value added versus the prior year, EVA makes the cost of capital very real, which encourages LBO-like cost cutting and the paring of capital budgets. Management incentives reflect a charge for the cost of capital, and bonuses only grow bigger if EVA increases. This means the company is doing a better job of covering the cost of capital: no excessive debt, no company at risk, but incentives that are similar to those provided by an LBO. It seemed so perfect.

Or so I thought.... As I worked on one EVA implementation after another, I noticed that many of my clients substantially reduced their investment in the business—even when overinvesting wasn't a problem. As a result, a number of them saw their growth slow down and eventually stall. Sure, for a few years they would see EVA jump higher as they cleared out cost inefficiencies and dealt with idle assets. But there is a limit to how high you can drive profit margins and asset productivity. If you cut too much fat, you eventually cut into the muscle. And without investment and growth, EVA stalled. Many companies became disenchanted and stopped using EVA after a few years. Those, like me, who were convinced of the efficacy of EVA, felt puzzled. We had thought EVA would become the universal model for management!

Just as I started connecting these dots, I left Stern Stewart, and a few years later I found myself at Credit Suisse after it acquired HOLT Value Associates. I joined the Buyside Insights Group in investment banking, where we used HOLT and other sophisticated equity valuation techniques to advise companies on what might happen to their share price if they made an acquisition or divestiture, bought back stock, issued convertible debt, or pursued virtually any other transaction that was influenced by equity valuation. Our group's role was most interesting.

The HOLT valuation framework[5] is based on the net present value of a real cash flow forecast derived from a prediction of fading cash flow return on investment, or CFROI, and real asset growth. The cash flow forecast is real—that is, before inflation—so it is discounted at a market-derived real discount rate. (Don't worry, there won't be a quiz on this.)

HOLT is a very sophisticated framework for valuation, which is to say that it's extremely complicated. It was designed for investors who, on average, are a fairly numerate lot, so the complexity is fine. But amid all the sophisticated complexity, HOLT has two features that, while absolutely insightful, are very simple. The first is that HOLT is "cash flow based," so it doesn't recognize depreciation as a cost, and assets don't decline in value as they get older. Indeed, HOLT actually increases the value of assets by inflation, over time.

The second HOLT contribution was that, in addition to using a return measure, HOLT explicitly forecasts an asset growth rate. Thus, it recognizes the importance of not only earning high returns, but also investing and growing an asset base, so long as the incremental CFROI is high enough. It is not simply about quality, or the percentage return; it is also about quantity—meaning the size of the asset base. This stood at odds with the capital spending cuts I saw at many of my EVA clients. During my nearly five years at Credit Suisse, I pondered the implications over and over.

Unfortunately, my reflection was cut short by the largest financial crisis since the Great Depression of 1929. Along with most of my group, I was suddenly left looking for a job. Surveying the carnage, I quickly realized there were few, if any, jobs for someone with my specialized skills and experience. So, I decided that my only near-term path was to start my own shareholder-value advisory firm. I managed to convince my friend and colleague John Cryan to join me as a cofounder, and together we managed to persuade Frank Hopson, my current partner, and Jeff Routh to join us.

It was March 2009 when we started the venture. The S&P 500 index bottomed at 57% below its 2007 peak on March 9, and nearly everyone in the business world was in a state of shock. We surmised that few companies would be interested in hiring us for any meaningful consulting projects until the crisis stabilized, so we set out to design a better mousetrap. John and I came up with all sorts of ideas about better ways to measure performance, while Frank and Jeff tested whether what we came up with actually worked in capital markets.

Armed with our knowledge of EVA and HOLT, and with the Capital IQ[6] database of financial and market information, we began testing our ideas. Our objective was to see if we could design a measure that was (1) simple enough to explain, even to those with no financial background, and (2) accurate enough for us to be confident that increases in it would consistently create value.

John, Frank, Jeff, and I thought hard about this new approach. We considered how to treat aspects of financial performance such as depreciation, R&D, leases, and taxes. From this process we created Residual Cash Earnings, or RCE, our standard measure of performance. Over time we customized different versions of RCE for various companies, including Varian Medical Systems and National Oilwell Varco, among others. Of the many performance measures that I have worked with over the last three decades, RCE remains the most useful and effective for corporate management applications.

Don Chew had been my partner at Stern Stewart. Although I don't claim to have reviewed every financial journal in existence, Don's *Journal of Applied Corporate Finance* is by far the most insightful, useful, and readable of those I have seen. He is a wonderful editor. Whenever I've written for the journal, Don pushes me to be sure I have thought through my points and my arguments and have explained them thoroughly. He is a pleasure to work with. When we invented RCE, Don gave me the opportunity to publish "Postmodern Corporate Finance,"[7] where I presented and then explained the potential uses and benefits of this new measure.

As I wrote in the article, postmodern architecture builds on the open floor plan style that evolved during the modernist movement while adding back ornamentation from earlier classical periods. In similar fashion, "postmodern" corporate finance builds on the principles of modern corporate finance. At the same time, it restores part of the emphasis on top-line growth that prevailed before the intense emphasis on returns on capital that was brought on by the ongoing shareholder value movement.

The most important difference between RCE and EVA is the treatment of depreciation. EVA recognizes accounting depreciation as a cost, while RCE does not. EVA reduces the capital on which management must earn a return by accumulated depreciation, while again RCE does not. To many, these probably sound like painstaking accounting details that can and should be left to the green-eyeshaded accounting team. I wish it were so. But the difference in the behavior that is motivated by RCE versus EVA is dramatic.

The significance can be illustrated with a simple example, which is depicted rather extensively in figure 7. What if your company invested $1 million in an asset that has a five-year accounting life? Let's assume that such assets typically stay in service for about seven years, that the asset generates EBITDA of $240,000 in the first year, and that this grows at 3% per year. The weighted average cost of capital is, say, 8%, which is pretty common these days with interest rates as low as they are.

Before going any further, forget accounting for a moment. Forget big-corporation finance. Let's take a very practical view. If you owned a small business and shelled out money to expand, you would be quite happy with a pretax cash return of 24% (i.e., $240,000 divided by $1,000,000), especially if this were expected to rise by 3% per year for seven years. And standard corporate finance tools back this up; the after-tax internal rate of return, or IRR, is over 14.7%—well above our 8% weighted average cost of capital. The investment seems desirable through both a practical and a theoretical lens.

What about the EVA lens? Since the asset has a five-year accounting depreciation life, there will be depreciation of $200,000 per year, which leaves taxable income of $40,000 ($240,000 of cash flow less $200,000 of depreciation). At a 21% tax rate, the taxes would be $8,400, which leaves $31,600 of NOPAT, or net operating profit after taxes. If we calculate the capital charge based on the beginning capital of $1,000,000 using an 8% weighted average cost of capital, we get a capital charge of $80,000. So, EVA in the first year is $31,600 of NOPAT less $80,000 of capital charge, or negative $48,400. Not a great motivator to make the investment if we are paying executives to increase EVA! At least for this investment, the EVA lens isn't very consistent with the practical or theoretical lens.

	$000s		Year 0	Year 1	Year 2	Year 3	Year 4	Year 5	Year 6	Year 7
Input Data	EBITDA	3%		240.0	247.2	254.6	262.3	270.1	278.2	286.6
	Depreciation			(200.0)	(200.0)	(200.0)	(200.0)	(200.0)		
	Pretax Profit			40.0	47.2	54.6	62.3	70.1	278.2	286.6
	Tax	21%		(8.4)	(9.9)	(11.5)	(13.1)	(14.7)	(58.4)	(60.2)
	Gross Book Value		1,000.0	1,000.0	1,000.0	1,000.0	1,000.0	1,000.0	1,000.0	1,000.0
	Accumulated Depreciation			(200.0)	(400.0)	(600.0)	(800.0)	(1,000.0)	(1,000.0)	(1,000.0)
	Net Book Value		1,000.0	800.0	600.0	400.0	200.0	0.0	0.0	0.0
Economic Value Added (EVA)	NOPAT			31.6	37.3	43.1	49.2	55.4	219.8	226.4
	Average Net Book Value			900.0	700.0	500.0	300.0	100.0	0.0	0.0
	EVA Capital Charge	8%		(80.0)	(64.0)	(48.0)	(32.0)	(16.0)	0.0	0.0
	EVA			(48.4)	(26.7)	(4.9)	17.2	39.4	219.8	226.4
	NPV		238.5	= 24% of investment						
Residual Cash Earnings (RCE)	Gross Cash Earnings			231.6	237.3	243.1	249.2	255.4	219.8	226.4
	Gross Operating Assets		1,000.0	1,000.0	1,000.0	1,000.0	1,000.0	1,000.0	1,000.0	1,000.0
	Average Gross Operating Assets			1,000.0	1,000.0	1,000.0	1,000.0	1,000.0	1,000.0	1,000.0
	RCE Capital Charge	10%		(100.0)	(100.0)	(100.0)	(100.0)	(100.0)	(100.0)	(100.0)
	RCE			131.6	137.3	143.1	149.2	155.4	119.8	126.4
	NPV		671.5	= 67% of investment						
Returns & Free Cash Flow	ROCE			3.5%	5.3%	8.6%	16.4%	55.4%	N/A	N/A
	FCF		(1,000.0)	231.6	237.3	243.1	249.2	255.4	219.8	226.4
	IRR	14.7%	= +83% over the 8% cost of capital (i.e. 14.7%/8%)							

Figure 7—EVA and RCE over Time

If we are trying to motivate managers to make value-adding investments, and if EVA pays them a smaller first-year bonus for making an investment that delivers a 14.7% IRR versus an 8% weighted average cost of capital, we have a problem. Corporate managers typically prefer a higher bonus—as they should—and they can achieve it in this case by forgoing the investment. What's more, it doesn't get any better in years two or three, as it takes until year four for the EVA contribution of this investment to be positive and to yield a higher cumulative bonus payment for the executive.

If we keep everything the same but increase the first-year cash flow from the investment, EVA breaks even in the first year when the IRR rises to over 20%. That's two and a half times the weighted average cost of capital. Investments of this nature that earn 12%, 15%, or even 18% internal rates of return over the life of the investments would have negative first-year EVA and would reduce the bonuses earned by executives tasked with improving EVA. In some cases, executives step up and say, "Though this project takes a long time to pay off, we are still making the investment in the future." But most of the time the investment *isn't* actually made. As the analysis shows, EVA stifles positive investment.

And this situation gets worse as the growth rate increases. The investment in our example generating zero EVA in year one delivers an IRR even higher than 20% when we increase the EDITBA growth rate above 3%. EVA not only stifles growth, it provides an even tougher hurdle for investments that deliver higher growth rates, since the IRR of projects that deliver zero year-one EVA would be that much higher than for lower-growth investments. This is unfortunate, but it may explain why tech industries, which often have higher than average growth rates, were less frequent adopters of EVA. The same is true in reverse. A mature industry with little growth, or even experiencing contraction, would face less of a "stifled investment" problem with EVA. Said differently, the mature cash cows that made good LBO targets were also fine platforms for EVA, but for companies with any sort of growth opportunities, EVA stifled that growth.

The root cause of these behavioral problems is depreciation. For the original purposes of accounting, which was to represent a reasonable view of profits and a conservative view of the balance sheet, depreciation makes sense. If I were a lender assessing the assets to back up my loan, I would like the idea of using depreciated net property, plant, and equipment. There is much less risk that I will be caught lending to a company with assets that are worth much less than book value. Accounting as a practice isn't wrong; it just wasn't made for measuring value creation.

Perhaps depreciation is best viewed from the perspective of an investor in a private company. Imagine that your neighbor Irma approaches you with a business idea. She wants to open a store selling work boots, and she explains all the reasons why she believes she will be successful. You don't like investing with friends, but you think Irma is smart and business savvy; further, you believe the idea might even work.

You and your spouse agree to invest $50,000 in Irma's new store. During the decision process, you evaluate alternative possible investments and how this might compare in terms of the upside opportunity and downside risk. You tell Irma you would be satisfied with earning 10% on your investment. Obviously, you'd like as much as possible, but you say you'd be satisfied with 10%. Irma says she understands your goal and appreciates the clarity.

A year later, Irma drops by and hands you a check for $5,000. You express your satisfaction along with your interest in how things will go the following year. At the end of year two, Irma hands you a check for $4,000, but is surprised at your dissatisfaction. When your spouse calls Irma's attention to your expectation of a 10% return on the investment, Irma responds that the accountants have depreciated the assets. The original investment for $50,000 amounted to a $40,000 net book value at the start of year two, she explains. She waxes eloquent about how accounting depreciation works, and then does the math out loud to demonstrate that the $4,000 check is, as she says again, a 10% return on investment. You and your spouse stare at Irma in silence, as if she had four heads.

A similar argument can be made in a corporation. Investors want a return on their investment. They are not concerned with depreciation and other noncash accounting charges. They just want a cash return on the cash they gave you. Residual Cash Earnings works this way.

The definition of Residual Cash Earnings is gross cash earnings (GCE), minus a capital charge calculated by multiplying the company's Required Return by its gross operating assets (GOA). GCE is essentially EBITDA after tax, except, where material, we add back R&D and lease expense. GOA represents the undepreciated investment in the business that must earn a return. It includes operating working capital, such as accounts receivable and inventory, plus gross property, plant, and equipment, as well as other operating assets, including capitalized R&D and leases when material. It is critical that we use gross property, plant, and equipment, *not* net. Since we are not charging for depreciation, we need to keep recognizing a capital charge based on the original cost, or gross property, plant, and equipment value. The formal definition of RCE also contains an inflation adjustment. But because inflation has been low for some time, we have not implemented this step in practice, to make the measure a bit easier to understand.

Let's go back to the $1 million investment discussed above. To determine RCE, we must first calculate GCE and GOA. Since depreciation is not a charge to RCE, the GCE would be $240,000 of cash flow less the $8,400 of tax, or $231,600. The Required Return in RCE is derived from the relationship of market values to GCE, and is higher than the weighted average cost of capital for most companies. If the Required Return were 10%, which is higher than the 8% weighted average cost of capital,[8] then the capital charge would be the $1,000,000 of GOA multiplied by 10%, or $100,000. So RCE would be $231,600 of GCE less $100,000 of capital charge, or $131,600. For managers who are being paid to increase it, RCE provides a positive signal to go ahead and invest in this value-creating project.

RCE measures after-tax cash flow, in the form of GCE in relation to a capital charge based on GOA, multiplied by a Required Return. The noncash depreciation charges are ignored, except to the extent that they shield taxes. The noncash reduction in asset values from accumulated depreciation is ignored, as well. With RCE, positive performance is recognized sooner and more evenly over the life of the investment. Notice in figure 8 that when the tax payments jump in years six and seven, RCE declines rather than increases, as is the case for EVA and ROCE.

Companies that are investing heavily in growth tend to look better from the perspective of RCE than that of EVA. The combination of high depreciation and high capital charges on assets that are relatively new weighs heavily on EVA. By contrast, companies that are making few investments, and that are essentially milking old assets, tend to look worse in RCE, mainly because it steps up the value of depreciated assets to gross book value and so recognizes their original costs.

Figure 8 illustrates the differences between EVA and RCE for this example:

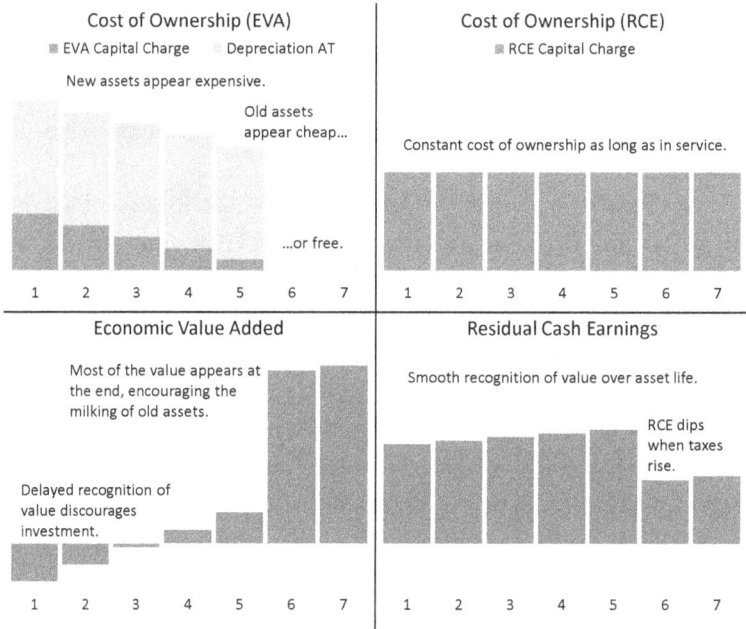

Figure 8—EVA and RCE Cost of Ownership

As can be seen in figure 8, RCE provides a smooth recognition of value over the life of an investment; by so doing, it presents decision-makers with the clearest possible incentive to undertake positive investments while discouraging the milking of old assets that are not expected to provide long-term value. More so than any other measure, when RCE rises, it does so because good actions were taken that benefit both the business *and* the share price. And when RCE declines, one can be confident it is because performance—as conceived of in terms of NPV—has also declined. Using RCE dramatically improves the ability of companies to consistently reward good performance and penalize bad performance.

Consider what happens with less effective measures, especially when they are linked to compensation. Most financial performance management in U.S. businesses revolves around performance measured against a budget. This way, goals can be set at the start of the year. For example, if the company uses EBITDA or operating profit, they can set goals expressed in terms of these metrics that reflect what they have agreed to at the start of the year. If a lot of investment has been made, the targets may be raised. Externalities can be incorporated, as well.

But, as we saw in earlier chapters, a big problem arises when performance targets are set on the basis of budgets: Doing so effectively eliminates any emphasis on delivering results in terms of true, multiyear improvements in performance for shareholders. Since poor value-creating business units tend to have dire outlooks, they also tend to be assigned modest goals that don't imply much value creation. At the same time, star businesses are often assigned "stretch goals." Ironically, in many cases the nonvalue creators earn as much bonus as the top value creators, or even more. Any possibility of getting managers to think about opportunities and accountabilities like owners do is cast by the wayside. The negotiation of the budget often has more impact on rewards than performance does.

Two steps are required to fix this and to focus behavior on true improvements in performance. First, stop measuring performance against budgets, and begin measuring against the prior year. Second, implement RCE, which provides a sufficiently comprehensive view of overall performance that improvement over the prior year is almost always a reliable indicator of value added.

The primary goal is to increase both total shareholder return (TSR) and RCE through balanced improvements in growth, margin, and asset efficiency. If the business has zero RCE margin, growth will not help, except to the extent that it leverages fixed costs and capacity, and improves the RCE margin. In this case, the focus of management is automatically shifted by RCE to margin and asset productivity improvements. For a business with a high RCE margin, the focus will be on investing aggressively in growth, even if some RCE margin has to be sacrificed. The goal is to grow RCE year-on-year and year-after-year. Sometimes RCE will decline in a single year following large investments. But this will pay off for managers only if in a later year RCE rebounds when the investment pays off. If it never pays off, management will be paid less—period. This absolute accountability focuses attention on making *all* effective investments and on culling investments in both capital and R&D that are not adequately promising.

The RCE measure is comprehensive and complete, and enables a manager to make tradeoffs, evaluate alternatives, and optimize performance. To better understand how and why RCE rises or falls, we developed the "Five Tools of Value Creation," which will be discussed in chapter 4. Two of the five tools are the Reinvestment Rate, which measures the amount of GCE that is reinvested back into the business, and Reinvestment Effectiveness, which indicates the amount of actual revenue growth delivered per dollar of investment. Both these measures are generally considered over three- or five-year periods, and can be incorporated into incentives. The use of these two measures over a multiyear horizon is designed to ensure that a manager who achieves RCE improvements while making good future investments will be paid more than one who simply delivers RCE while cutting investment.

The RCE approach will always encourage management to pursue the optimal balance of growth and returns. Figure 9 shows "Iso-TSR" lines that indicate the relative value of improving either returns or growth, given the current state of each. The main message of the figure is that for companies already earning returns that are well above the cost of capital, but achieving modest growth rates, incremental growth tends to be perceived by the market as more valuable than increasing the already high returns. Conversely, for companies experiencing rapid growth in sales and even earnings, the market—at least at some point—is likely to respond more positively to increases in returns than to further growth. Another way of thinking about this growth-return tradeoff is that, merely by virtue of management's focus on one of these two goals in the recent past, pursuit of the other becomes likely to create more value.

Iso-TSR Line Illustration

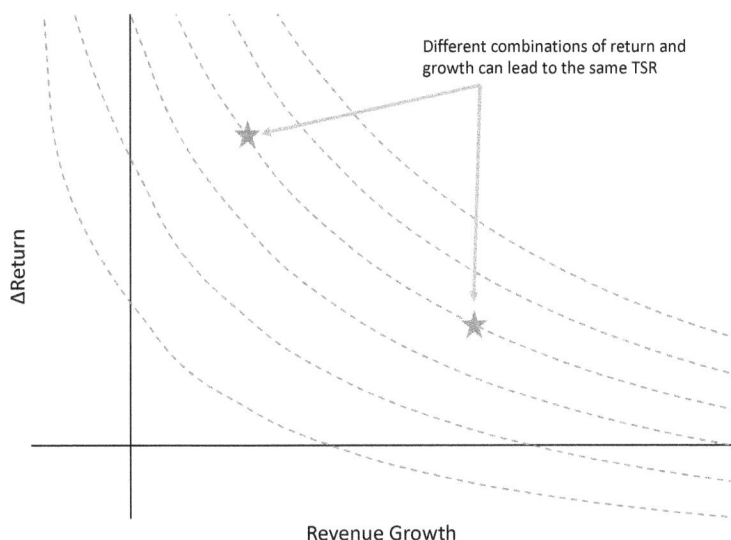

Different combinations of return and growth can lead to the same TSR

ΔReturn

Revenue Growth

Figure 9—Balancing Growth and Return

People often question whether giving up returns for growth can really lead to better TSR. So, my colleagues and I studied the facts. As reported in my paper "Don't Be Too Preoccupied with Return on Capital,"[9] sacrificing returns to achieve higher revenue growth worked for most companies over the full decade of the study, which ran from 2000 through the end of 2009. The study sample included the 1,000 largest nonfinancial U.S. companies as of 12/31/2009, excluding those not public for the entire 10-year period of the study—for a total of 765 companies. Although only 14% of the companies had both higher revenue growth and lower return on capital in the second half of the decade, 57% of these higher-growth, lower-return companies generated TSR above the median. Among these were several well-known companies, including Oracle, PepsiCo, CVS Caremark, and Procter & Gamble.

Oracle illustrates this well. During the first half of the decade, the company's return on capital hovered between 33% and 36%, while its growth averaged only 3%. And Oracle's TSR underperformed the NASDAQ in those five years. During the second half of the decade,

Oracle invested heavily, acquiring Peoplesoft, BEA Systems, Seibel, and Hyperion; growth surged to an average of 18% while return on capital collapsed to the 15%-to-25% range. This investment in growth delighted investors, and TSR outpaced the NASDAQ by 73%. Figure 10 illustrates the year-by-year performance trends.

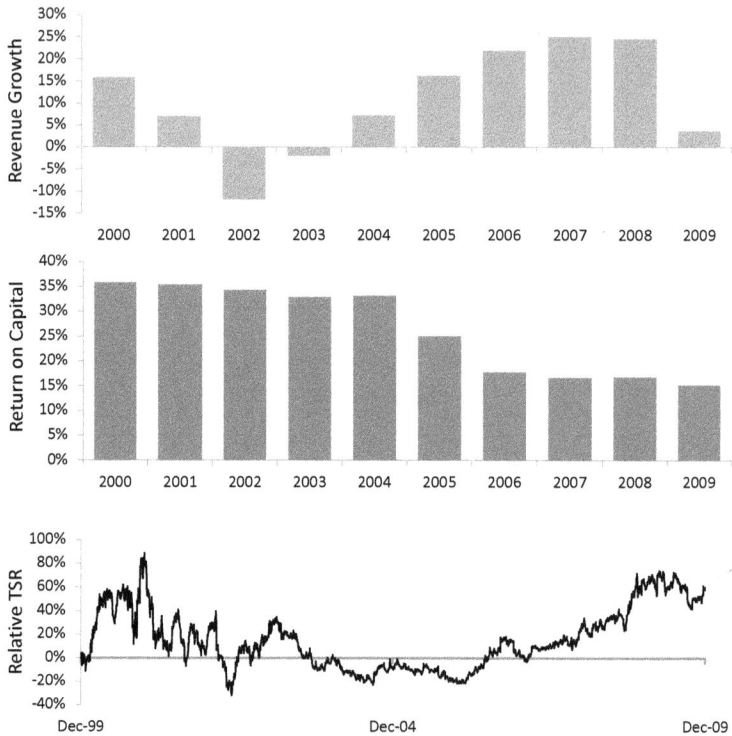

Figure 10—Oracle Growth, Return, and TSR

An overemphasis on growth or return often reflects the corporate culture. Some companies, such as Mylan and Alliance Data Systems over the last five years, have been so concerned with growth that they never seem to deliver solid returns. Other companies, like The Gap and IBM also over the last five years, have been so protective of their high returns that they have forgone growth. In both cases, these companies' TSR has suffered. Yet a number of companies have succeeded in balancing the two objectives to deliver superior TSR, for example Microsoft and Electronic Arts over the last five years.

One Important Adjustment to RCE

To ensure that RCE is comprehensive and encourages the right behavior, in businesses where R&D is critical, an adjustment may be needed. In these situations, RCE should be defined by excluding the R&D expense from the calculation of Gross Cash Earnings and adding the capitalized R&D investment to Gross Operating Assets. The standard approach is to accumulate the prior five years of R&D spending and treat it as an asset. In some businesses with longer investment cycles, it is better to use more than five years as the weighted average life, so as to reflect the longer expected payoffs from the R&D. At the same time, it's important to recognize that the weighted average life of a company's R&D investments is often considerably shorter than the average life of its *successful* R&D investments, since unsuccessful R&D investments tend to get weeded out earlier—and the earlier the better.

By capitalizing R&D we seek a better relationship between movements in RCE and TSR and, perhaps more important, better decisions by management. For example, sometimes managers squeeze R&D budgets to meet short-term EPS and other goals. They are, in essence, sacrificing the long-term value of the business to meet these short-term objectives, which is generally not in the best interest of shareholders. At other times, the pursuit of steady growth in EPS leads management to spread out R&D spending over multiple accounting periods, despite the evidence that investing more aggressively early on, or less evenly in general, may yield better results.

A case in point was Monsanto in the late 1990s, which had implemented EVA with R&D capitalized as an investment. At the time, I was the Stern Stewart project manager assigned to the company. As an interesting aside, Monsanto simultaneously hired the Boston Consulting Group (BCG), which uses HOLT. As a consequence, the ultimate measures and strategic direction turned out to be more of a hybrid than would have been recommended by either Stern Stewart or BCG alone, and were closer to what we advocate today as RCE. (The leadership of Monsanto was ahead of its time.)

During our work with the company, Monsanto faced some tough decisions regarding the timing of R&D and product-launch expenditures in its Searle pharmaceutical business unit. If they accelerated expenditures, EPS would suffer. If they spread the expenditures out over multiple accounting periods, the launches would be delayed, and the time from launch to patent expiry would be shortened. A *Wall Street Journal* article[10] documented the story. The following are excerpts:

> *Third-quarter results will be weighed down by a 40% increase in research spending at Searle, Monsanto said. That unit currently has five drugs in advanced-testing stages, when development costs are particularly high.*
>
> *"In our judgment, aggressive funding is warranted to make sure that [new] products reach the market quickly," with speedy regulatory approvals and broad public acceptance, Chairman Robert B. Shapiro said in a prepared statement. "The costs associated with these activities have depressed current income," he said.*

In response to this news, a NatWest Securities analyst, Mark Wilamuth, said he would lower his 1997 earnings-per-share estimate to $1.20 from $1.28 and his 1998 per-share estimate to $1.40 from $1.60. But how did the market respond to this information? Monsanto closed $1 higher at $39.6875 on the day of the announcement.

Undoubtedly, many companies would benefit from employing a similar accelerated investment strategy, but they seem to be too preoccupied with meeting the short-term EPS consensus of security analysts to pursue it. This is not to say that all R&D spending is always good. The two virtues of treating R&D as an investment are (1) the enhanced incentive to invest without regard to short-term EPS implications, *and* (2) the enhanced accountability for delivering a return on the R&D over time. If a company invests millions in R&D that is unsuccessful, it will have to bear a capital charge on the capitalized R&D for five or more years. But by increasing both the incentive to invest and the accountability for delivering returns, we encourage decision-making by management that is more aligned with the interests of owners.

Some say that a focus on EPS growth doesn't dissuade management from making the right decisions on R&D spending. Many managers may be out there who are willing to forgo short-term praise and financial rewards to do the right thing for the long-term success of their business. But why have a system that requires management to override their own best interests? Why not use incentives that make "the right thing" for managers and shareholders one and the same?

The same case can be made for other investments that are treated as period expenses in accounting. Among these are marketing expenditures aimed at building long-term brand value, training expenditures that seek to improve employee skills, and information systems expenses that are intended to augment long-term capabilities. For many companies, these expensed investments are growing, which creates a growing distortion of their accounting statements. In each of these cases, if the item is material and important, better behavior can be motivated by treating the item as an investment. It is much harder to do any capital market research on these items, since there are no consistent accounting standards for their disclosure as there is for R&D.

So, in RCE we don't depreciate fixed assets, and we capitalize R&D only when it's material. Is that it? No, we must perform one more standard accounting adjustment to define RCE. Some companies make extensive use of operating leases. So, to normalize the measurement of leased versus owned assets, we add back the rent to GCE, and we add the present value of lease commitments to GOA. Note that this doesn't make RCE the same between leased and owned assets—it simply applies the same treatment. Leases can be quite strategic, as discussed in chapter 12, and our treatment recognizes this.

The importance of customizing measures for the characteristics and needs of a company cannot be overstated. Consider something as simple as whether cash should be included in the asset base when measuring returns and economic profits. Most performance measurement seeks to separate operating and financing elements. So, in theory, the "operating cash" needed to run the business should be included in the asset base, and excess cash should be considered essentially negative debt. But if the primary objective is to motivate operating decisions that convert working capital and underutilized fixed assets to cash, as is often the case, then it may be best to exclude all cash from the asset base. As a result, as soon as an asset is converted to cash, it is recognized and rewarded. If cash is left in the asset base, no credit is given when assets are converted to cash.

But if the company has historically been a chronic underinvestor, and the goal is to promote operating-asset investment, then maybe cash should be left in the asset base. This way, whether management reinvests it or not, it incurs a capital charge. That will tend to motivate investment but may also overencourage distributions. Also, some companies have trouble getting subsidiaries to sweep cash up to the parent. Yet by including the cash in the asset base of the subsidiaries, this encourages transferring cash to corporate.

Naturally, there is no single right answer that applies to all companies and situations. Therefore, the customization of RCE for a particular business involves the specification of adjustments to GAAP accounting, which in turn requires the careful consideration of key financial measurement issues. In the interest of simplicity, though, such adjustments to accounting should be made *only* when the benefits far outweigh the complexity. A full evaluation of data availability and objectivity, behavioral implications, and materiality should guide the prioritization. As discussed further in chapter 9, multi-business companies also need to specify the methodology for transfer pricing and also, more generally, that for treating shared costs and assets.

Notes

1 Bryan Burrough and John Helyar, *Barbarians at the Gate: The Fall of RJR Nabisco* (New York: HarperBusiness, 2008).

2 Michael C. Jensen, "Corporate Control and the Politics of Finance," *Journal of Applied Corporate Finance* 4, no. 2 (1991): 13–34.

3 "Leveraged Buyout," Wikipedia, December 28, 2018, accessed January 15, 2019, https://en.wikipedia.org/wiki/Leveraged_buyout#1980s.

4 Robert D. Hershey Jr., Special to the *New York Times*, "Congress Is Moving Closer to Acting on Buyout Curbs," *New York Times,* December 5, 1988, accessed January 15, 2019, https://www.nytimes.com/1988/12/05/business/congress-is-moving-closer-to-acting-on-buyout-curbs.html.

5 For more on the HOLT framework, see Bart Madden, *CFROI Valuation* (Burlington, VT: Elsevier Science, 1999); *see also* David Holland and Bryant Matthews, *Beyond Earnings: Applying the HOLT CFROI and Economic Profit Framework* (Hoboken, NJ: Wiley, 2018).

6 Capital IQ is a database produced and marketed by S&P Global: https://www.spglobal.com/marketintelligence/en/solutions/sp-capital-iq-platform .

7 Gregory V. Milano, "Postmodern Corporate Finance," *Journal of Applied Corporate Finance* 22, no. 2 (Spring 2010): 48–59.

8 Gregory V. Milano, Steven C. Treadwell, Jeffrey L. Routh, and Joseph Theriault, "A Fresh Look at the Required Return," *Buona Fortuna!*, February 13, 2012.

9 Gregory V. Milano, "Don't Be Too Preoccupied with Return on Capital," *SSRN Electronic Journal*, 2010.

10 Peter Fritsch, "Monsanto Warns R&D Spending May Depress Third-Quarter Net," *Wall Street Journal*, September 29, 1997, accessed January 15, 2019, https://www.wsj.com/articles/SB875312098246726500.

FOUR

The Five Tools
of Value Creation

SOMEONE ONCE EXPLAINED to me that he had identified over 400 key business performance indicators. This, of course, calls into question how "key" each of these indicators is. If 399 of the metrics increase and one declines, what does it mean? If the one is sales growth, and it drops significantly, it could be pretty bad despite the other 399 indicators' being positive or neutral. Alternatively, if most of the metrics decline, but a few key ones rise, it could still be a pretty good outcome for the company. If, say, 223 measures rise and 177 decline—or some more balanced mix like that—what does this tell you? The point is that when there are too many metrics, the picture becomes muddled. We need a hierarchy that allows us to balance various inputs in order to optimize a decisive measure.

When it comes to performance measurement, corporate finance executives tend to layer measures on top of measures to ensure that nothing escapes measurement. Don't do it—the use of too many measures will distort the signals needed to make decisions. If you managed a baseball team, you'd view success in a game as winning, not producing runs or limiting opponents' runs. If all you cared about was runs scored, would you be happier with a 1–0 win or a 7–9 loss? What about team batting average? The ratio of strikes to balls of your pitchers? Number of errors? All these matter, but only to the extent that they help you win.

As conveyed in chapter 3, the performance measure that best indicates success in terms of value creation is Residual Cash Earnings, or RCE. When RCE rises, value is created because the increase in cash earnings exceeds the required return on incremental investment. Even moving from a negative RCE to a less-negative RCE creates value by destroying less.

Let's use this insight to reconsider the sales decline example above. In most cases, when a sales growth rate declines from 8% to –5%, it's not good. But sales growth alone isn't what's important—it's the change in RCE. Using the example in figure 11, we see that value can be created by shrinking revenue, as long as the lost revenue was destroying value. Perhaps the company did a thorough analysis of RCE by customer (as will be discussed in chapter 9) and found a group of customers who were contributing negative RCE. By discontinuing business relations with these value-destroying customers, we forgo sales and Gross Cash Earnings. But so much capital was tied up—perhaps in woefully underutilized production capacity, inventory, accounts receivable, and collateral—that the RCE contribution was negative. When the contracts are discontinued, sales drop by $50 million and GCE declines by $5 million, which is determined after considering the effects of such reductions on fixed as well as variable costs.

Year 1: Shrinking Revenue by Discontinuing Customer Contracts with Low Margins and High Asset Intensity

$millions	Prior Year	– Discontinued Contracts	= Current Year	
Sales	1,000	(50)	950	↓
Sales Growth			-5.0%	
Gross Cash Earnings (GCE)	300	(10)	290	↓
GCE Margin	30.0%	20.0%	30.5%	
Gross Operating Assets	2,000	(400)	1,600	↓
Asset Intensity	2.00x	8.00x	1.68x	
Gross Business Return	15.0%	2.5%	18.1%	↑
Capital Charge @8%	(160)	32	(128)	
Residual Cash Earnings (RCE)	140	22	162	↑
RCE Margin	14.0%	n/a	17.1%	
ΔRCE			22	∨

Figure 11—Eliminating Unprofitable Customers

Since firing customers can be a tough sell to managers, a more tactful approach can be to raise prices and let customers decide if they want to continue transacting at this higher price. This method, of course, curbs demand and can recalibrate the RCE equation to yield a positive output.

The critical result in figure 11 is that fully $400 million of Gross Operating Assets disappears; when this happens, returns go up by 3% and, more important, RCE rises by $22 million. The company is better off without these customers—let someone else who is simply focused on earnings serve them. Although this is a hypothetical example, it is a situation that many companies find themselves in. Unfortunately, some companies are so consumed with concerns about growth and absorbing fixed costs that they can't bring themselves to say no to the client or adjust pricing to spur customer attrition. They are understandably proud of their historical growth track record and are unwilling to tell investors that sales have declined. But regular reviews of customer profitability and proactive pruning of customers that destroy value are both essential to delivering continuous improvement in RCE.

Let's imagine now that this same company uses the freed-up capital to invest in organic and acquisitive growth the following year. As shown in figure 12, it invests a total of $1.4 billion in highly asset-intensive and high-margin activities that deliver incremental revenue of $250 million and Gross Cash Earnings of $160 million. The Gross Business Return on this investment is 11.4%, which is lower than the 18.1% of the existing business but well above the required return of 8%. This drives RCE up by $48 million, but drags the Gross Business Return down from 18.1% to 15.0%. Although the opening paragraph of this chapter indicates that a decline in returns is usually not great, in this case it's a *good* thing; the return on the incremental investment, at 11.4%, is higher than the required return of 8%, even if not as high as the existing business. RCE helps us peer through the muddle of figures and metrics to see whether value has been created.

Year 2: Growing by Investing in Positive RCE Projects with Lower Gross Business Returns

$ millions	Prior Year	− Discontinued Contracts	= Current Year	
Sales	**950**	**250**	**1,200**	
Sales Growth			*26.3%*	
Gross Cash Earnings (GCE)	**290**	**160**	**450**	
GCE Margin	*30.5%*	*64.0%*	*37.5%*	↓
Gross Operating Assets	**1,600**	**1,400**	**3,000**	
Asset Intensity	*1.68x*	*5.60x*	*2.50x*	
Gross Business Return	**18.1%**	**11.4%**	**15.0%**	↓
Capital Charge @8%	(128)	(112)	(240)	
Residual Cash Earnings (RCE)	**162**	**48**	**210**	↑
RCE Margin	*17.1%*	*19.2%*	*17.5%*	
ΔRCE			**48**	√

Figure 12—Reinvesting in Positive RCE Projects

It is helpful in business to have several performance drivers in the scorecard. This way we can readily assess why RCE increases or decreases. Over the years, my colleagues at Fortuna Advisors and I developed what we call the Five Tools of Value Creation. It's a take-off on the five-tool baseball player who can hit for average, hit for power, run the bases with speed, throw accurately, and field his position. Three of our five tools drive current value creation (current ΔRCE). The other two provide reliable indicators of how well the company is preparing for and investing in future value creation (indicators of future ΔRCE).

Three Tools that Drive Current Value Creation

Three measures, when viewed in combination, can provide a complete, fundamental picture of why RCE changes. But, again, each only represents one facet of performance and must be combined with the other two in order to determine if the net effect is desirable—that is, produces higher RCE. The three measures are sales growth, Gross

Cash Earnings Margin (GCE Margin or GCM), and Gross Operating Asset Intensity (or asset intensity). GCE Margin is an indicator of P&L efficiency and pricing power, while asset intensity reflects capital productivity. Together with the required return, these three measures are sufficient to understand why RCE increased or decreased during the year.

Consider a business with $1 million of sales last year, a GCE Margin of 30%, and asset intensity of 2.00x. What was its RCE last year? Assume an 8% required return. These are the steps to work this out:

Step 1.   Calculate Gross Cash Earnings, which is sales of $1 million multiplied by the 30% GCE Margin, or $300,000.

Step 2.   Calculate Gross Operating Assets, which is sales of $1 million multiplied by asset intensity of 2.00x, or $2 million.

Step 3.   Determine the Capital Charge, which is the 8% required return multiplied by the $2 million of Gross Operating Assets, or $160,000.

Step 4.   Calculate RCE by subtracting the $160,000 Capital Charge from the Gross Cash Earnings of $300,000, which yields an RCE of $140,000.

We have just calculated the base year in the first column of figure 11. Now comes the fun part: In the first year after the base year, sales declines 5% to $950,000, which in and of itself seems bad. But GCE Margin rises from 30.0% to 30.5%, and asset intensity declines from 2.00x to 1.68x, which both seem positive on a stand-alone basis. A lower asset intensity implies less investment and, therefore, a lower capital charge per dollar of revenue. With growth moving against us while margin and asset intensity move in our favor, we need some way to determine if this change in performance will add or subtract value. Of course, we use RCE. We follow the same math to determine the RCE in year 1 and the change in RCE from the base year.

Step 1.   Calculate Gross Cash Earnings, which is sales of $950,000 multiplied by the 30.5% GCE Margin, or $290,000, which is a decline from the base year.

Step 2.   Calculate Gross Operating Assets, which is sales of $950,000 multiplied by asset intensity of 1.68x, or $1.6 million.

Step 3.   Determine the Capital Charge, which is the 8% required return multiplied by the $1.6 million of Gross Operating Assets, or $128,000.

Step 4.   Calculate RCE by subtracting the $128,000 Capital Charge from the Gross Cash Earnings of $290,000. RCE is $162,000, which is an increase of $22,000 of RCE over the base year.

The same math can be applied to the year 2 information in figure 12. The benefits of 26.3% growth and an increase in GCE Margin to 37.5% are tempered when asset intensity jumps to 2.50x, but the net RCE effect remains positive. So, it's good!

Ultimately, what matters is the increase in RCE. But Revenue Growth, GCE Margin, and asset intensity all help diagnose RCE's movements, as well as inform our strategy to improve RCE. One client hadn't paid a lot of attention to its balance sheet before we were engaged. While Revenue Growth and GCE Margin looked decent, each year the asset intensity, already high, was increasing. In the end, the increase in the capital charge more than offset the improvements in Gross Cash Earnings, so RCE declined. We collaborated to determine that their capacity utilization had been declining as they added new technology assets without selling or disposing of the older assets that were being replaced. They also had been virtually giving away contract terms, including extended payment terms, to secure new orders. Without any price adjustment for the lenient terms, working capital ballooned, which dragged down RCE.

We collaborated with the client to develop a plan to improve asset productivity by better managing capacity, shedding idle assets, negotiating contract terms with greater care, and using a series of other tactics designed to better balance Revenue Growth, GCE Margin, and asset intensity. In each of the next three years, RCE improved, along with the share price.

This lack of concern for capital productivity is common and a real drag on value creation. A different client had a habit of hoarding assets for use as collateral to borrow against. We explained that if they monetized the assets by selling them or, in the case of accounts receivable, collecting them, they wouldn't need the loan in the first place.

Some have asked why I use asset intensity instead of one of the more commonly used asset turnover measures. A solid link has been established between GCE Margin and asset intensity in determining the RCE Margin, which tells us the average RCE contribution of each dollar of sales. In the first example above, if we multiply the 2.00x asset intensity by the 8% required return, we calculate the capital charge as a percentage of sales, as shown in figure 13.

	Dollars	Margin
Sales	1,000	
Gross Cash Earnings (GCE)	300	*30.0%*
Gross Operating Assets	2,000	
Asset Intensity	*2.00x*	
Capital Charge @8%	(160)	*(16%)*
Residual Cash Earnings (RCE)	140	*14.0%*

Figure 13—Asset Intensity and Margins

In this case it's 16% (i.e., 2 × 8% = 16%), which can be subtracted from the GCE Margin of 30% to determine the RCE Margin of 14%. The capital charge as a percentage of sales sets the minimum GCE margin needed to have positive RCE. Said differently, there is a maximum asset intensity that sets the RCE break-even, given a particular level of GCE margin.

As will be discussed in chapter 7, the RCE Margin, or RCM, combines the GCE Margin and asset intensity tools and indicates the RCE of each dollar of sales growth. This makes it a perfect tool for evaluating the tradeoff between growth and capital productivity when determining a strategic position. The higher the RCM, the more valuable each dollar of sales, and the more a company should invest to fuel growth. More on that later.

Two Tools that Drive Future Value Creation

In early 2011, a client situation prompted me to develop a new way to measure future investment. I detailed this new method in an article entitled "Are You Reinvesting Enough?" in *CFO* magazine.[1] The client faced desirable investment opportunities, but the CFO chose not to cut her substantial share repurchase program to fund the new investments. Instead, she decided to finance the new outlay by slashing investments in two other businesses, both of which were growing well and earning strong returns. So, she missed an opportunity to step up the rate at which the company profitably reinvests, which would have driven its share price higher over time.

My article introduced the concept of the "Reinvestment Rate," which quantifies the percentage of Gross Cash Earnings that is reinvested in the business. To calculate the reinvestment rate, add capital expenditures, acquisitions, research and development, and other investments (including changes in working capital), and divide that sum by Gross Cash Earnings. Top-line growth is, obviously, an important driver of TSR, as has been discussed. What may be less intuitive is that sustained growth is typically the result of having a higher reinvestment rate. My colleagues and I have studied the overall market and many sectors and industries, and have consistently found that the companies with the highest reinvestment rates have delivered higher median compound annual growth rates (CAGR) in revenue. In the original article, our research study sample was the largest 1,000 nonfinancial U.S. companies, excluding those that were not public for the full decade ending in 2009.

It may be easy to see that high reinvestment rates drive more revenue growth. However, is value really being created? Our capital market research has demonstrated time and again that the highest reinvestment-rate companies typically deliver better TSR. In the original study, the benefits of reinvestment are so significant that over 200 of the 277 companies that reinvested more than 100% of their cash flow for the full decade delivered higher TSR than the median of the 0%–50% reinvestment group. This outperformance by high-reinvestment companies is particularly noteworthy, considering the tough economic environment of the decade ending in 2009.

Because the reinvestment rate is an important driver of TSR, we made it the fourth tool of what eventually became the Five Tools of Value Creation. The goal is not to maximize the rate of return, but rather to balance the pursuit of higher returns with adequate reinvestments to fuel business growth. Although larger companies may find it difficult to match the reinvestment rates of small companies, many large companies would benefit from a higher reinvestment rate, even if the average rate of return declines (as in the Oracle example shown in figure 10 in the previous chapter).

Our research findings indicate that this is *not* a superficial stock market effect whereby investors arbitrarily assign higher multiples to high-reinvestment companies. In fact, it is quite the contrary. While high reinvestment typically boosts TSR over time, it does not increase average price-to-earnings multiples or enterprise value-to-EBITDA multiples. Nor does high reinvestment boost valuation at a point in time. Instead, it drives value appreciation over time by improving growth prospects, and usually RCE, too. Unfortunately, in an odd paradox, executives who are too fixated on current valuation multiples usually seek to maintain their current strong operating metrics. To avoid risk they tend to underinvest, which limits stock upside.

Indeed, most executives at companies with low reinvestment rates understand and agree with our research findings that high reinvestment rates add value. But many claim they don't have sufficient opportunities for profitable reinvestment. One CFO defended his position by stating that he "never turns down positive net-present-value investments." But on closer inspection, we found that the company's culture and internal processes together put excessive emphasis on avoiding bad investments. For upper middle-level managers, there appeared to be an asymmetry between reward for success and punishment for failure: the managers tended to feel they received only small amounts of praise for good investment outcomes, but major disciplining for bad ones.

This asymmetry comes on top of, and no doubt reinforces, a natural behavioral bias known as "loss-aversion." When coupled with processes that disproportionately punish losses, this encourages indecision and inaction. It also leads to less experimentation, even in situations where the costs are relatively small and the benefits potentially large.

Such risk-averse corporate cultures are common. Given these internal and external influences, all but the highest-return investments are habitually shelved. In many companies, arbitrarily tight capital expenditure budgets set a strategic tone of restraint that, in turn, sets the bar very high for operating managers. And because of this tendency of these "high-return cultures" to produce low reinvestment-rate outcomes, such cultures need to change if top executives want to provide adequate support and incentive for desirable growth investments.

But is the reinvestment rate likely to be more valuable for companies that are already earning high internal cash-on-cash operating returns than for companies with low returns? In our research, we found that whether you have high, medium, or low returns, TSR is positively related to higher rates of reinvestment. As we would expect, however, high-return companies get a larger benefit from reinvestment than low-return companies. On the other hand, lower-return companies need to be more careful since their success rate with reinvestment—a subject to be discussed in detail later—tends to be lower than for high-return companies.

Some may question the causality in our findings that high-reinvestment companies typically achieve higher revenue growth and higher TSR. Are the successful companies the only ones that can afford to reinvest more? Do the "good" industries skew the data, making reinvestment appear desirable for all? We have conducted extensive research in our client studies of their individual industries, including healthcare, industrial, energy, technology, and other sectors. The results are consistent across the board.

Hard question: Are you reinvesting enough? Management teams should assess their companies' reinvestment rates both on an ongoing basis and as part of the annual planning process. During this process, they should consider capital expenditures, R&D, marketing, and even acquisitions as means of building future value. It also helps if they examine the reinvestment rates across different business units to see if enough reinvestment is occurring where the returns and opportunities are highest. More on this in chapter 9.

A few practical steps can be taken to ensure that the reinvestment rate remains at the level likely to maximize value. Most important, try to create a culture in which positive feedback on investment success is at least as strong as negative feedback on unsuccessful investment. Recognize that a willingness to fail is essential if you want managers to invest in clearly valuable projects despite facing uncertain conditions. And in performance reports and analyses, avoid measuring investments as a percentage of sales. Instead, be sure to measure and discuss the reinvestment rate as a percentage of Gross Cash Earnings, which is "pre-investment" cash flow. By thus linking reinvestment with cash profitability, management effectively signals and reinforces their company's intent to invest heavily in its most profitable businesses.

For a few years we were content to use just four tools of value creation—until we ran into a challenge when evaluating a certain client's financial and share price performance. The client had strong RCE that stemmed from a desirable combination of a high GCE Margin and relatively low asset intensity, both in comparison to peers. Some of the company's businesses offered products at premium prices that provided a big boost to GCE Margin. Other of its businesses used advanced manufacturing processes that enabled them to achieve their sales volumes with substantially less capital invested than peers, which provided an asset-intensity advantage. Overall, when the company's high RCE Margin was multiplied by its fairly large sales figure, management was producing a very high level of RCE—one measured in billions of dollars.

What's more, the company had an industry-leading reinvestment rate, which, as discussed above, tends to lead to strong revenue growth as well as TSR. The client seemed to invest more as a percentage of GCE than any of its competitors. Yet, despite all these signs of success, its top-line growth was anemic. Its managers were investing billions and seemingly getting little for it. It became clear that their investments weren't very effective.

While looking for a simple way to evaluate and portray this aspect of performance, we came up with our fifth and final tool of value creation. We started by considering some version of incremental return on investment, but RCE and the three drivers of current value creation already told us pretty much everything we need to know about incremental returns. Our aim was to capture a distinct and new aspect of performance—one that was not being reflected in the other four tools.

In the end, we developed a simple measure we called Reinvestment Effectiveness, defined as the three-year increment of sales (measured in dollars) as a percentage of the amount of investment in capital expenditures, R&D, marketing, acquisitions, and working capital (also measured in dollars). In other words, how many dollars of sales growth are you getting per dollar of investment?

A "minimum acceptable" rate of Reinvestment Effectiveness can be determined as a function of the GCE Margin. The formula is simply the required return divided by the GCE Margin. A company with a GCE Margin of 15% and a required return of 10% must have Reinvestment Effectiveness of at least 67% (10%/15%) to generate enough sales and GCE to overcome the incremental capital charge. To check this, assume we invest $150,000 at Reinvestment Effectiveness of 67%, so the incremental sales are $100,000. Since the incremental GCE is 15%, GCE is $15,000, which is equal to the capital charge (10% of the $150,000 investment). At a Reinvestment Effectiveness above 67%, the investment would drive RCE higher; below this level, RCE would decline, since the incremental GCE would be less than the incremental capital charge.

Having told you this, it's important that I also stress that there is no precise answer to how much Reinvestment Effectiveness is enough. Companies with exceptionally high RCE Margins can get by with a Reinvestment Effectiveness of 0.30x or even 0.25x; companies with lower RCE Margins will need a much higher Reinvestment Effectiveness to drive improvements in RCE.

Now, let's consider Amazon again, as we did in chapter 2. Over the five years through 2017, Amazon had reinvested a whopping $99 billion back into the business, which is a 94% reinvestment rate when divided by the cumulative Gross Cash Earnings over the period. Its largest investment category was $67 billion in R&D, followed by $32 billion in capital expenditures and $14 billion in acquisitions—primarily the Whole Foods acquisition. Offsetting these investments was a reduction in operating net working capital of $14 billion. Note that Amazon actually invested $113 billion but had $14 billion of it funded by structuring its operating working capital policies such that current liabilities are increasingly worked off more quickly than its current assets are replaced. In other words, it gets paid before it pays—and that helps fund its growth investments. Its working capital policies effectively paid for Whole Foods!

Amazon's reinvestment rate is above the median rate for the S&P 500 over this period. But to see how well Amazon has performed, we must look at the company's reinvestment effectiveness. During this period, its revenue increased by $117 billion, which, when divided by the investment of $99 billion, implies a reinvestment effectiveness of 118%.

In summary, Amazon has been reinvesting 94% of its Gross Cash Earnings back into the business; it had a reinvestment effectiveness of 118%; and its RCE Margin has averaged 14.1% over the five-year period. It's no wonder that its RCE increased more than fivefold from $5.4 billion in 2012 to $27.7 billion in 2017. During this period, Amazon's five-year TSR was 366%, or 3.4 times the 107% TSR of the SPY ETF that tracks the S&P 500.

Some say, "Sure, Amazon invests a lot—but will they ever generate a profit?" Indeed, Amazon seems to be a valuation conundrum to those who follow accounting net-income and EPS trends. Some say it is unprofitable; irrational investors are simply wowed by its story and its service. It's easy to see how those who cherish EPS statistics can draw such conclusions from graphs like that in figure 14.

Even in 2017, as the company's EPS finally turned meaningfully positive, its average price-to-earnings multiple, using daily share prices and the last four quarters of reported EPS, averaged over 200x. Many observers see that as one of the biggest con jobs of our time. Such a view, which continues to be widespread even to this day, remains in thrall to the myth of EPS and accounting convention; and in so doing, it has completely missed one of the most remarkable episodes of value creation in our time.

But when looking through the RCE lens, we see Amazon's massive R&D expenditures as *investments*, and we also view its heavy capital expenditures on a cash basis. With these two simple alterations to basic accounting practices, we see the true value that Amazon is creating. It isn't unprofitable at all! In fact, it is hugely profitable; it's just that it is reinvesting most of its profits back into the business, and a large proportion of those investments are in a form that accountants require to be expensed. This preponderance of expensed investments makes it harder for investors to understand the profitability. But such investments also end up providing a massive tax shelter, as contrasted with investments in capital equipment, for example, where the tax benefits are usually realized more gradually, over time.

Price and EPS for Amazon.com, Inc.

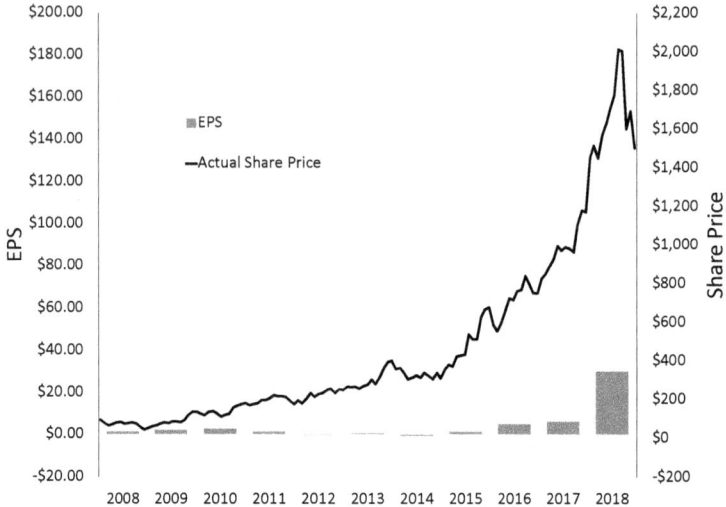

Figure 14—Price vs. EPS for Amazon

Let's pause for a moment and explain the RCE framework for valuation. Valuation through the RCE lens is based on a methodology similar to discounted cash flow. Enterprise value is estimated as Gross Operating Assets (GOA) plus the present value of RCE. When RCE is zero, no value is being created or destroyed, and estimated enterprise value equals Gross Operating Assets, no more and no less. When RCE is positive, the enterprise value is expected to rise as the company delivers returns above the required return demanded by investors—and value is destroyed by companies and their investments in which RCE is negative. One simple way to come up with an estimate of the present value of RCE is to capitalize RCE as if investors were pricing in a future in which RCE remains at the current level. Moreover, when calculated across the full market, such simple estimates of enterprise value based on capitalized RCE correlate remarkably well with actual enterprise values.

How does this work for Amazon? As shown in figure 15, the share price has tracked Amazon's RCE-implied share price quite well.

RCE Implied Share Price for Amazon.com, Inc.

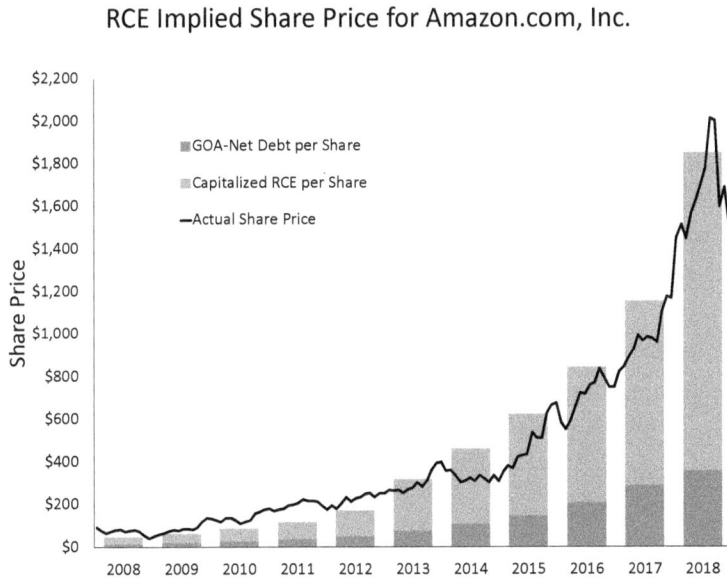

Figure 15—RCE Implied Share Price for Amazon.com

There is no con job—Amazon has in fact created significant value, and the market has recognized it. At times, the share price has been a bit below the price implied by RCE; at other times it has been a bit above it. It's natural for there to be expectations of improving or declining RCE when positive or negative news surfaces. But, over time, investors have generally followed the capitalized RCE valuation pretty well—even before RCE was created, which is an important point. It's not that thousands of investors are out there calculating RCE. Not at all. But savvy investors *do* care about growth, margin, and asset intensity. They prefer cash flow to profits, and they *do* see R&D as an investment in the long-term growth, viability, and cash generating capacity of the business. RCE captures each of these performance attributes in one easily calculated measure. This is what gives us confidence that if a company grows its RCE, its share price is likely to rise, even if its EPS doesn't.

Bringing Together the Five Tools of Value Creation

We designed the Five Tools of Value Creation to capture the aspects of financial performance that drive share prices in as simple a framework as possible. We don't need 400 key performance indicators; we just need five. Current value, or simply ΔRCE, is driven by revenue growth, GCE Margin (also known as Gross Cash Margin or GCM), and asset intensity. Future value is driven by the reinvestment rate and Reinvestment Effectiveness. The goal is to drive positive ΔRCE through the Five Tools of Value Creation, with reinvestment, innovation, excellence, and a long-term focus. The relationship of these measures is shown in figure 16.

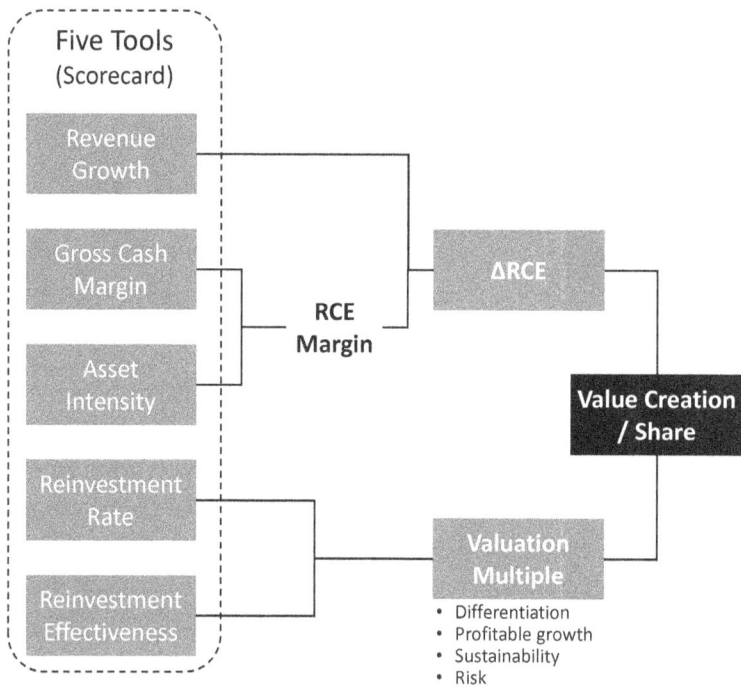

Figure 16—The Five Tools of Value Creation

We help our clients customize the five tools and then, in performance scorecards and planning documents, show how they feed into and help evaluate both RCE and ΔRCE. With one client, we asked how they could expect to generate their forecasted growth with what was a particularly meager capex budget. The company would have needed twice their peak historical Reinvestment Effectiveness to achieve its planned growth for the investment. To be fair, in some cases a new type of investment is conceived, with much higher or lower Reinvestment Effectiveness, and in other cases there is meaningful underutilized capacity that can support growth. But at the very least, Reinvestment Effectiveness helps managements consider whether they are making logically consistent predictions.

The interaction of the five tools can be insightful in many other ways, too. For example, in the case of another client, growth was slowing but they were still investing heavily in the future. Reinvestment Effectiveness had dropped off, which suggested a need for reevaluation. It turned out that many of the new investments supported products that were more differentiated and expected to have higher GCE Margins than the baseline company average. So, when we considered how this other key variable was interacting with the lower Reinvestment Effectiveness, we were able to determine that such investments would be adequate to still drive RCE improvements.

A decline in Reinvestment Effectiveness can sometimes be acceptable. An example is when a company has a high concentration of new acquisitions that cost relatively more than past organic investments per unit of growth. This can still be value-increasing, if it provides sufficient growth and GCE Margin, over time, to deliver positive RCE improvements. Another case is a switch to more R&D investment, which takes time to generate sales and would reduce short- or medium-term Reinvestment Effectiveness. In the long term, this will still pay off if the R&D is successful and RCE increases.

As with anything new, it can take time to see the trends and interactions among the five tools. Yet the only way to get there is to use them. Discussions during operating performance reviews and plan evaluations should actively use the five tools as part of the dialogue until it becomes natural. Once the team gets there, the clarity used when discussing performance and projections will greatly enhance understanding of what is happening and what needs to be done.

It is important to track the reinvestment rate and Reinvestment Effectiveness, since improving RCE is more valuable when it can be done while investing effectively in the future, rather than at the expense of it. A general theme of this book is that many managers are inclined toward short-term thinking, profit and cash flow "squeezing," and underinvestment. By including the reinvestment rate and Reinvestment Effectiveness on an equal footing with revenue growth, gross cash margin, and asset intensity, managers can be encouraged to balance both the short and the long term.

Alternative for When Revenue Is Less Meaningful

In some companies, revenue fluctuates with commodity prices that are simply passed through to the customer by contract. For example, many chemical companies are exposed to volatile input costs related to energy prices and various feedstocks. So, even as revenue rises and falls with these changing costs, this volatility typically won't flow through to EBITDA or RCE.

Such companies have learned over the years to look at returns on capital rather than margins, since the latter may be irrelevant because of the pass-through structure. For these companies, the standard Five Tools of Value Creation lose some of their explanatory power as they are influenced by the revenue fluctuation.

Figure 17 shows one way of adapting the drivers to such a situation. The changes in RCE are driven by the same reinvestment rate that is used in this case to drive the growth in Gross Operating Assets. This is combined with the RCE Return, which is simply RCE divided by Gross Operating Assets, to determine the current and future growth in RCE. The RCE Return can also be portrayed as the spread between Gross Business Return and the Required Return.

It's also worth noting that this pass-through approach is more akin to the HOLT framework, as discussed in chapter 3, which drives cash flow forecasts from Cash Flow Return on Investment and inflation-adjusted gross asset growth.

Of course, we could define the RCE drivers per store for a retailer, per aircraft or passenger mile for an airline, per barrel of oil equivalent (production or reserves) for an oil and gas company, or even per employee for a professional services firm. It works well as long as the drivers are few enough in number to be understandable and mutually exclusive enough to each reflect discrete aspects of performance. By customizing the Five Tools of Value Creation for the specific business model, the framework becomes more useful.

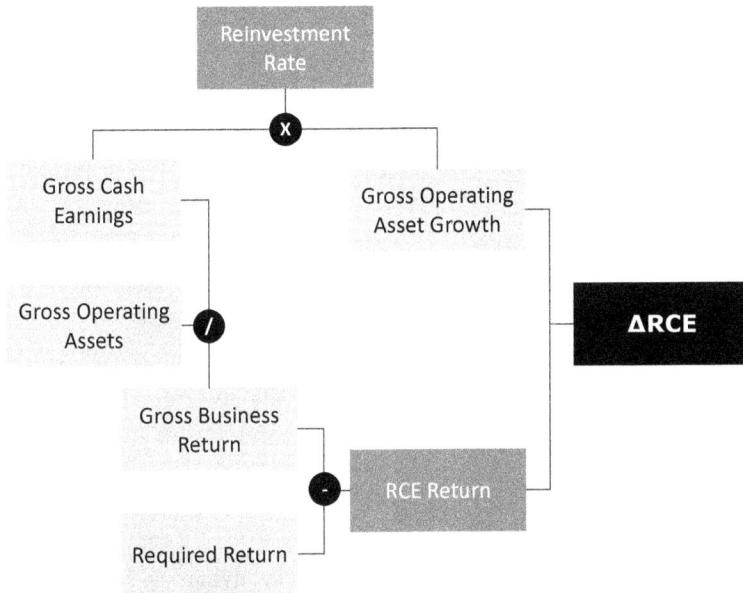

Figure 17—RCE Drivers for Revenue Pass-through Businesses

Moving Further Down the Measurement Hierarchy

The focus should, of course, be on improvements in RCE, with the five tools providing the next layer of performance insights. All companies have secondary performance drivers that feed into these tools and calculations, so understanding and linking these inputs to the five tools can sometimes be useful. This is, naturally, very different than large scorecards with hundreds of loosely related metrics.... The following are examples of a few key lower-level metrics:

Based on the job a person has, they may need to measure days of sales outstanding (DSO), inventory turns, production yields, or similarly important localized measures. If you are responsible for customer collections, DSO is a fairly important indicator of how well you are performing. To determine DSO, simply divide the accounts receivable balance by total annual revenue, and multiply by 365. Of course, the DSO may be rising in a way that is not the collection department's fault (sure it's not). No, really. Maybe, during the last round of negotiation, the customer requested to pay in 120 days, and your sales team responded by negotiating such a meaningful price increase that it more than covered the increase in capital charge that was expected to result from the extended payments. Although companies routinely measure DSO, when evaluating the performance of customer collections, what you really want to measure is the actual DSO versus the expected or contracted DSO. Then you hope that your negotiation team managed to achieve prices that reflect any financing your company is providing to the customer through the extended payment terms.

Extended credit terms are essentially a loan and should be evaluated as a financier would evaluate a borrower. If the customer seems "too willing" to accept a substantial price increase in return for the extended payment terms, perhaps they are unable to secure financing elsewhere, and you should be on your guard and alert to this possibility.

Similarly, procurement and inventory management folks may benefit from tracking inventory turnover, which is simply the annual cost of goods sold divided by the inventory. It reflects the number of times per year, on average, you turn over inventory. It may seem that it's always good to have less inventory, or higher inventory turns, since this will make the capital charge lower in RCE. Yet the optimal inventory level is not necessarily the lowest. The value-maximizing level should be thought of as the one where any further reductions would cause a manufacturing slowdown that results in either a cost increase or a decline in sales volume attributable to stock-outs. Either of these problems could cost you more in Gross Cash Earnings than you gained by reducing inventory and the capital charge. The larger your profit margin, the more inventory you should hold, since any lost sales will cost you in RCE.

Manufacturing yield can also be a useful measure for those trying to improve the efficiency and effectiveness of the production process. But, again, a higher yield is *not* always better, especially if it takes considerable investment and cost to achieve a small improvement.

Scores of such measures are available—maybe some 400 of them— that can each provide an important signal to particular operations departments and corporate functions. But as shown in the examples in this chapter, each must be used with care. To consistently make the best decision, it's important to understand and take into account how all of RCE's key inputs feed into the final RCE output.

Notes

1 Gregory V. Milano, "Are You Reinvesting Enough?," CFO.com, March 4, 2011, accessed January 15, 2019, http://ww2.cfo.com/accounting-tax/2011/03/are-you-reinvesting-enough-2/.

PART II

SETTING GOALS AND DEVELOPING BUSINESS PLANS

FIVE

Setting Aspirational Goals

IF AN INTERVIEWER were to ask LeBron James how he expected his team to do before a game, he wouldn't hedge and say, "We're probably going to lose" just to impress everyone if they happen to win. With his average of 27.5 points per game in the 2017–18 season, he would have been unlikely to say, "I hope to score at least 6 to 8 points tonight," seeking praise even if he scores just 15. People who follow sports have an absolutist mentality—"they won" or "they lost." Over a full season, it's "they were champions"—or they weren't. Of course, some teams have better chances than others, but few athletes plan for mediocrity. Even those teams that are expected to finish last in their division aim to improve on their situation.

The 2015–16 Premier League soccer season was an excellent case in point. But before we get to that, consider that European sports don't have all the competition levelers we have in the United States. They lack salary caps and significant revenue sharing. They don't conduct drafts that reward the worst teams with the best draft picks, as we do here in America. Europe's best teams have the most success; they attract the most fans; they make the most money; and they can afford the best players. It's capitalism. If you listened to U.S. sports-league executives, you would think the only way to have commercial success is to install competitive parity. Every time a team gets an edge, these executives believe they need to remove it by setting salary caps or rewarding failure with better draft picks and other subsidies. European football is a talent-concentrated sport with only a few teams that have a real chance of being named champion in each league in a given year. According to Total Sportek's international sport popularity ranking, which is based on 13 well-thought-out factors, soccer is the most popular sport in the world. Its fan base of over 4 billion people is far ahead of the 1 billion fans of the next most popular sport, basketball. Baseball and American football rank 11 and 12, respectively, on the list of the top 25 international sports. Maybe ensuring competitive parity isn't that important to fans.

Against this backdrop, the achievements of Leicester City Football Club are remarkable. In the summer of 2015, the betting odds for Leicester to win the Premier League were 5,000 to 1—and rightfully so. It seemed they had no chance. In England, the lowest three teams in each league are "relegated"—that is, forced to trade places with the top three teams from the league below. What an awesome concept! If you underperform, you are *demoted*—as opposed to what happens in the United States, where we shower the worst teams with top draft picks and revenue sharing. It's as if we were trying to find ways to *reward* failure—a really bad idea.

As the prior Premier League Season drew to a close in the spring of 2015, Leicester was struggling. With a mere nine matches left, they had a record of four wins, seven draws, and 18 losses; so they were in danger of relegation. But the team had other ideas. They won seven, tied one, and lost only one of the last nine games, managing to avoid relegation. It was impressive, to say the least, but the idea that Leicester might win the Premier League championship the following season was far from anyone's mind. Thus the 5,000-to-1 odds.

To upset the apple cart, during the offseason the team replaced the manager who led them to their great finish that spring with Claudio Ranieri. Many fans were puzzled by the move, but it worked out about as well as it could have. Ranieri and his Leicester club did more than merely stay in the Premier League—they won it all the very next year! Since 1992 when the Premier League was created, only five teams had won the league championship. Now there was one more. Leicester City stunned everyone.

The Leicester coaches and players undoubtedly tried hard to stay grounded and avoid overconfidence. Publicly, they never boasted about their chances of winning, but deep down they believed they had a shot, and they played their hearts out all the way to the final week.

They set their sights high and achieved what almost nobody deemed possible. They went from near-worst to best in a single season.

Sports offers many such examples. That's why we watch. If the favorite always won, it wouldn't be interesting at all. All sports fans have had times when their team was expected to lose. Although they know a win is not likely, they know it's possible. They watch because every once in a while, they get the elation that comes from an upset. The experts hold up their logic, show film clips from previous games, and trot out myriad statistics to support their claim. And then the underdog wins anyway—what euphoria! When it happens, we can't wait to talk smack to the doubters in the office on Monday.

The same is true in business. Every year certain management teams, though underestimated within their industry, somehow achieve an outcome the experts didn't see as possible. The only difference is the experts are on CNBC and in *The Wall Street Journal* instead of on ESPN. Can your corporate team be one of these upsets, and what does it take?

Let's look at it from another perspective. Say your company is the favorite. Sure, there are other companies that threaten your industry lead, but your management team is the best and is expected to sustain the advantage. How do you avoid an upset? What does it take to maintain a lead and avoid being Microsoft's IBM? Or being Google's Yahoo (or, heaven forbid, Ask Jeeves)?

It all starts with aiming high. Few success stories in sports or business begin with a goal to be mediocre. We don't want to set up unrealistic aspirations; but from wherever we are, we *do* want to stretch higher. We want to move up the rankings and inspire ordinary people at all levels of the organization to achieve extraordinary outcomes.

Most executives understand that they need to aim high to achieve success. This is why it's so confounding that the preponderance of them use annual budgets and plans developed by their subordinates as tools for setting performance targets in their incentive plans. Once we tell the head of a business unit or functional department that we're going to use their plan as a benchmark for success, we have limited their motivation to aim high.

This is a hugely important point in the context of the overall message of this book.[1] Given whatever level of performance a manager actually achieves at the end of the year, if the budget was set at a higher level of performance at the beginning of the year, they will look worse against it—and most often earn less money. If they seek to earn more, as they should, they have an incentive to plan for mediocrity. The technical budget development term for this is "sandbagging." You know it well, for you have seen it many times—though doubtless only by others. But despite the common awareness of the problems that arise when using budgets as the basis for setting targets, most companies still do it.

In chapters 13 and 14, I will provide a more complete view of what's wrong with executive compensation, and will offer more-comprehensive solutions for fixing it. But for now, suffice it to say that incentives should *not* be linked to performance against a budget or a plan.

Once planning, forecasting, and budgeting are freed from the shackles of the incentive target-setting process, forecasting and budgeting can become more useful for actual planning. To begin the planning process, a good start is to set "stretch goals." These goals should be a bit uncomfortable, so that they motivate strategic ideas that will transcend the status quo, since we don't want our managers to *just* extrapolate what we do now. We don't want mere incremental improvements here and there; we want game-changing strategic ideas—even if they cannibalize what we're already doing. Why wait for someone else to disrupt the industry when *we* can do it ourselves and keep the benefits to ourselves (and our shareholders)?

In practice, achieving the right level of difficulty when setting stretch goals is a bit of a balancing act. We want to expand our thinking and strive beyond what seems readily achievable, but we also must be careful not to set goals so high that our team views them as unrealistic. Frustrating managers with unachievable benchmarks can be every bit as counterproductive as sandbagging.

Consider the manager of a baseball team who wants to motivate a hitter. The manager knows that Ted Williams was one of the best hitters of all time and that he had a .406 batting average in 1941. Indeed, between 1876 and 1941, 28 players batted over .400 for a season. (For those less familiar with baseball, a batting average indicates the percentage of the time a player gets a hit per at-bat.) The manager could try to motivate the hitter by encouraging him to hit like Ted Williams and bat .406 in the upcoming season. Yet the hitter will know that no major league baseball player has had a .400 or higher batting average since 1941, and so he almost certainly will view the goal as unrealistic. The goal will likely be dismissed and have no positive effect on his motivation.

Maybe there is a better goal. Let's assume that the hitter batted .275 last season (27.5% of at-bats resulted in a hit). The manager may explain to the hitter that the top hitter in major league baseball in each year from 2008 through 2017 had a batting average of between .336 and .365, for an average of .349. So, perhaps the manager should encourage him to strive to close about one-third of the gap between his current average and the overall .349 average of these batting champions. Or, in other words, he should aim for a batting average of at least .300. This will seem much more feasible than batting .400, and will most likely raise *both* the player's eagerness to meet the goal *and* his expectation of being able to achieve it.

Striving for a stretch goal may or may not be the best way to motivate a baseball player. I don't know, as I've never coached baseball players, at least none over the age of 12. But I do know that striving for a stretch goal is a great way to motivate most business leaders.

One way to think about setting goals is to consider the expected probability of achievement. In this context I am not talking about an exact numeral probability, but more a general sense of difficulty felt by the manager to whom the goal is assigned. The first type of goal to consider is the sandbagged goal. This occurs when a business unit's managers roll out a laundry list of strategic and competitive obstacles that make success more difficult and then propose a profit budget or plan that the managers claim is tough, but is in fact quite achievable (if not indeed "soft"). When creating such budgets, the managers also typically fail to describe the positive things that will help them achieve success, lest the benefits of these items be rolled into the budget (as well as the incentive plan target). These sandbagged budgets are met or exceeded most—let's say 70% to 80%—of the time.

Next, we have the "most likely" budget. This would be a higher level of profit achievement, such that the manager truly believes that the actual performance is equally likely to end up above or below the budget—not what they say they believe, but what they actually believe. These most-likely budgets are, by definition, met or exceeded about 50% of the time. My experience, having sat through a host of conference sessions led by financial planning and analysis experts from all around the globe, is that this is the outcome the experts are usually looking for.

In fact, I have heard such planning and analysis experts say that it's just as bad to end up *above* your profit budget as below it. "Errors are errors," they say. "If you don't hit the budget, you didn't plan right." That may be valid for measuring the planning department, but to the manager or owner of a business, more is always better. Earning more than the budget shouldn't be viewed as negative, even if it arouses suspicions of sandbagging. On the other hand, costs are more likely to get out of control if they weren't planned for in advance. And the same applies to unplanned and ill-advised capital expenditures. In this sense, the experts have a point.

I prefer to think of the main purpose of plans as financial planning itself—that is, providing both the business units and headquarters with reliable estimates of spending and capital requirements. But because of the temptation they offer for sandbagging, such plans should *not* serve as the basis for performance evaluation or incentive compensation. For example, I would much prefer to plan for $100 million of profit and achieve $80 million than to plan for $60 million and achieve $70 million. In other words, I would prefer that my business earn $80 million rather than $70 million, regardless of the plan or budget.

Setting Stretch Goals

This leads us into the discussion of setting aspirational goals. Seeking to achieve a goal that is maybe only 20% to 40% likely to be achieved requires more than merely the status quo plus a few incremental improvements here and there. Not that these incremental improvements are bad, but more is required to consistently exceed investors' expectations, and this tends to make a management team a little less comfortable. "Where are we going to find more improvements? Maybe we should take that research we did and use it to improve the product and drive market share or pricing. Maybe we should push into that new region we have been talking about to secure new customers and more sales. Or maybe we should get off the dime and acquire that smaller competitor that has new products and brands or is in that region we seek to be in." Sure, there is risk in new products, new regions, and acquisitions, so we need to be careful to balance risk and return. But the conversation is taken much more seriously when we have to find a way to close the gap to a stretch goal than with sandbagged goals that are almost automatically achieved.

Companies that effectively use stretch goals to drive their planning and managerial processes tend to be more creative, more resourceful, and more driven. They typically invest more and grow more. And they are highly results-focused in every stage of the planning, decision-making, and execution processes. This all results in more value creation.

Although stretch goals can work as part of an annual budgeting process, they are more effective as the start of a longer-term, three- to five-year planning process. Even though RCE tends to show the benefits of new organic and acquisitive investments sooner than return on invested capital or economic-profit metrics, large strategic investments still take time to devise, develop, execute, and show up in results.

One technique for setting aspirational goals is to derive them from the market. Remember that the net present value of RCE links back to corporate valuation. Normally, we forecast financial performance, convert the forecast to RCE, and calculate the present value of RCE to determine the valuation of the forecasted performance. For goal setting, we do this process in reverse.

The expected RCE can be calculated and linked to the drivers of revenue growth, margin, and other key variables, to indicate a reasonable path to achieve investor expectations. If everything stays the same, we would expect that should management achieve this forecast, the share price will grow at the cost of equity that is implied by the Required Return.

The first step is to determine the average future RCE improvement that is implied by the current valuation. Usually we start with either the RCE from the prior year or, if the current year is expected to be very different, the RCE implied by consensus forecasts for the current year. If we then make the simple assumption that RCE remains flat, it is easy to determine the valuation implied by this flat RCE. If this valuation is significantly higher or lower than the company's current market cap, then we need to adjust the RCE forecast to reflect a straight-line performance decline or improvement that equates the company's implied value with its actual valuation in the market.

Figure 18—Amazon RCE Expectations

Consider, for example, the expectations for future RCE improvement for Amazon (as of December 2018), shown in figure 18. Using these numbers, we can then solve for a combination of growth, margin, and investment by year that exactly corresponds to the RCE trend and that seems plausible versus current performance. Preparing such a forecast is a blend of science and art. If we assume too much growth, then margins may need to decline in a seemingly random way to achieve the RCE forecast. If we don't assume enough investment, asset intensity may decline rapidly while Reinvestment Effectiveness skyrockets—both in ways that fail the smell test. When a combination of growth, margin, and investment is settled on that feels balanced and plausible, we refer to this as the "investor expectations" forecast.

For Amazon, then, the RCE growth rate required to achieve the "investor expectations" forecast is much lower than the actual historical growth rate, and is indeed a decline. If the historical rate of RCE growth is achieved in the future, TSR will likely be very high, as it has been in the past. The share price declined in the fourth quarter of 2018, and it seems investors are betting they cannot keep up the RCE growth trend.

Thus far, this analysis reflects investor expectations that will typically *not* include enough improvement to be considered a stretch goal. Sometimes, though, the performance already baked into a share price can seem to management like a stretch. In these cases, the stock price may be "too high." Not many executives are comfortable thinking, or even worse saying, that their share price is too high. Logic, however, tells us that we should expect our price to be too high about as often as it is too low. But many executives don't see it that way, which is why this analysis is so useful. In chapter 8, we will address the capital deployment strategy implications of share prices that seem to reflect either overly aggressive or pessimistic expectations.

Many companies set aspirational goals that imply growth above what is embedded in the share price. The simplest approach would be to arbitrarily pick a number. For instance, in the Amazon example shown in figure 18, the company's RCE is expected to decrease by about $1.4 billion per year. Note that this doesn't mean sales and profits are expected to decline, but that the capital costs are expected to rise faster than the GCE, perhaps due to the very large ongoing investments in airplanes and other elements of the company's in-house distribution network. Management could choose to set a stretch goal at, say, $5 to $10 billion per year. Unfortunately, picking an arbitrary number doesn't give us much sense of achievability.

A much better approach would be to strive for top-quartile TSR over, say, the next three years. Averaging the last 100 three-year cycles, rolling back monthly from December 2018, we find that the 75th-percentile company in the S&P 500 delivered annualized TSR that was about 8.1% higher than that for the median company. This number could alternatively be derived from the Russell 1000 or an industry peer set. For example, the 75th-percentile consumer discretionary company delivered 9.4% more annual TSR than the median consumer discretionary company, but in utilities this gap was only 3.8%. It is no surprise, of course, that in some industries performance varies more, and it takes a greater level of outperformance to be top-quartile. Bear in mind, though, that generating an extra 3.8% TSR per year in a heavily price-regulated—and, often, rate-of-return-regulated utility—environment may be a lot tougher than it seems.

In any case, the process for setting aspirational goals begins by increasing the starting share price for the above analysis by growing it at the cost of equity, plus a premium corresponding to the 75th percentile, which we then discount at the present cost of equity. Let's use 8% for the example that follows.

Consider a company with a $20 share price and a cost of equity of 10%. We would first grow the share price out three years at 18%—that is, the 10% cost of equity plus the 8% premium required to be top-quartile on TSR. This gives us $32.86, which is the expected price three years from now if we achieve 18% share price performance.[2] We would then discount this back to the present at 10% to get a value of $24.69. Finally, this would be used in an analysis similar to the above investor expectations example to set aspirational goals for growth, margin, and the other key variables. This is a useful process because it sets a goal for how much investment and return are required to produce the RCE growth that is expected to be needed to become a top-quartile TSR company. If everything stays the same, we would expect that if management can achieve this forecast, the share price should grow at a level that is expected to be top-quartile (as shown in figure 19).

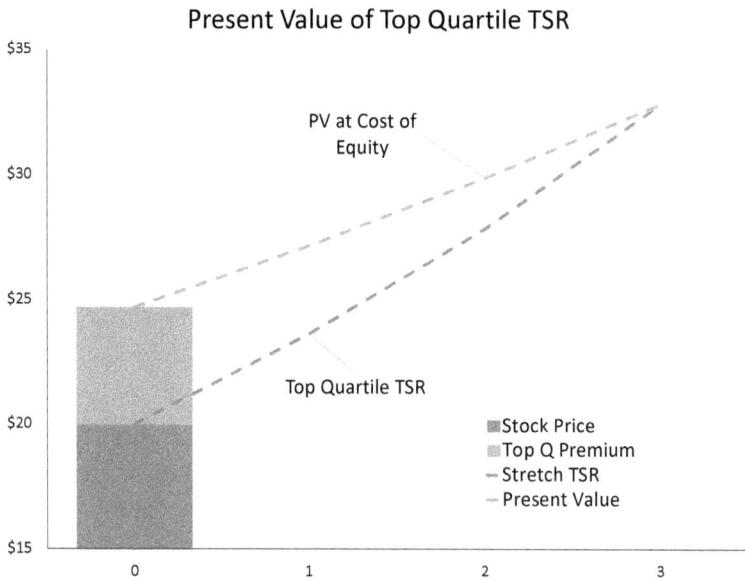

Figure 19—Top-Quartile TSR

This approach has the virtue of being objective and explainable. Not that we need to explain all the math, but it seems better to tell your investors "we analyzed the level of RCE improvement that we believe is needed for us to be a top-quartile stock," as opposed to "we increased investor expectations by X because we said so."

As a kick-off to the planning process, these aspirational goals can be allocated by business. And during the planning process, the business-unit management can be tasked with building a plan to achieve some combination of the five tools that deliver the aspirational business goal. Management may not always be able to get there, but gaps between the sum of these plans and the aspirational consolidated goal can potentially be filled through acquisitions. This and other loose ends will be discussed in chapter 11.

Consider a company with three business units that has been through the above process and has set a consolidated aspirational goal of improving RCE by $25 million per year. Let's initially assume the business units all have similarly modest expectations for improvements in growth and profitability. In such a case, we can simply allocate the aspirational goal for RCE improvement based on current value, which for each of the units we might roughly estimate as its gross operating assets plus the capitalized value of its RCE. Take the largest business unit A, which in the example has GOA of $1.4 billion, RCE of $40 million, and a required return we will assume to be 10%. The present value of repeating $40 million of RCE indefinitely is simply $40 million divided by 10%, or $400 million. Add this to the GOA of $1.4 billion, and we get a rough-and-ready valuation of $1.8 billion. Business unit B is smaller, but has a higher RCE. Business unit C has much more GOA but has negative RCE. Figure 20 depicts the simple valuation along with the allocation of the goal: to improve RCE by $25 million per year at the consolidated company.

For each business, we now have an aspirational goal to serve as a starting point that management can strive for when planning. How much can the businesses grow, and which sort of investments are needed to deliver that growth? What are the pricing, cost-efficiency, or capital-productivity opportunities? The aspirational stretch goal is designed to make them uncomfortable and encourage thinking about big opportunities that, despite the risks associated with pursuing them, could yield significant value.

Note that this is only one of many ways in which we can allocate an improvement goal. We could also allocate it by revenue, for growth-oriented businesses, or by GOA for capital-intensive businesses. Sometimes the business units don't face the same growth and profitability opportunities. In the above example, business *C* may have been struggling against new competitors the last few years, and experienced declining RCE. In such cases, corporate management may view simply maintaining the current RCE to be commendable performance; but in that event, more of the corporate-wide expected improvements will need either to be assigned to other units or perhaps to be accomplished via acquisition. This process requires careful consideration.

Goal Allocation Across Business Units

$ millions	Bus. A	Bus. B	Bus. C	Total
RCE	40	50	(30)	60
Capitalized RCE (@ Required return of 10%)	400	500	(300)	600
Gross Operating Assets	1,400	400	600	2,400
Simple Valuation (GOA + Capitalized RCE)	1,800	900	300	3,000
Allocation Key (% of Value)	60%	30%	10%	
Aspirational Goal for RCE Improvement per Year	15.0	7.5	2.5	25.0

Figure 20—Allocating Aspirational Goals

Once we deviate from the value allocation in the figure, subjectivity and judgment inevitably come into play. But there are two important reasons why this subjectivity may be more acceptable than the typical subjective negotiations that go on in annual budgeting. First, one very important objective, which we will return to later, is the separation of pay from budgets, plans, and even the aspirational goals that we've just been discussing. Each manager wants to improve his or her RCE as much as possible, regardless of whether the improvement is higher or lower than goals, plans, or budgets. So, when a CEO asks business-unit managers if they believe it would be reasonable to plan for achieving more aggressive goals, the managers may say yes or no—but they all know that if the units achieve more, the CEO as well as the managers will make more. There is no incentive to sandbag or to demand anything other than realistic stretch goals.

The second reason this subjectivity is more acceptable—and can actually be valuable—is that it provides useful information that will be applied to capital deployment decisions. This will be more fully discussed in chapter 7, where we will consider the best ways to manage the portfolio of businesses. For now, suffice it to say that the goal is to deploy capital where expected RCE improvements are largest and most likely to be realized. Planning a corporate portfolio strategy for a business unit should, of course, begin by considering its past performance. Perhaps the unit should be sold if it has persistently declining RCE and if management is essentially throwing up its arms, saying there is "no way" to improve RCE, given the business, its capabilities, its competitors, and the alternative strategies considered. Maybe we need to monetize the value of the business by simply selling it to an owner with more valuable synergies that may be willing to pay more than the business is worth to us. Then we can redeploy the capital into business activities where we can improve RCE. Or, alternatively, maybe the business is fine and we just need to find a new management team for the unit.

With all that said, this process of setting aspirational goals that are 20% to 40% likely by trying to achieve the RCE growth associated with a 75th-percentile TSR company is far from foolproof. Some businesses have a lot more, or less, opportunity, so management can adjust the aspirational stretch goal to calibrate it to an appropriate level of difficulty. Still, the process is useful in understanding what is needed over the long term to stimulate thinking beyond the status quo and thus to exceed expectations.

Notes

1   Michael C. Jensen, "Integrity: Without It Nothing Works," HBS Working Knowledge, December 17, 2009, accessed January 15, 2019, https://hbswk.hbs.edu/item/integrity-without-it-nothing-works.

Jensen has identified inadequate budgeting as possibly the single most important failing of incentive compensation systems in U.S. companies. Indeed, he puts the budget at the heart of what he views as a lack of "integrity" that ends up reducing corporate efficiency and value.

2   Note that the full 18% should be used even if the company pays dividends, though this overstates the expected share price appreciation, since it keeps it consistent with the 10% discount rate.

SIX

Continuous Improvement

INVESTORS SOMETIMES REMARK, "That's a great company but it's not a great stock." This can have different meanings, but it often refers to a large, highly profitable company that is well regarded and trades at a high valuation. So, it is a great company that's valued accordingly, but the investor doesn't see much room to earn a good return. Indeed, many great companies have had stagnating or even fading share prices for extended periods.

Consider Microsoft, by all accounts a great company. As of mid-2018 the company was worth about $850 billion and had over 120,000 employees. For decades it has played a major role in transforming the usability and accessibility of computers for everyday consumers and employees around the globe. In August of 1997, Microsoft even invested $150 million in Apple preferred stock, an investment that some described as saving its competitor. Indeed, this cash infusion helped ensure that the world would benefit from all the innovation that Apple has produced since then. Microsoft went public on March 13, 1986, and over a nearly 14-year period (ending on December 27, 1999), investors realized a 59% compound annual return on their investment—enough to turn $10,000 into over $6 million. Microsoft was clearly a great company *and* a great stock.

But then Microsoft's share price languished for more than a decade. A dollar invested in its stock on December 27, 1999, wouldn't be worth a dollar again for more than 14 years. Zero return over such a long period is by all accounts a pretty bad return on investment. But there is absolutely no doubt it was still a great company. To management's credit, over the four and a half years from the day the stock finally crawled over that 1999 peak to the end of 2018, the stock has delivered returns of 24% per year. Once again, Microsoft was both a great company *and* a great stock.

The message to corporate executives should be clear: It's not enough to be a great company. To also be a great stock requires continuous improvement. Whether an investor has a short horizon—say, a day or a week—or a longer horizon of several years, the objective is to earn a decent total shareholder return (TSR). So, what does it take to deliver strong TSR and to be a great stock? In 2016, we published a comprehensive article[1] that reported the findings of our study of the drivers of TSR in technology companies. This study was particularly noteworthy, since so many believe that the kind of economic analysis discussed in this book doesn't really apply to the valuation of the tech sector, with its economic idiosyncrasies. We proved them wrong.

We studied the operating and stock market performance of no fewer than 169 publicly traded tech companies with ending market capitalization of at least $1 billion that were listed from 2004 through 2015. We collected data for the companies on eight different performance metrics for the 12-year period starting in 2004 and running through the end of 2015. As listed in figure 21, the metrics included five widely measured and monitored performance indicators as well as three cash-value measures that were developed by Fortuna Advisors.

Widely Used Measures

(1) Sales Growth
(2) Gross Margin
(3) Operating Margin
(4) EBITDA margin
(5) Return on Equity (ROE)

Cash Value Measures

(6) Gross Business Return
(7) (change in) Residual Cash Earnings (ΔRCE)
(8) Residual Cash Margin

Figure 21—Measures Used in Tech Study

Our next step was to divide our 12 years of operating data and performance measures into 10 rolling three-year periods with endpoints in each year from 2006 to 2015. The first period runs from 2004 to 2006, the next from 2005 to 2007, and so on. Then, for every one of the eight operating measures, we assigned each of the companies to one of three performance tiers—high, medium, and low. For example, the companies with the highest cumulative average growth rates in three-year sales were put in tier 1, and those with the lowest sales-growth rates went into tier 3. For each performance metric, we then compared the median TSR of the high-performance companies in tier 1 with the median TSR of the low-performance companies in tier 3. This difference gave us a sense of the importance of each metric as a driver of TSR in tech.

It was the change in RCE (ΔRCE), as a percentage of beginning assets, that turned out to be the strongest driver of TSR, as reflected in the large difference between the median TSR of the best ΔRCE performers (tier 1) and the worst (tier 3). When we aggregated the 10 rolling three-year periods in our sample, the top ΔRCE companies had median annual TSR that was over 14% higher per year than that of the bottom ΔRCE companies.

The next two most value-related metrics were sales growth and ROE, in that order. This makes sense, since growth and return tend to be the two most important drivers of RCE, which of course clarifies the tradeoff between growth and return. The clear message from these findings is that if you want your tech company to be a great stock, improve your RCE. Typically, this requires a combination of sales growth and improved returns.

Many investors have been bedazzled by exotic tech valuation metrics, such as value per click or per eyeball. So, they are usually surprised to hear that RCE is the *most* important driver of tech TSR. Sure, some tech companies attract extraordinary valuations for a host of reasons that don't show up in current RCE improvements. Sometimes it's a general expectation of future RCE improvements. At other times it's a technology or market breakthrough with no clear sign of how the opportunity will translate into profitability. Often the results grow into the valuation. But sometimes these optimistic valuations turn out to be inflated and will revert to a more normal level over time. But if these gyrations happen in all industries, they seem to happen more often, and to a greater degree, in tech and related industries like biotechnology.

Nevertheless, when we examine the whole tech industry over time, we find that improving RCE is what drives TSR. Just as in other industries, then, the objective should be to grow RCE. Continuous improvement in RCE leads to strong TSR the vast majority of the time, and more so than any other metric I've studied.

When presenting to corporate management teams and at conferences, I have found that the words "continuous improvement" often trigger defensive reactions that are rooted in perceptions of and concerns about volatility and cyclicality. A participant might ask, "How can you expect me to improve every year when the market is highly variable?" Often, they describe this variability as being driven by volatility in commodity prices, exchange rates, demand, and other factors.

Perhaps what is most surprising is that these comments don't just come from business leaders in volatile or cyclical industries, such as energy or commodity chemicals. Even those in relatively stable businesses tend to be overly concerned about the effects of volatility. Reflecting on these trends and conversations, I've become convinced that these perceptions of volatility and cyclicality largely derive from managers' tendency to view their own company's historical trends as a broadly applicable, industry-wide frame of reference or benchmark.

In the case of highly volatile businesses, which routinely experience both up- and down-swings in profits amounting to 5% or even 10% of sales, managers are likely to need to respond decisively to such swings. When upturns happen, managers need to find available capacity, keep customers happy, and simultaneously maintain a reasonable level of structure and organization. And the downturns are often more demanding, since a reduction in orders can beget a whirlwind of layoffs, shortened shifts, asset sales, and just about every type of crisis management imaginable. The relative calm when profits shift by only 2% of sales seems almost like a vacation.

But now let's consider another leadership team—one that operates in a highly stable business that has never seen a profit swing of more than 2% of sales. When it does swing 2%, it feels like a momentous event, even though the same level of volatility seemed like a vacation in the prior example. Attempts to explain how such volatility is relatively low are met with resistance. The truth is, regardless of the actual absolute amount of volatility that a business faces, many managements think of their business as being volatile. Hence their skepticism about the term "continuous improvement," which they mistakenly perceive as implying the need to improve every single year.

I have advised many oil and gas exploration and production companies, and the volatility they experience is positively gut-wrenching. On June 30, 2014, for example, the price of a barrel of West Texas Intermediate oil was $106. Just over 19 months later it bottomed at $26—a decline of over 75%. How many companies can survive a 75% decline in their selling price? And for many oil and gas service and equipment companies, it turned out even worse. In some cases, sales volumes and prices dropped so low that it was no longer economical to keep producing. Hundreds of thousands of employees lost their jobs, and hundreds of billions in market capitalization disappeared. *That's* volatility.

Nonetheless, even companies facing very little volatility can find it difficult to improve every year. I don't expect any company to improve smoothly every year, for much the same reasons that I don't expect a company's stock price to go up every year. But what *is* important is not that a company always improves, but that its management is always striving to do so. Some external factors will get in the way some years. And internal factors will have to be dealt with, as well. But if we are developing and executing sound strategies, RCE will improve over time—and TSR will follow.

The U.S. Declaration of Independence recognizes the "pursuit of happiness" as an unalienable right. It doesn't say that all U.S. citizens *will* be happy, only that they have the right to pursue happiness. Along these lines, maybe we should describe the corporate goal as the "continuous pursuit of improvement."

A corporate focus on multiyear continuous improvement can also help reduce the pressure exerted by relatively minor short-term concerns that otherwise end up excessively consuming management's time and attention. Consider a fire in a supplier's plant that shrinks supply and causes a temporary spike in commodity prices, resulting in a short-term increase in your costs. You know that in a few months the plant will be back on line and the commodity price will revert. So long as the spike isn't threatening the survivability of your company, why waste much time worrying about it? Companies that are too focused on achieving quarterly goals risk being consumed by every variance, small or large—even those that are temporary. Sure, they will be able explain why all the factors that hurt the company's performance were out of their control. But is this really a justifiable use of management's time? In most cases, the answer is no.

This is not to say you shouldn't take action to mitigate the effects of such spikes. Maybe there is a substitute commodity that, though usually more expensive, could be used during the price-spike period. Maybe some of the effects can and should be temporarily passed on to your customers. But when making such a decision, you should take care to avoid a temporary cost recapture that ends up either reducing long-term revenue or raising long-term costs. For example, if customers feel they are being price gouged, they may stay away for a long time. There is a gas station near my home that raised prices excessively, to my mind, after hurricane Sandy. Seven years have passed since then, and I still haven't gone back. While there may be no legal penalties associated with this type of predatory pricing, the loss of business is likely to be a far bigger cost.

And because managements are often faced with tradeoffs between near-term and longer-term revenues and costs, it may be more accurate to describe the corporate objective not as continuous improvement, but rather as *cumulative* improvement. Of course, we want management to make continual efforts to identify and achieve improvements. In other words, we want the managerial *inputs* into the value-creation process to be continuously provided and improving in quality if not quantity. But when evaluating the measurable *output* of the value-creation process—say, in the form of RCE—cumulative improvement may be the most reliable and realistic description of the goal. For, even after we take into consideration the ups and downs of the business, and if we do all the right things, our RCE may in fact not get bigger every year. Yet when we look back in a few years, we will end up reporting a significant cumulative increase in the measure.

This brings me to a recurring, and critical, question raised in this book: Would you, as the CEO of a public company, be willing to take actions that are almost certain to be negatively received by investors in the short run but, once the new initiatives pan out, are likely to drive your share price up significantly in a few years? Say the stock would drop from $20 down to $18 or $17 over the next few months but will have risen to between $30 and $40 in two or three years. Would you still take your proposed actions? Most will recognize the inherent value of such a tradeoff when it's posed hypothetically. But, in practice, many managers are all too willing to forgo such investments to avoid even a relatively small reduction in value over the short term.

We cannot eliminate cyclicality or volatility, but we *can* do our best to ensure that each peak is higher, and each trough shallower, than the last. Figure 22 shows how this plays out over time.

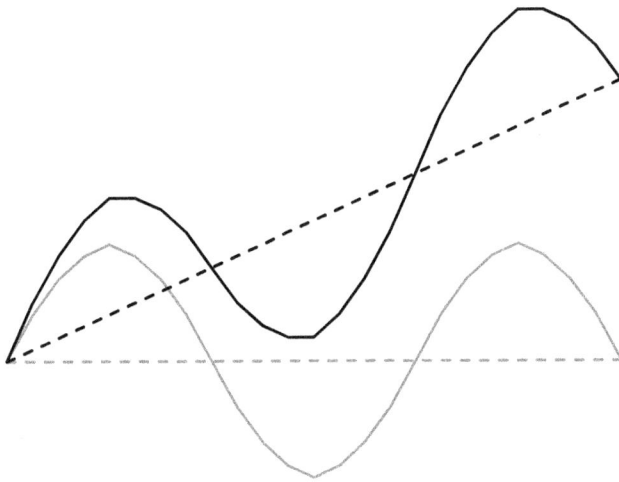

Figure 22—Continuous Improvement in a Cyclical Business

If our goal is to maximize results *this year*, we will focus too much attention on dampening cyclical effects to meet our quarterly or annual goals or investor guidance. Sometimes this leads to cutting deals that really don't yield enough value over the long term. For example, say that your customers are offered unusual discounts to place an order at the end of a fiscal year or quarter that otherwise would have occurred at the start of the following period. Overall, the shareholders make less money, but in the short term management hits a quarterly number. An owner wouldn't do that.

If, by contrast, the goal is to maximize performance three to five years from now, business managers will spend more time identifying, evaluating, and implementing investments and efficiencies that have enduring effects throughout the cycle. Longer-term managers buy assets at the bottom of the cycle when they are selling for a fraction of the price, compared to short-term managers who want to buy capacity only at the peak, at a time when they don't know what else to do with all the cash they are generating. Longer-term managers also take the other side of the bad year-end deal above: They accept unusually large shipments (at big discounts, thereby reducing their own cost of goods sold) at times when it's convenient to support the quarterly accounting figures of their short-term-focused supplier.

It sounds simple, but the continuous-improvement mindset requires a constant, deliberate effort to develop and maintain. First, it requires a good understanding of where we are now in the business and market cycle versus peers as well as the broader capital market on every important dimension of growth and efficiency. And this requires overcoming "recency bias" that, as we discussed previously, can lead managers to extrapolate recent conditions as if they were to continue indefinitely.

Second, we need to also understand the elements of performance at the top and bottom of the last cycle. Did we do relatively better when times were good or when they were tough? This sounds like a straightforward metric, but to understand it requires a thorough understanding of the company's business model in terms of fixed and variable costs—and this includes consideration of financing costs such as interest and even dividends, which are not contractual but behave like fixed costs.

Unfortunately, many companies make predictably poor decisions as a result of neglecting to incorporate cycles into their plans and forecasts. An example would be a very large capacity-expanding investment when demand is at its peak and circumstances appear most favorable. By making such an investment, a company ends up in a tough situation in the next downturn, and this can accelerate the decline in its share price and potentially damage its reputation with investors.

At the top of the business cycle, many companies also voluntarily absorb more risk by insourcing services or acquiring suppliers to reduce costs. But inadequate attention is often paid to the reduction in flexibility that comes from converting these variable costs to fixed costs. Since the cost savings are typically estimated based on smooth forecasts with relatively constant growth and margins, when a downturn eventually arrives these companies are faced with costly excess capacity. When companies buy these services externally, they can simply scale back on them. But when services and the like are insourced, they bear the burden of fixed leases and equipment as well as of full-time staff who are much harder to flex up and down.

Third, and most important, we need to identify the desired future state of the company. Without worrying about how to get there, which elements of the business model should be changed over the next three to five years? How big should we be? How profitable? How much should we invest? We can start by understanding what competitors do better than our own company. Are their products and services of higher quality? Is their response time quicker to customer needs? Do they produce at a lower cost? Which of these benefits would be useful to adopt? Where can we leapfrog them? Which attributes would be adequately valued by customers to warrant the effort?

And if we consider the needs of customers—as of course we should—are there better ways to serve them? Sometimes they don't even know what they need because they haven't thought of it; but perhaps we can find a way to improve their experience. None of us knew we "needed" an iPhone, but that didn't stop Apple.

Once the desired future state is established, the path needs to be considered. And this is where goal-setting ends and planning starts. We know how high we want to stretch and we've set some general parameters about what "there" looks like. Now we must develop and weight alternative paths to get there—and then develop a plan, which is the subject of the next chapter.

As you may recall from chapter 3, we recommend setting performance targets based on the prior year's RCE. Some have questioned whether continuous improvement motivated in this way can be sustainable—consider a manager faced with a target based on exceptionally good performance the year before, for example. But this *actually* serves to unlock the true performance potential of a business.

There likely *is* a limit to how high margins can go, and asset intensity can fall, as a result of competitive forces; at large scale, organic growth alone usually isn't sufficient. But there isn't a limit to how much profitable growth can be achieved if management is creative and has the right incentives.

Managers in these situations are motivated to move beyond incremental improvement and to find alternative solutions to adding value, whether that means acquiring, moving into adjacent markets, seeking out value-adding synergies, or pursuing other more-innovative strategies (Berkshire Hathaway is a good example of a company that consistently does this). And this is exactly how great companies regularly exceed expectations.

The pursuit of continuous improvement is very different from the typical incrementalism of managing quarter to quarter and extrapolating annual budgets. The benefits are clear, but the obstacles to getting there are many. Company leaders face the pressures of providing guidance to investors and analysts, running quarterly earnings calls, and dealing with the increasingly rapid news cycle. Adding to and complicating these challenges are the counterproductive incentives provided by today's prevailing practices of performance measurement and compensation.

Developing a continuous improvement mindset in a large organization is hard work. It begins with a firm and explicit commitment by top management to the task of creating long-run value. It involves reconfiguring goals, management processes, and especially management incentives, to emphasize "more is better"; and it demands constant communication, training, and coaching of at least those near the top of the organization and, in most cases, even some up and down the ranks. But if it involves changes in financial decision-making and processes, the expected outcome is nothing less than a fundamental change in corporate culture.

Notes

1   Gregory V. Milano, Arshia Chatterjee, and David Fedigan, "Drivers of Shareholder Returns in Tech Industries (or How to Make Sense of Amazon's Market Value)," *Journal of Applied Corporate Finance* 28, no. 3 (2016): 48–55.

SEVEN

Business, Product, and Service Portfolio Strategy

AN IMPORTANT ROLE of the senior executive team at most corporations is to manage the portfolio of businesses or activities. In some companies, for example GE or Siemens, these portfolios include a diverse group of businesses. Other, more-focused companies manage a portfolio of various product lines, brands, customer groups, geographies, or some other logical segmentation of the businesses. Still, everyone manages a portfolio of business activities.

Many of us were first exposed to portfolio management via the Boston Consulting Group (BCG) Growth/Share Matrix, shown in figure 23, which was intended to illuminate both opportunities and problems.

		Relative Market Share	
		High	Low
Market Growth	High	Star	Question Mark
	Low	Cash Cow	Dog

Figure 23—The Boston Consulting Group Growth/Share Matrix

Products with high market share in a fast-growing market were labeled *stars* because they had a high market share in growing industries. But they also required a lot of fresh investment to maintain their growth status. Well-managed stars can be significant drivers of TSR.

These days the term "cash cow" has taken on many new meanings. As used by BCG, it designated products with high market share but whose overall market growth was relatively low. These products were expected to have minimal opportunities for investing in growth, so the cash they generate can be thrown off, or "milked," in order to fuel growth elsewhere.

Before we move on to the low-market share side of the matrix, consider the differences between *stars* and *cash cows*. They both have high market share and are expected to throw off a lot of operating cash flow, but in the case of the stars, the value-maximizing strategy tends to be reinvesting to fuel profitable growth. For the cash cows, by contrast, the suggested strategy is to minimize reinvestment and to milk the cash for other uses. This is a significant difference, so the person or team managing the portfolio needs to have an extensive understanding of the rate of past, current, and future market growth. What if you were in the cell phone business and trying to forecast market growth right before Steve Jobs introduced the first iPhone? Or what if you produced vinyl records just before the compact disc was released? To strictly apply the matrix, we need to firmly understand what is happening in our own industry. Despite the best of intentions, it's often hard to know what's coming. As a result, many cash cows have been mistaken for stars—and far too much was invested in expected growth that never materialized. Perhaps even worse, many stars received too little growth investment and lost market share because they were thought to be cash cows. How do we avoid such strategic errors?

Four clear steps can reduce this risk. First, consciously develop a mindset that avoids rigidly applying successful strategies from the past; instead, your management should be flexible and nimble in considering what may work in the future. Second, keep your organization's ears to the ground. Avoid an exclusively internal focus—stay close to customers, follow your competitors' innovation plans, and monitor adjacent industries that could encroach on your business. (Incidentally, these tasks are best carried out in the business unit, *not* the corporate planning department.) Third, undertake each year a thorough qualitative and quantitative portfolio review at the start of the business planning process, and be sure to seek new information to understand what has changed. Finally, be responsive to unexpected innovations when they occur. Develop roadmaps for responding to potential changes by considering expected innovations, preparing response strategies, and quickly executing to mitigate the disruptive effects of such changes. You will still be surprised at times, but less frequently than in the past, and your team will be able to respond more quickly when it counts.

Let's go back to the BCG Matrix. It's rarely still used in its original form, but it will be discussed here because it provides a useful backdrop for making some important points before recommending a new approach. The two boxes on the right, "question marks" and "dogs," are for products that have relatively low market share. The easier ones to deal with are the dogs—products with a low market share in a slow-growth market. Alas, most managements get it wrong. As I wrote in 2011 in a CFO.com article titled "Are You Wasting Time on Poor Performers?"[1] it is common for executives to devote more attention and financial capital to fixing poor-performing products and businesses, while at the same time mistakenly assuming that stronger products and business units will "take care of themselves." This mistake can be in response to investors' challenging executives with tough questions about the company's unsuccessful products and business units. In other cases, it may be personal pride that motivates executives to improve disappointing projects during their tenure.

But is shareholder value really maximized when the corporate office devotes a higher proportion of time or capital to turning around poor-performing products and business units? Or would the shareholders be better served by exiting their losers and focusing executive effort on investing in and growing the revenue and value of the winners?

To help answer this question, we examined long-term shareholder return trends in capital markets, to develop a pragmatic perspective on where corporate resources should be devoted. At the time of the study, the then-current members of the S&P 500, excluding those not public for the full period, were evaluated over the 10-year period from 2001 through 2010 on the basis of their cumulative TSR.

The high performers whose returns are shown at the far right of (both parts of) figure 24 delivered outstanding value creation. And when we grouped all companies into performance quartiles (based on TSR), the top-quartile performers, as shown in the graph at the right, delivered dramatically higher average TSR (+709%) than those at the bottom (−35%). A favorite consulting maxim says that roughly 80% of value creation comes from 20% of activities. We will broach this in more detail later, but for now it's worth noting that the data in the figure neatly follows this dictum: Of the total value of all quartiles (877%), the top quartile (or 25%—close enough for our purposes) represents 81%. This is only one data point, of course, but it supports the idea that value creation tends to be highly concentrated.

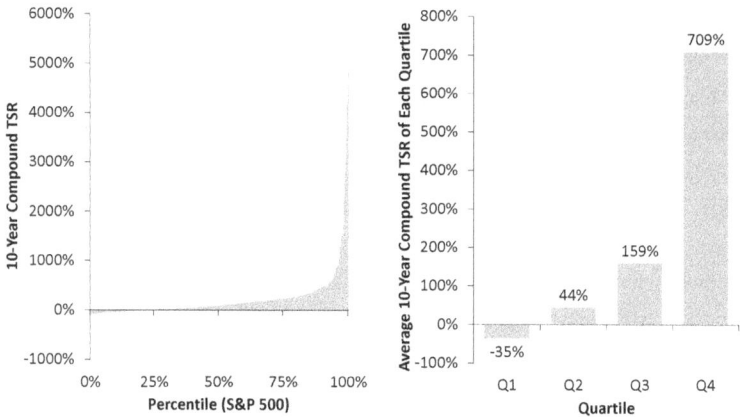

Figure 24—Average TSR by S&P 500 Quartile 2001–2010

But how do these companies achieve such outstanding results? Doing so requires sound strategy and outstanding execution; in most cases, these top-quartile companies successfully reinvest a substantial percentage of their cash flow in capital expenditures, R&D, acquisitions, and other investments that lead to strong, top-line revenue growth. They typically deliver a strong cash return on capital, as well.

To apply these findings in a given organization, consider a hypothetical company with four business units, each valued at $100 million at the start of 2001. We then assume that each of the business units grows in value at the average TSR of one of the four quartiles in our study. In other words, the value of the top business unit *A* grows by

709%, B grows by 159%, C grows by 44%, and D declines in value by 35%. Figure 25 demonstrates the change in value of our hypothetical company. The star business unit A grows over 10 years to be worth over eight times its starting value, representing 63% of the value of the company in 2010. This value *creation* in A is 20 times higher than the value *destroyed* by the bottom business D.

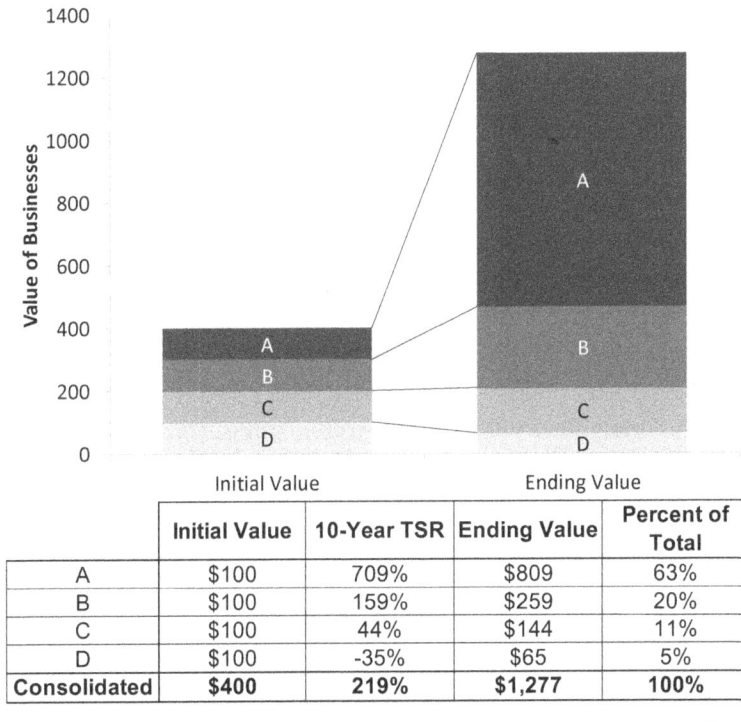

	Initial Value	10-Year TSR	Ending Value	Percent of Total
A	$100	709%	$809	63%
B	$100	159%	$259	20%
C	$100	44%	$144	11%
D	$100	-35%	$65	5%
Consolidated	$400	219%	$1,277	100%

Figure 25—Change in Value of Hypothetical Four-Business Company

What does this mean for the priorities of executives? If a lack of corporate attention and investment causes the top business to deliver only 90% of its potential, then $71 million of the $709 million in expected growth vanishes. For sure, A would still be a great business, but this $71 million shortfall wipes out twice as much value as the entire $35 million in value destroyed by D.

In many client situations, my colleagues and I have observed that executives overseeing multi-business companies often limit the potential of their star businesses by underinvesting in their future. Capital allocation can become a bureaucratic process in which negotiations, a misplaced concern for fairness, and fear of change lead to an indiscriminate smearing of capital, R&D, and marketing resources across the company's business units with far too little attention to the differences in value creation opportunities. Maximizing shareholder value involves *focus*, which is to say it often requires investing substantially more in strong products and businesses than in the weak ones. This will be discussed extensively in chapter 9.

Sometimes the only effective way to divert attention from a *dog* business is a sale or spinoff. There is often a hesitancy to sell, since these poor businesses don't fetch much in the market, so executives often prefer to try to "fix" performance first and then consider a divestiture. Unfortunately, the reluctance to sell these businesses often exacerbates the problem by delaying the true potential value of the *stars*. In the example above, it may be beneficial to sell business *D* at the outset, even at a substantial discount, if needed. This may help focus management's attention and investment on business *A* and so avoid giving up millions more in potential value. Some managers, though, worry that the write-off from taking such a loss on a sale will tank EPS and cause their stock to crash. In most cases, luckily, investors have already baked the book loss into the price, and the stock actually increases due to the signal that the company is taking action. This is yet another reason why an RCE outlook is more accurate and comprehensive than focusing on EPS alone.

The products in the final quadrant of the BCG Growth/Share Matrix are characterized as *question marks*, or what are sometimes referred to as *problem children*. These products are in high-growth markets but have been unable to amass a meaningful market share. You can't develop a true default strategy for these products without first understanding why they are where they are—which is why the "question mark" nomenclature is perhaps more fitting than "problem children."

For example, a product could be relatively new and innovative, with a low market share that is expected to be temporary. Products facing this situation are hardly "problem children"; they are in fact future *stars*, and in the best of cases they present the most likely opportunities for success. Often, the ideal value-creating strategy for such products is to reinvest in their development and growth at a very high rate—often with a reinvestment rate of well over 100%. That is, more than 100% of the cash flow they generate is plowed back into growth. The extra cash needs can be met through debt financing, issuing equity, or using cash generated from other products. For stand-alone companies, where such products are the company's only business, it can be difficult to maximize value. This is why such businesses often make great acquisition targets for large competitors that are replete with *cash cows* and yet lacking effective areas for reinvestment.

At the other end of the spectrum, some products that show up as *question marks* have been around for quite some time but, even with the best of efforts and intentions, have been unable to gain the customer traction needed to attain significant market share. Perhaps they have a weak or unappealing brand, or they are perceived as low-quality or lacking reliability. Or maybe there is nothing wrong with the product, though tactical execution has been ineffective.

In principle, having low market share in a fast-growing market should provide the opportunity to beat market growth. The key to determining the right strategy is to figure out what has caused the underperformance. Given the potential size of the upside, it is worth considering alternatives to revitalize the product, increase growth, and move it into the *star* quadrant. Possible improvements to the product, the positioning, and brand identity, as well as to distribution and other aspects, should be considered. In some cases, incremental improvements aren't worth much, so the best path is to leapfrog the product with a new and better offering that cannibalizes the existing product but has a better chance of delivering above-market growth and market-share gains.

The BCG Matrix has revolutionized strategic thinking, though many experts have identified problems with it. Some of the criticisms relate to how it is often implemented in more of a backward-looking rather than forward-looking manner. It is imperative that the market-share and market-growth indicators are based on forward expectations, not the past. Of course, evaluating the past can be important in ensuring that the forecast of the future is grounded in reality. Big changes from past to future should be expected *only* when their causes are fully understood and considered probable.

The BCG Matrix was developed as a process to reallocate cash internally between businesses. But it poses unnecessary constraints on growth because it ignores the ability to finance externally through debt or new-equity issuances. It also has the potential to encourage overinvestment, since it similarly ignores the possibility of distributions to shareholders.

But potentially the biggest problem with the original matrix is that it doesn't factor in actual profitability. The originators made assumptions about what the likely profitability would be in each quadrant and used that to inform the strategy. But, of course, we will find products in commodity businesses that are in the *star* quadrant, yet whose average rates of return through a business cycle are hardly attractive. Investing in these products could well be value-destroying. And there are *dogs* that produce decent cash flow and perhaps should be treated more like *cash cows*, especially if such businesses command such a low-valuation multiple that the proceeds from a disposal would be worth significantly less than the option of continuing to harvest the remaining cash flow.

Before I propose a new, improved, two-by-two strategic matrix, which will be discussed below, consider first how an investor studies a portfolio of stocks. And the same principles, by the way, are at work for any investor holding a portfolio of fixed-income securities, real-estate assets, commodities, or even cryptocurrencies. I use the stock example because it's more akin to managing a portfolio of operating businesses.

At its core, the goal of stock investors is to hold shares in companies that will rise in value, with consideration for both stock-price appreciation and dividends. Of course, they won't get them all right, but if they pick more stocks that outperform than underperform the rate of return of the overall market, their portfolio will likely perform well. The same is true inside a company. If we're in management, we want to have our capital invested in products and businesses that we expect to rise in value. As discussed in chapter 6, it's not about investing in good companies. It's about investing in companies that improve more than the market already expects them to. Think of the cumulative RCE trend of each product or business as its stock price performance. We want to hold products and businesses that are expected to be able to meaningfully increase RCE; and if we achieve that, the overall company's stock price is highly likely to rise.

Countless factors drive a company's RCE, and hence its share price. But if we use the simplest portrayal, RCE increases either when revenue grows or when the RCE margin improves, or both. It is critical to understand that the higher the RCE margin, the more valuable the growth is. Let's say companies *X* and *Y* both add $1 million in revenue, but that company *X* has an RCE margin of 10%, as compared to just 2% for company *Y*. In that case, whereas company *X* would add $100,000 in RCE, the RCE increase for company *Y* will only be $20,000. Of course, it's better for company *Y* to grow its RCE by $20,000 than to have no growth at all; yet the important point here is that the identical revenue growth of company *X* generates five times as much RCE improvement as the revenue growth of company *Y*—and that's likely to translate into five times the value creation per dollar of growth.

If these two businesses were part of the same corporate business portfolio, we would want to be sure we funded *all* the growth available in company *X*, even if we have to curtail the growth investment budget in company *Y* to do so. Unfortunately, as discussed above, far too many companies "peanut butter" spread[2] resources across their portfolio and thus end up underfunding their best opportunities. This is one of the most important reasons why spinoffs of smaller, faster-growing businesses tend to create tremendous value. As part of a large corporate infrastructure, promising businesses often find it hard to attract the resources needed to fuel all their available growth. The leaders of all the other more-established businesses in the corporation sometimes complain, "Why do *they* get to invest 10% of sales in growth, but *we* only get 4%?" You see the problem....

The negotiations and backroom deals that occur during capital budgeting often hinge on fairness and balance, which aren't words the average stock-market investor can even spell. Imagine Warren Buffett investing equally in 10 companies because he didn't want the leaders of the lower-performing companies to feel he was being unfair. What's worse is when internal cronyism diverts resources to *favor* the subpar businesses. Say business unit *X* has more valuable growth opportunities, but the head of business unit *Y* was the college roommate of the chief operating officer; so though business unit *Y* may create scarcely one-fifth of the value, it very well may end up getting as many or more investment dollars.

Of course, nobody will ever say they are allocating more resource to a business because the leader is a close friend. They always have some strategic sounding mumbo jumbo like, "Susan, I know you and your team are really delivering and you have some exciting plans and investment opportunities, but this year we will need you to be team players while we plow untold millions into shoring up the faltering strategic position of Harry's business unit." The affronting manager continues, "They have taken a hit lately and their business built this company 50 years ago. How would it look if we didn't do everything we can to fix it? In the end we may be throwing good money at bad investments, but we've got to try. Maybe we can fund your growth plan next year…." These situations, as regrettable as they are, happen all the time.

The Tradeoff between Growth and Return

Because value is created by the combination of growth and return, we should dispassionately allocate more resources to the best growth and return opportunities. To build a better two-by-two matrix, we need one dimension to capture growth and the other to capture return. Simply using market growth is inadequate—we need to augment this with some sense of whether we can gain market share. A basic methodology is to combine market growth with market share, where lower market share relates to a greater opportunity to capture more. The higher the market share, the more limited are the opportunities to increase it; in fact, it may be hard just to maintain market share if it's already high.

A table can be created in which a company's (or product's) growth score is derived based on its market growth, plus an increment determined by its current market share as a percentage of the market leader's. An examination of historical growth versus the ratio of market share to the leaders' share for our product and peer products can be used to estimate a useful table for a product market or industry.

For example, consider figure 26, which is based on apparel retailers[3] currently in the Russell 1000 that were public for the full period of 2000 through mid-2018. The graph relates the one-year percentage change in market share to the initial market share at the start of the period as a percentage of the leader's share at that time. As this is just an illustration, this graph shows whole companies, but some of these companies have multiple brands, and better insights would come from an analysis of market share and revenue growth by brand. But even in this case, it is easy to see how low-market-share companies tend to gain share while higher-market-share businesses tend to lose it.

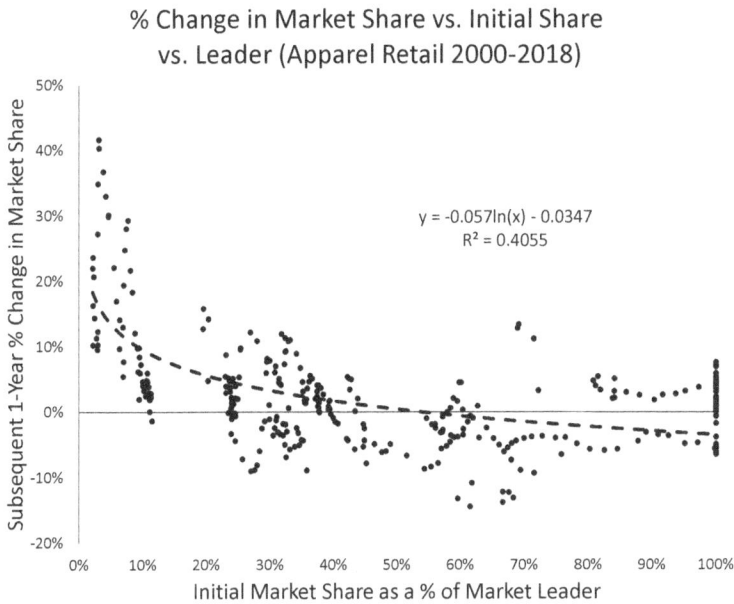

% Change in Market Share vs. Initial Share vs. Leader (Apparel Retail 2000-2018)

$$y = -0.057\ln(x) - 0.0347$$
$$R^2 = 0.4055$$

Initial Market Share as a % of Market Leader

Subsequent 1-Year % Change in Market Share

Figure 26—Percentage Change in Market Share vs. Initial Share as a Percentage of the Leader Share

The next important growth characteristic is market growth. In many product categories there are experts who forecast growth, in some cases with decent accuracy; but the longer the forecast, the less reliable it is. It's important to use such forecasts but also to examine past experience before management makes a judgment about what they expect in terms of forward growth in a market. It is essential to recognize that, though there are many credible inputs from forecasting experts, in the end management must make its own judgment. There is no escaping this responsibility, especially given that 10 "experts" will give 10 different answers.

How about 22 experts? As of September 2018, Apple was the most valuable company in the world, so, given the amount of money at stake, it is scrutinized by many highly skilled sell-side analysts. For the quarter ending September 2019 (a year from the time I wrote this), there are 22 analysts following Apple who have made revenue forecasts. They range from $59.7 billion to $65.4 billion, with fairly good dispersion across this range. The consensus estimate for the current quarter is $61.1 billion, so the projected growth rates from this level range from –2.3% to +7.0%. If you were collecting such data for Apple and some peers in order to estimate market growth, it would be a challenging decision to settle on an expected market-growth rate.

Fortunately, when we "average" the experts' forecasts, we tend to get much better predictions. Not perfect, but much better. This is really just what's known as "the wisdom of crowds," whereby the average answer of a group tends to be better than that of any individual in the group—since each of their unique perspectives, along with the errors they entail, is mitigated by the averaging process.

The wisdom of crowds is compelling. In the book *Out of Control*,[4] Kevin Kelly describes how in 1991 Loren Carpenter led a group of about 5,000 computer graphics conference attendees who were given a wand with a red and a green side. Carpenter and his team used cameras to pick up the average signals from the crowd. The two sides of the room were able to control paddles and play the then-popular game of Pong. To take up something harder, they began flying an airplane. I suspect few, if any, of the computer graphics crowd knew how to fly, so undoubtedly many got it wrong. But on average, they directed the aircraft controls correctly and fly they did. (I highly recommend the book.)

Back to our apparel industry example. In figure 27, we see for the aggregate apparel industry both the one-year consensus revenue growth forecast and the actual growth that occurred. The forecasts are derived by adding up the average revenue forecasts of the analysts following each company, as of each historical quarter going back over 60 quarters.

The graph has a lot going on. In stable times the analysts do a quite good job of estimating growth. And the median of analysts' forecasts over time of 5.1% is very close to the actual median of 5.0%. But when big swings happen, the analysts are a step behind. In mid-2006 they forecasted 5.9% market growth—actual was 6.7%— but a year later they were still forecasting 4.7%, and actual dropped to 0.2%. By the end of the third quarter in 2008, they still predicted

4.1%, almost as if they didn't want to recognize reality; Q3 growth dipped to –3.6%. Finally, by the first quarter of 2009, they forecasted a decline of –3.5%, but nope; the market had now turned, and the actual apparel industry growth turned out to be a positive 1.7%. Two quarters later, the predicted growth turned positive at +2.6%, yet the actual growth that quarter was a whopping 7.2%.

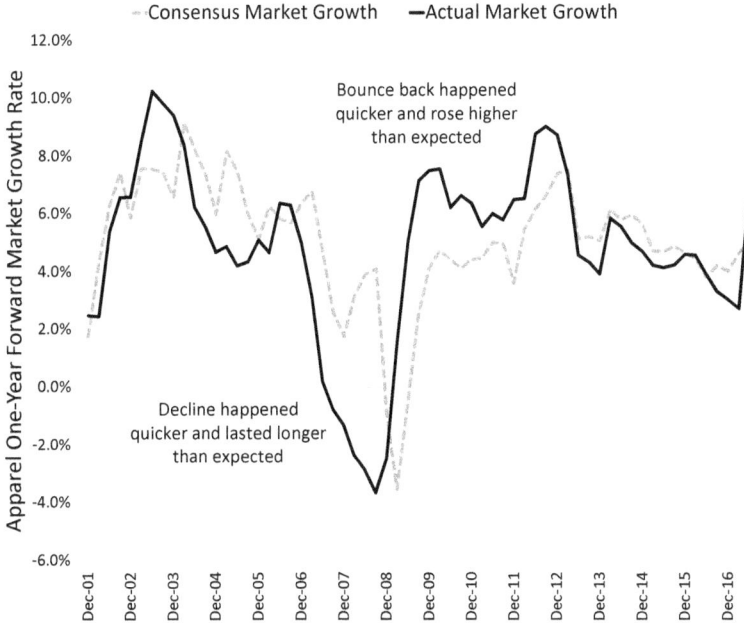

Figure 27—Historical Apparel Market Growth

This is not to blame the analysts—it's normal human behavior! As discussed earlier, behavioral economists refer to this as recency bias. It can be hard to avoid such innate biases, which is why it is recommended that rules-based decision processes be implemented wherever possible.

To bring together market growth and market share into a grid for use in assessing market opportunity, like that in figure 28, we simply combine the historical market growth at various percentiles with the typical growth achieved as a function of market share (that is, as a percentage of the market share of the market leader). The white box at the upper left, for example, is simply the sum of the 9.7% above and the 10.3% to the left. Typically, apparel companies with such a small share in such a fast-growing market achieve as much as 20% revenue growth.

		Market Share as a Percentage of Market Leader's Share										
		9.7%	5.7%	3.4%	1.8%	0.5%	-0.6%	-1.4%	-2.2%	-2.9%	-3.5%	Market Share Growth
		Min	20%	30%	40%	50%	60%	70%	80%	90%	Max	% of Leader Share
10.3%	Max	20%	16%	14%	12%	11%	10%	9%	8%	7%	7%	
8.5%	90%	18%	14%	12%	10%	9%	8%	7%	6%	6%	5%	
6.8%	80%	16%	13%	10%	9%	7%	6%	5%	5%	4%	3%	
6.4%	70%	16%	12%	10%	8%	7%	6%	5%	4%	4%	3%	
5.8%	60%	15%	12%	9%	8%	6%	5%	4%	4%	3%	2%	
5.0%	50%	15%	11%	8%	7%	6%	4%	4%	3%	2%	2%	
4.7%	40%	14%	10%	8%	6%	5%	4%	3%	2%	2%	1%	
4.2%	30%	14%	10%	8%	6%	5%	4%	3%	2%	1%	1%	
3.2%	20%	13%	9%	7%	5%	4%	3%	2%	1%	0%	0%	
0.5%	10%	10%	6%	4%	2%	1%	0%	-1%	-2%	-2%	-3%	
-3.6%	Min	6%	2%	0%	-2%	-3%	-4%	-5%	-6%	-6%	-7%	
Market Growth	Historical Percentile											

Market Growth (left vertical axis)

Figure 28—Growth Score Based on Market Growth and Market Share

The shading in the figure indicates those combinations of market growth and market share that would be expected to have a below-average revenue-growth opportunity. It is important to note that actual growth may well be different from the growth opportunity, but for characterizing the market, the growth-opportunity score is what is needed.

This growth score needs to be compared to a score that reflects pricing, efficiency, and productivity. The ideal measure for that purpose is Residual Cash Margin (RCM), which is simply RCE as a percentage of revenue. Several advantages accrue from the use of RCM, versus return on capital or similar return measures. The product of RCM and revenue is RCE in dollars, so RCM directly tells us, as discussed above, how much value is created by each increment of revenue growth. It is straightforward to determine if giving up some RCM to achieve higher growth will lead to more RCE dollars, or, alternatively, if giving up some growth to achieve higher RCM adds value. And of course, since RCE is determined on a cash basis relative to a required return on assets shown at their original cost, there is no bias either against investment or in favor of milking old assets well beyond their useful life, as discussed in chapter 3.

One important benefit of using RCM is that it is agnostic about the value-maximizing level of asset intensity. That means RCM works just as well for asset-intensive businesses as for asset-light ones. An asset-light business, like a pure service company, will have very few assets, so any measure of return is likely to be astronomically high—and it may seem that more assets should be invested. But alas, in such a business there is really no capital investment opportunity, so the signals are misguided. With RCM, it doesn't matter if a business is asset-intensive or asset-light; in both cases, asset intensity is simply treated as a cost in determining RCE and RCM.

With the revenue growth score and the RCM in hand, we can now introduce the Fortuna Advisors Growth/RCM Matrix. Products and businesses can be placed into the two-by-two matrix, based on whether they are above or below average on the growth score and RCM, as shown in figure 29.

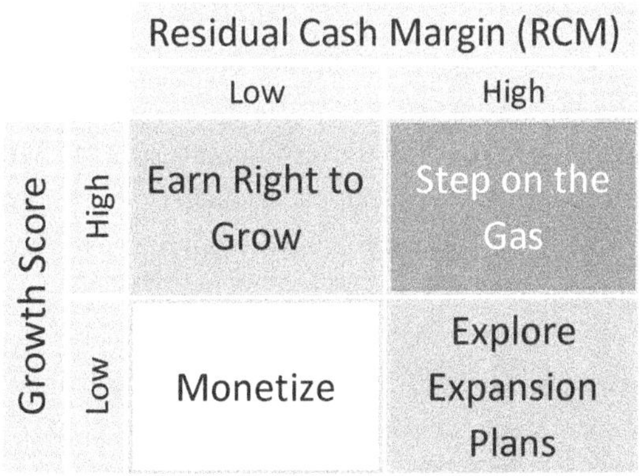

Residual Cash Margin (RCM)

		Low	High
Growth Score	High	Earn Right to Grow	Step on the Gas
	Low	Monetize	Explore Expansion Plans

Figure 29—The Fortuna Advisors Growth/RCM Matrix

As we have found in our client work, the most value, by far, is created by the products and companies in the upper-right quadrant ("Step on the Gas"), where both the growth opportunity and the profitability are above average. As shown next in figure 30, high-revenue growth and RCM products typically deliver the best TSR, so we really need to step on the gas. We examined the TSR of the largest nonfinancial companies listed in the United States at the end of 2017 and sorted them based on whether their three-year revenue growth and RCM were each above or below median.

The median TSR of the companies in the *step-on-the-gas* quadrant was 66%, which was over 3½ times the median TSR of the companies in the *monetize* quadrant at 18%. The longer the time horizon, the more this gap widens.

		Three-Year Average RCM	
		Low	High
Three-Year Growth CAGR	High	41%	66%
	Low	18%	33%

Figure 30—Median Three-Year TSR vs. Growth and RCM (2015–2017)

Those companies above median on growth but below on RCM had median TSR of 41%, which is somewhat better than the 33% median TSR achieved by the companies that were above median on RCM but below median on growth. Not to overemphasize this, but it shows that growth has been somewhat more important than profitability among this broad population of companies over this period. This finding can and does vary by industry, and for many industries the findings can be different at various points in the economic and market cycle.

Several important strategic insights should be considered in each quadrant of the Fortuna Advisors Growth/RCM Matrix, further discussed below.

Step-on-the-Gas Products and Services

Step-on-the-gas products in the upper-right quadrant should receive the highest priority for resource allocations and command the most attention from management. The opportunity to create value is the greatest, but the chance to fall short of the potential is greatest, too. Avoid the temptation to get caught up in spending all your time fixing "problem products." Unless the problems are threatening the survival of the company, far more of the potential difference in the success of a leader will be determined by how they manage their *step-on-the-gas* products.

A *step-on-the-gas* product typically consists of a well-differentiated product in a fast-growing market that is highly meaningful to consumers. For example, consider the iPhone, which introduced impressive new technological features that revolutionized and significantly expanded the smartphone market. At the Macworld convention on January 9, 2007, Steve Jobs introduced the world to the iPhone, and it became available a few months later. Between 2007 and 2018, Apple introduced no fewer than 11 models, each with new features...and a higher price tag. Total iPhone units sold soared from 1.4 million in 2007 to more than 216 million in 2017. Talk about stepping on the gas!

To determine how best to *step on the gas* requires an understanding of the potential sources of differentiation. For example, does the product (or service) have superior features and capabilities that are useful and important to the customer? Or do customers simply like being associated with the product as a symbol of status and prestige? If so, the product may be said to be differentiated, which allows the possibility for premium pricing—customers will pay more for it.

There are also other sources of differentiation, for example process efficiencies. Say a product is more readily available or has faster delivery thanks to a logistics advantage (*cough*—Amazon). This would be an example of a process improvement creating a functional benefit that drives differentiation. But not all process efficiencies result in differentiation.

Say, instead, that a product is made through a more-streamlined process that allows it to be available at a price discount while still maintaining comparable profitability with competitors. In this case, we're dealing with a cost advantage—not exactly a product differentiator, though this still allows for the ability to profitably grow market share. In any case, many types of differentiation and other comparative advantages abound, but it is critical that these all be evaluated in an objective and disciplined manner.

Everyone thinks they have a differentiated brand, but these days we have credible ways to assess how differentiated a brand really is in the collective eyes of the consumer audience. One useful source of brand assessment insights, which will be discussed in detail in chapter 11, is BERA Brand Management, a firm that Fortuna Advisors began working with in 2017. BERA developed one of the largest brand-equity assessment platforms in the world, capturing one million consumers' perceptions across over some 4,000 brands. Such perceptions are then used to explain and quantify not only how brands grow, but, perhaps more important, how brand growth translates into financial performance, including valuation. Tools like BERA provide managements with a strict, fact-based ability to interpret and apply insights on the sources of brand differentiation.

Differentiation is always defined by the customers' being willing to pay a price premium due to their perception that the value to them of the product or service is higher than that of competing offers—in short, differentiation is defined by relative consumer value. We can assess it in two ways: first, by surveying consumers and asking questions that can quantify differentiation; and second, by analyzing changes in both market share and relative pricing data to determine whether our product is priced at a premium, at parity, or at a discount. If a product is not priced at a premium or is growing market share, it is not differentiated.

Once the sources of differentiation are understood, management needs to explore how robust these differentiators are, whether (and the extent to which) competition is encroaching and so could neutralize the differentiators, and whether any other external or internal trends are on the horizon that could reduce the company's potential for profitable growth. The first priority for investment must be to reinforce and extend the sources of differentiation, and to be prepared to leapfrog existing products with new and improved offerings despite the potential for cannibalizing current sales.

We were all impressed with the first iPhone, and would continue to be awestruck by how it changed the world of mobile telephony, even if nothing followed it. But from a commercial perspective, each successive new iPhone created the opportunity to reach a higher and higher plateau, even though that plateau wasn't visible when it all began. The pipeline of new iPhones and upgraded versions keeps producing, and though some versions have underperformed, the volumes attained would have been considered so wishful that they would have sounded laughable in 2007. We have no way of knowing what Steve Jobs really thought the potential was, back when the original product development project began, but it's hard to believe he expected annual sales of 216 million units as a reasonable forecast. It was the relentless pursuit of continuous improvement in the iPhone user experience that led Jobs and his successors to greatness, and this required a constant and massive ongoing innovation investment in a product that was already remarkable, to make it even better.

The next priority for *step-on-the-gas* products, after investing in sustaining and expanding the sources of differentiation, is to actually step on the gas. And that requires marketing expenditures, including traditional media such as TV, radio, and print ads, along with an increasing investment in newer marketing methods, such as social media, email campaigns, and Internet ads. Perhaps an investment to expand a sales force can help drive sales in areas that are underserved, as the industrial supply company W. W. Grainger did when it hired over 500 mobile territory sales representatives to reach customers far from its stores. This was a large increase in annual expenses, and the benefits took time to pay off with each new wave of representatives hired. But, overall, it created substantial value by accessing new customers and making new, and highly profitable, sales.[5]

When considering these growth and investment plans, it is important to use the Reinvestment Effectiveness metric introduced in chapter 4. Many companies underinvest in growth even when they have strong revenue growth projections. This reluctance to commit more capital can stem from an excessive focus on period free cash flow, for example. Such forecasts typically imply a higher level of Reinvestment Effectiveness—which, again, is the increase in revenue divided by the amount of investment over three or five years—than the company has achieved in the past. But though it's possible that such new levels of Reinvestment Effectiveness will be realized, unless a new source of differentiation is discovered, such underinvestment will likely lead to underperformance against growth forecasts. Conversely, low rates of both projected revenue growth and Reinvestment Effectiveness can provide an indication of, and so help prevent, overinvestment in capacity in relation to projected sales growth. Such overinvestment often takes the form of building too much production capacity, or by what we used to call, when I worked in engineering, "unnecessary gold plating." (Engineers enjoy impressing other engineers.)

To effectively make such tradeoffs requires the integration of the P&L budget and the capital budget, as will be discussed in chapter 9.

Explore-Expansion-Plan Products and Services

Explore-expansion-plan products, which occupy the lower-right quadrant in figure 29, have above-average profitability, as indicated by a high RCM. But they don't score highly in growth because of either low market growth or a high market share that is more likely to decline than increase. As a result of such high RCM, even small increases in growth for these products and services tend to be highly valuable, while small losses in share can be very costly. So, it is worth taking the time to try to find new strategic paths to growth either by trying to expand the market, as Apple did with the iPhone, or by finding applications in adjacent markets.

But seeking to generate growth from a product with a low growth score is fraught with risks—for example, extending a brand to an adjacent product can end up having a negative effect on consumer perception of the brand. To avoid such possibilities, it's best to start by considering lower-risk expansion plans and then introducing risky alternatives only if the opportunity is significant enough to drive a desirable risk-return relationship.

The lowest-risk strategy is to pursue growth in existing and adjacent markets. A dominant market leader sometimes can drive the size of the market higher by publicizing new uses and expanded fulfillment of customer needs. As long ago as 1972, McDonalds launched its breakfast menu, a very successful market-expanding strategy that originated with a franchisee who showed founder Ray Kroc a sandwich made with eggs Benedict.

Brand extension is most feasible when there are potential customers who prefer a competitive product with different attributes but are open to a switch if adequately enticed to do so. Adjacent subcategories can be tapped with brand extensions, such as when Cheerios was extended to Honey Nut Cheerios, to address the sweetened cereal customer, along with Multi-Grain Cheerios, Very Berry Cheerios, and the rest of the current 16-product Cheerios line. Each of these product proliferations undoubtedly cannibalized some sales of the original Cheerios, but most of these new products probably brought in many new customers, too. And if Cheerios had stood still, it would likely have lost share to other products introduced by competition.

Market extensions into new geographies can be fruitful. For many years, Guinness was viewed as a cold-weather beverage, probably due to the strong taste, thick viscosity, and a warmer suggested serving temperature. The theory was that, in warm climates, consumers wanted beer with a light taste, a watery flow, and a virtue of being best served extremely cold. The company decided to try a big push into Africa, which seemed unlikely. As of 2018, the company now boasts in an advertisement that among their top 10 countries by volume are Nigeria (#4), Cameroon (#5), Kenya (#6), Ghana (#7), and Ivory Coast (#9). All these countries are ahead of Canada (#10), known in ads as the country that "invented ice." Sometimes we need to overcome our preconceived notions when we consider brand and market extensions.

The farther the subcategory is from the core market, the riskier the extension, and that risk manifests itself both in terms of the potential failure of the new extended product offering and also in potentially negative feedback effects on the core product. The company can end up worse off than before the investment. It is important to perform adequate pretesting but also to have a process for small, regional introductions that are rapidly and progressively scaled up if successful feedback is received, but with an eye toward swiftly canceling the experiment if enough negative feedback emerges. The landscape is littered with unsuccessful brand extensions, including Harley-Davidson cake-decorating kits, Chicken Soup Pet Food for the Pet Lover's Soul, and Zippo, the women's perfume that comes in a container that resembles a lighter.

One common obstacle to the success of *explore-expansion-plan* products is a focus on percentage performance measures, such as profit margins and rates of return. The whole reason we are exploring an expansion is the high profitability of the product, and many successful expansions will create value but may bring down the average when blended in with the high margins and rates of return. So, the type of growth often involves giving up some margin and return in exchange for growth; to make this tradeoff, we can rely on the RCE decision framework, as illustrated earlier.

Products and Services that Need to Earn the Right to Grow

Products in the upper-left quadrant of figure 29 are labeled *earn-right-to-grow* due to their below-average RCM in an environment with an above-average growth score. Unfortunately, management teams often grow such products rapidly because they *can*, not because they should. Growth should be slowed on such products while the product management team considers ways of improving RCM. And if RCM can indeed be improved, then management will have earned the right to invest in growth. If not, then their top priorities should be continuously focused on cost efficiency and capital productivity, or on divestiture (as we'll see the next section).

An exception to this occurs when a product is new, does not have economies of scale, and has not yet advanced down the learning curve with regard to production efficiencies. In such cases, it may be OK to grow, yet careful monitoring is required to ensure that the situation improves over time.

It is easy to see the challenges faced by multi-business companies. It's culturally difficult for senior leadership to encourage some of their product management teams to step on the gas while telling others to wrack their brains to come up with expansion plans for products having low-growth scores. Still other product management teams are told *not* to grow, but instead to focus on cost efficiency and capital productivity. Imagine how confusing it can get if products across these quadrants share sales teams and production facilities!

Nevertheless, products with negative RCM, or such low RCM that growth adds little value, need to prioritize improving RCM even if it means losing market share. The likelihood of success in improving RCM depends on the reasons for RCM's being low to begin with. If the product is undifferentiated, no opportunity will arise to drive premium pricing, so the only possible path to a high RCM is to be the low-cost producer. This pure focus on minimizing cost and capital often seems more achievable than it is. Only when unique production or distribution methods are employed can a sustainable cost advantage be achieved and protected. Otherwise, cost and capital reductions will simply be matched by competitors, and prices will be "competed down" to eliminate the surplus value.

A company has a greater chance of success when its products are differentiated and are already commanding premium pricing, but also when RCM is low because of inefficient cost structures and unproductive asset utilization. The identification and implementation of industry best-practices in manufacturing, logistics, and service can bring cost and capital levels in line, and the benefits will flow directly into an improved RCM.

The only big risk occurs when the high-cost profile is achieved not because of inefficiency but rather because of the higher-cost nature of the product or service, especially when the higher cost is driven by attributes that produce the differentiation. Consider a restaurant where extra waitstaff improves service, a key element of differentiation relative to other local eateries. Perhaps leaving more space between tables improves the ambiance, which is positively perceived by patrons, but this reduces the number of tables and the amount of sales per dollar of capital. Maybe the investment in higher-quality ingredients, such as fresher vegetables and better cuts of meat and fish, improves the most important differentiator—the quality of the food. With all this differentiation, the restaurant may attract more patrons who are willing to pay higher prices, generating maybe 50% or even 75% more revenue per patron—but its costs will be much higher, too. In such a situation, a blind focus on cost control might lead to a reduction in staff, an increase in the number of tables, and even a downgrade in the quality of food ingredients. These efforts may dramatically reduce differentiation, and as a result, revenue may decline more than cost. It is imperative, therefore, that cost inefficiencies be distinguished from desirable investments in differentiation.

Because these *earn-right-to-grow* products are frequently the most misunderstood, they often have the most misaligned strategies applied to sell them. Traditional strategic thought says if you are in a fast-growing market, "then just grow!" A common assumption has it that growing markets must be profitable, but this is certainly not always the case, at least not for all products in such markets. By balancing the emphasis on growth and return, the Fortuna Advisors Growth/ RCM Matrix helps managers identify and appropriately drive success in such product areas.

Products and Services that Should Be Monetized

The combination of being below average on both the growth score and RCM provides little hope for success in most circumstances. At times opportunities will present themselves to rejuvenate a brand, reimagine a technology, or restructure inefficient manufacturing and distribution processes. Yet for every home run it seems there are far too many strikeouts, especially when the turnaround is undertaken within a large, multi-business company. Even when business-unit turn-arounds work, they often come at the expense of neglect of the most successful businesses, so it's like winning a battle but losing the war.

As mentioned above, sometimes the only way to divert manage-ment attention away from this type of business is a sale or spin-off. The private equity industry is far better suited to achieving successful turnarounds, thanks to its much more powerful incentive and gover-nance structures, as well as to their ability to reduce public transparency along with the short-termism that comes with the quarterly earnings cycle. Nevertheless, private equity buyers don't like to pay premium prices, so management often hesitates and instead holds onto poor performers to "fix" them and improve their value. This prolongs the drain of value by distracting management from maximizing value in their *step-on-the-gas* products and businesses.

The situation must be studied on a case-by-case basis. In most companies, though, management will find that selling these businesses helps them to focus on the areas where they can create more value, even if the sale happens at a price below what management really thinks the business could be worth. And beyond the immediate benefit of exiting an inferior business, divestitures can simplify the company, reducing overheads and enabling simpler management processes.

Notes

1 Gregory V. Milano, "Are You Wasting Time on Poor Performers?," CFO.com, accessed July 8, 2011, https://fortuna-advisors.com/2011/07/08/are-you-wasting-time-on-poor-performers/.

2 A term used in allocations where resources are spread evenly across segments.

3 For this simple illustration, data was gathered from CapitalIQ for Foot Locker, L Brands, Ross Stores, The Gap, The TJX Companies, and Urban Outfitters.

4 Kevin Kelly, *Out of Control: The New Biology of Machines* (London: Fourth Estate, 1995).

5 If these sales and marketing efforts pay off, volumes will increase, so there may be necessary investments in production capacity, logistical capacity, and even supplier capacity. This should be intentionally decided on after considering adding new volume to reduce the risk of unnecessarily adding idle capacity. Unutilized capacity increases fixed-cost and capital charges per unit, and can dramatically reduce overall RCE, valuation multiples, and share price.

PART III

ALLOCATING STRATEGIC RESOURCES

EIGHT

Capital Deployment Policies

OVER THE LAST few decades, the cost of capital has become a commonly used benchmark for considering investment, performance management, and valuation decisions. These days, instead of blindly pursuing growth at any cost, many companies invest in buildings, equipment, technologies, brands, and human talent with the expectation of earning an adequate return on their investment. And corporate finance principles define an "adequate return" as the cost of capital.

I began my career as a flight control system design engineer, and a colleague once said to me, "too much is no good." We were working together on some design changes to an experimental plane, the X-29, and he was describing how nearly every attempt by his team to offset control system design deficiencies tended to overshoot and leave them facing the opposite problem. For example, if the aircraft tended to have too much lift when coming out of a specific maneuver, the design fix tweaked the algorithms in the flight control computers too much and tended to leave the aircraft with insufficient lift. Fortunately, my colleague was working on a simulator, and these bugs were repaired before the plane ever flew.

So it has been with the cost of capital. The intended application of the cost of capital was as the discount rate to be used when calculating net present value of a long-term forecast of free cash flows. Many users of this analytical framework realized that the spread between the average return on capital and the cost of capital, over the life of an investment, was generally associated with net present value. That is, when the average return on capital exceeded the cost of capital, the NPV tended to be positive, and vice versa. As a result, many financial analysts, both at operating companies and at investment advisory firms, devised a shortcut whereby they would present this spread between return on capital and cost of capital as the most important variable in their performance scorecards. If the return spread was positive, they took this as an unambiguous sign that value was being created.

The implications of measuring this return spread were positive at first, but the increasing focus on ensuring a wide and expanding positive gap between the company's return on capital and its cost of capital has, in many cases, gone too far. Indeed, as with my flight control system design colleague, "too much is no good." Far too many management teams are overly risk averse, which discourages new investment, and they often have become so preoccupied with beating the cost of capital by maximizing their return on capital that they tend to underinvest in the future of their business. The result, more often than not, is a high near-term return on capital, but a slowdown in capital investment, a decline in revenue growth, a weakening of differentiation and long-term prospects, a drop in valuation multiples, and, ultimately, poor total shareholder returns.

These managements have the right intentions, but the outcome too often differs from their expectations. They habitually blame this outcome on the fickle stock market, but in fact *they* created a value-creation problem by underestimating the influence of investment and growth on TSR. They hear, and heed, the calls from investors for more financial discipline, reduced capital spending, and a higher return on capital. They listen to what investors say, and over time they view capital expenditures and acquisitions as unfavorable necessities that should be minimized.

This excessive focus on percentage rates of return and the resulting underinvestment has led many companies to experience rising cash balances, which leads to questions from investors about what to do with all the cash. To add to this, historically U.S. corporate tax law has exacerbated the problem by essentially giving companies a tax break by not taxing cash held overseas, trapping hoards of cash in foreign subsidiaries—though the Tax Cuts and Jobs Act of 2017 largely fixed this part of the problem.

While it may be no coincidence, this emphasis on rates of return, the deemphasis on investing in the future, and the surplus cash situation all developed at the same time that corporate America became infatuated with the stock buyback. Perhaps the biggest discrepancy between reality and common perception involves the impact of share buybacks on shareholder value. Quite a few academic research papers show that, on average, when a company announces a share buyback, its share price rises. If you believe stock markets are highly efficient, then this evidence alone is enough to convince you that buybacks are good for the company and its owners. No doubt, the stock market is very effective and accurate over time. But having lived through the junk-bond bubble, the Internet bubble, the real-estate bubble, and other less-pronounced bubbles, I am unwilling to believe it is accurate and efficient enough to base strategy development and decision-making solely on short-term stock market reactions to corporate announcements.

The cases made for buybacks abound. Some investors and other commentators ask questions such as, "why don't companies buy back more stock in their own company, which they know, rather than buying stock in other companies they don't know?" It is easy to see how these buyback arguments are attractive to managements and boards alike. This is especially so when the very same share price reaction research is used to show that acquisitions, on average, destroy value—as demonstrated by the tendency of share prices to drop on the announcements of such deals.

These days, many managements devote considerable attention to ensuring that their teams can deliver earnings per share (EPS) that meet or exceed the consensus estimates of brokerage analysts. In almost all cases, buying back stock lifts EPS, since the number of shares declines and earnings hardly change. Bankers use this angle to pitch share buybacks as a financial strategy, making it particularly appealing to managements who use EPS as a primary measure in their incentive compensation plans. After all, why *not* aim to improve the single most discussed measure of company performance?

Taxes have also played a role. In years past, buybacks had better tax treatment than dividends, at least for the combined company and investor. However, the Jobs and Growth Tax Relief Reconciliation Act of 2003 eliminated this tax difference. Oddly, buybacks accelerated, growing nearly fivefold from 2003 to 2007. And over the five years through the end of 2017, total buybacks by the 353 members of the S&P 500 in the 2018 Fortuna Advisors Buyback ROI Report[1] amounted to $2.5 trillion, 64% more than was distributed in dividends by these companies. Total buybacks and dividends were $4.0 trillion, which is 106% of net income over the period. Many experts claim that corporate America is underinvesting in the future, and these figures suggest that this may be because investments are being crowded out by an obsession with distributing cash as dividends and buybacks.

The strategic reality is quite different when we observe what investors do rather than what they say. A rigorous study of the performance of companies over time shows that those who deploy more of the cash earnings they generate to buy back stock deliver lower TSR to shareholders.[2] Our original research on this was based on the 1,000 largest nonfinancial U.S. companies as of 12/31/2009, excluding those not public for the entire period of the study. For the five years through 2008, the companies were separated into quartiles based on the amount spent on buybacks as a percentage of Gross Cash Earnings. Those directing more of their cash earnings to buybacks had lower median TSR, and each quartile showed successively worse TSR as the buybacks increased, as shown in figure 31.

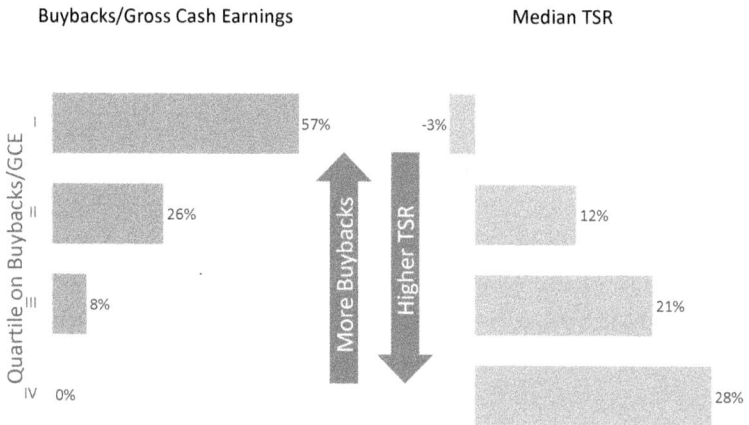

Figure 31—Buyback Rate Inversely Related to TSR

How can this be? Investors say they want most companies to buy back stock, and yet those that listen tend to do worse for shareholders. To unpack this, let's reflect on the case of stock buybacks at a small private company. Consider a restaurant where you are one of five owners, and one of the other owners seeks to exit the business and pursue a different career path, as illustrated in figure 32.

$000s	Situation Before Buyout			Situation After Buyout		
	Baseline	Value Increases	Value Declines	Buyout	Value Increases	Value Declines
Partner 1 (you)	$200	$240	$160	$200	$250	$150
Partner 2	$200	$240	$160	$200	$250	$150
Partner 3	$200	$240	$160	$200	$250	$150
Partner 4	$200	$240	$160	$200	$250	$150
Partner 5	$200	$240	$160			
Equity Value	$1,000	$1,200	$800	$800	$1,000	$600
Debt	$0	$0	$0	$200	$200	$200
Total Restaurant Value	$1,000	$1,200	$800	$1,000	$1,200	$800
Individual Investor Returns		20%	-20%		25% *More Upside*	-25% *More Downside*

Figure 32—Restaurant Buyback Example

If you buy out the fifth partner, the restaurant will borrow the money to pay for the repurchase of the departing partner's shares. The remaining partners, then, will each own one quarter of the now somewhat leveraged business. If the purchase price is fair, and if the value of the business stays stable, the value of your stake in the restaurant won't change. This can be seen by comparing the *baseline* and *buyout* columns in the figure.

When you and your remaining partners get together to decide whether to buy out the departing partner, and at what price, your main consideration is the forward prospects of the business. You're likely to be keen to buy out your partner if you and your remaining partners see a solid future with strong profit growth over the next few years. If your confidence turns out to be justified, you will realize a better upside than you would have with five partners, since the extra value creation will be shared by four owners instead of five. This can be seen in the figure by comparing the two *Value Increases* columns. The return rises from 20% to 25% because of the leverage effect of the debt and the reduced share count.

By contrast, perhaps a renowned chef is rumored to be launching a new restaurant down the block, and you and your partners think your restaurant may have seen its best days. In this case, you don't want to buy the partner out at anything but a very low price. You dread the thought of looking back in a few years to see your ownership worth a fraction of what you paid, as the decline in value would then be shared by fewer partners (as shown in the two *Value Decreases* columns). In this scenario, the leverage effect of the reduced share count causes the negative return to decline from –20% to –25%.

For public companies, a stock buyback should be contemplated the same way. Share price increases after a repurchase will reward the remaining shareholders, since the gain is now divisible by fewer shares. The converse holds for a drop in share price: Just as with gains, losses are dispersed across fewer shares, meaning the company now is stuck with a higher concentration of the losses. When this happens, expect to hear groaning along the lines of: "the company repurchased 100 million shares of stock when the price was $60, and now that it's $40, they could have repurchased 150 million shares for the same amount."

So, the first lesson is that investors should prefer more buybacks when the upside seems better (when the stock price seems low), and they should want management to avoid buybacks when the stock price seems high and therefore when the prospects for further share price growth are diminished. Unfortunately, this is the opposite of what most companies do. As shown in figure 33, buybacks tend to be higher when stock prices are high relative to history, and vice versa.

There are various explanations for why companies do a poor job of timing buybacks. One culprit is the conventional corporate approach to capital deployment, whereby certain uses of capital are prioritized and management successively allocates available cash to different possible uses.

The traditional approach follows a sequence similar to the following prioritization. First come urgent financial needs. For companies that are overleveraged, the initial priority is to pay down debt and establish enough liquidity to ensure that the company remains viable. Next, companies typically consider organic investment and, if any money is left over, they may consider acquisitions as well. Next, or possibly before acquisitions, the company considers dividend increases. Finally, any money left is used for buybacks. This seems wonderfully logical—

but unfortunately, capital is typically left over for buybacks only when the company is generating the most cash, which is also when the stock price is usually peaking. This capital deployment strategy often backfires because it ignores the business and market cycles and concentrates buybacks in times when the share price is the highest.

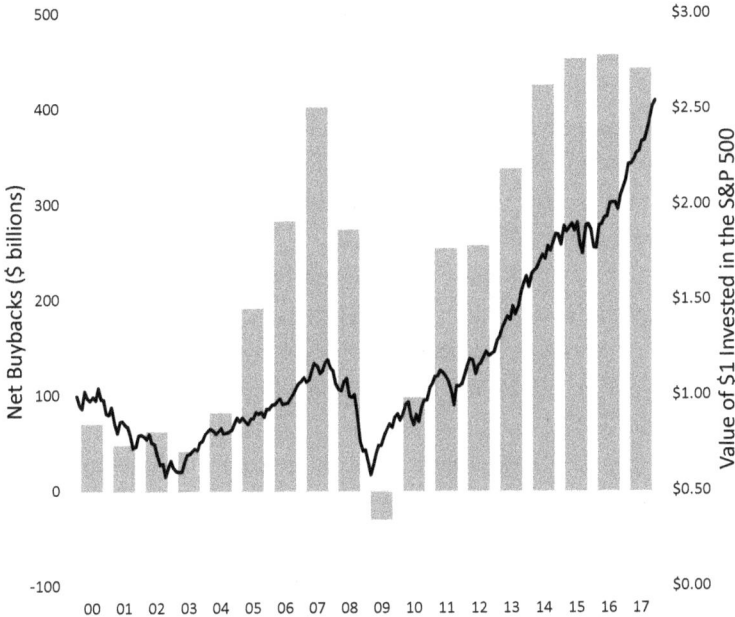

Figure 33—Net Buybacks for the S&P 500

The desire to deliver strong quarterly EPS improvements also motivates buybacks at the peak of the market cycle. Generally, as we approach the top of a market cycle, we also approach the top of an economic cycle. So, though revenue and profits are still very high, the rate of growth slows down. Corporate leaders who have become accustomed to seeing strong quarterly EPS growth don't really want the party to end, so as growth in net income slows down, their motivation remains strong to buy back shares to maintain EPS growth. Once again, this tends to drive up the volume of buybacks at the worst time for the remaining shareholders: when the price is highest.

The decision-making challenge at hand is complex and fraught with all sorts of behavioral biases. We don't really want management to sit on excess cash, since this can serve as a slush fund to absorb errors and can even lead to poor discipline and subpar investments, which can invite activist investors. And the cash may be more valuable in the hands of another management team that faces more desirable or plentiful investment opportunities. Nor do we really want the company to disgorge its cash when there may be better things to do with it internally, now or in the future. We need a consistent means of comparing past and future buybacks to other past and future uses of capital; but unfortunately, investments tend to be evaluated using rates of return and NPV, while buybacks are evaluated, if at all, based on EPS accretion/dilution statistics. So, how do we compare an investment that is expected to earn a 17% IRR to a buyback that is expected to improve EPS by $0.02?

What's worse, EPS accretion generally considers only the near-term decline in share count from the buyback. It doesn't consider the potential net income, had the capital been invested. In other words, factoring EPS accretion alone ignores the opportunity cost of buying back stock.

This capital deployment dilemma led me to develop a new measure of a buyback program's return on investment, which I refer to as Buyback ROI. This measure was specifically designed to address the above-mentioned need to make direct comparisons of buybacks to other uses of capital, such as buying equipment or making acquisitions. Buyback ROI reflects the annualized rate of return, determined by comparing the capital deployed to repurchase shares to the dividends saved, plus what the shares would be worth at the end of the period.

Consider a company that uses $100 million to buy back five million shares at $20 dollars a share. To keep it simple, let's assume they don't pay dividends. If at the end of the year the share price is $18, the buyback doesn't look too good. The decline in value of $2 represents a negative 10% Buyback ROI. Just like the restaurateurs who didn't want to sell high and watch the value of their restaurant fall, public shareholders don't want management to buy at $20 in advance of a $2 share price decline. Had management waited, it would now be able to buy back more shares at $18.

When calculating Buyback ROI using public information, we would like to use the monthly number of shares and the average share price that is reported in the quarterly 10-Q report. But, as of this writing, this data is not captured in the Capital IQ database, so we relied on the quarterly amount deployed to buy back shares in the statement of cash flows. Our standard approach is to use the average daily closing price each quarter to estimate the number of shares purchased, which may be a bit high or low, depending on how well managements time their buybacks within the quarter. Of course, all the evidence points to poor buyback timing by many managements, so our assumption may indeed make the situation look better than it really is. But it could go the other way, too.

Some say this approach is too exposed to the whims of fickle markets and unexpected share price movements. This is true, but how is this different from acquiring a public company? Is the price paid in an acquisition to be ignored because of market quirks? Of course not, so it shouldn't be ignored in a buyback. In fact, it is quite possible for management to estimate a rough intrinsic value and then to distinguish when a share price is generally high or low. This is especially true in an environment in which the company's share-price high during a given year is often 40%–50% or more above the low for the year.[3] But despite how reasonable it seems to try to time buybacks better, managements are notoriously bad at determining when their own share price is (too) high or low.

Coming back to Buyback ROI—we can disaggregate the measure into the two main drivers of whether a buyback actually creates value. The first Buyback ROI driver is Buyback Strategy, which tells us whether a company bought back shares during a period when its share price was generally rising. Buyback Strategy reflects the total shareholder return, based on share price appreciation and dividends over the period.

Predictably, companies with rapidly rising share prices tend to have higher Buyback ROI. So, naturally, it's a good Buyback Strategy to repurchase shares when the share price is rising. In such situations, reducing the share count tends to push the share price even higher, since the quarter-by-quarter increase in market capitalization is spread across fewer shares. Similarly, companies with falling share prices tend to deliver a low or negative Buyback Strategy, because the decline in market capitalization is also spread across fewer shares, accelerating the decline in the per-share price.

The second Buyback ROI driver is Buyback Effectiveness, which is simply the compound difference between Buyback ROI and Buyback Strategy and reflects how well buybacks were timed, based on price fluctuations within a given period.[4] Companies that tend to buy back more when the share price is below the overall trend, and less when it is above, buy back more shares for the same amount. In other words, their buybacks are more effective. It should be noted that Buyback Effectiveness is positive whenever Buyback ROI is higher than Buyback Strategy.

After developing these new measures of buyback success, *Institutional Investor* magazine chose to publish our Buyback ROI Ranking in its November 2012 issue. Yet, even five years later in 2017, in an article titled "The Most and Least Effective Buyback Programs,"[5] author Stephen Mintz wrote: "In fact, return measurements that are typically applied to capital expenditures, mergers and acquisitions, and virtually every other use of corporate capital are rarely used to measure the value of buybacks, even though they consume equal or greater amounts of corporate capital." We agree.

The magazine decided to have us determine the Buyback ROI ranking, based on the trailing two years, or eight quarters. While we considered using a longer period to elicit more robust findings, the editors preferred a shorter period to show results that were more current and more relevant to their readership. We ranked only those companies that spent an amount on buybacks that was at least 4% of their ending market capitalization, or at least $1 billion, so as to exclude those where the findings might be less meaningful. The first ranking showed an average Buyback ROI of 9.7%, with an average Buyback Strategy of 10.7% and an average Buyback Effectiveness of −1.0%. Overall, these buybacks didn't create or destroy much value, as their Buyback ROIs were probably not far off the average cost of capital; if your shareholders want to earn a 10% return and you deploy capital at 10%, you neither create nor destroy value.

Though it seemed neutral on average, at the extremes the results were quite different. Sunoco, the energy company, led the table with a whopping Buyback ROI of 115.4%. It was a great time for it to buy back stock, as shown by its Buyback Strategy of 34.2%, which was amplified by good buyback timing, as indicated by a Buyback Effectiveness of 60.5%.

To understand the relationship between Buyback Strategy, Buyback Effectiveness, and Buyback ROI, it is helpful to see the math, as shown in Figure 34.

$$(1 + \text{Buyback Strategy})\qquad (1 + 34.2\%)$$

$$X\ (1 + \text{Buyback Effectiveness})\qquad (1 + 60.5\%)$$

$$= (1 + \text{Buyback ROI})\qquad (1 + 115.4\%)$$

Figure 34—Sunoco Buyback ROI as of 2012

In that inaugural 2012 ranking, the top 18 companies all had both positive Buyback Strategy and positive Buyback Effectiveness, meaning they timed their buybacks well, as the price was generally rising. And the bottom 18 were all negative on both Buyback Strategy and Buyback Effectiveness, indicating both that it was a bad time for them to pursue buybacks generally, and that, based on the price movements within this period, they also timed them poorly. While at the time of this writing it seems hard to explain, Netflix was last on the list with a Buyback ROI of –51.9%. After that, however, Netflix delivered very strong share price performance and its Buyback ROI improved considerably.

These rankings continued on more or less a quarterly basis in *Institutional Investor*, but then *Fortune Magazine* picked up the ranking for 2017 and requested a few changes. Most important, the period evaluated was extended to five years, or 20 quarters. This decision was made collaboratively with the editorial staff, but we at Fortuna Advisors felt fully on board. The longer period would provide a more robust impression of how companies were performing on buybacks, with less influence from market volatility.

On May 1, 2017, Ryan Derousseau's article "Stocks that Dodge the Buyback Blues"[6] appeared in print and in a longer format on *Fortune's* website. The strong stock market over the five years ending in 2016 drove median Buyback Strategy up to 16.6%, which created a better environment for buybacks to be successful. Unfortunately, the

ability to successfully time buybacks got worse and average Buyback
Effectiveness dropped to –4.3%. Almost a third of the median positive buyback strategy was consumed by poor buyback timing, and
median Buyback ROI diminished to just 11.2%. These returns were
still slightly positive for shareholders, but could have been improved
with better timing.

The second *Fortune* article, "Why Stock Market Buybacks Should
Make Investors Nervous,"[7] again authored by Ryan Derousseau, was
published on April 20, 2018. It showed that median Buyback ROI rose
from 11.2% in the prior ranking to 13.8% for the five years ending
in 2017. By sorting companies into high, medium, and low groups
based on their buybacks over the five years as a percentage of recent
market capitalization, we were able to measure whether companies
doing more or fewer buybacks had better median Buyback ROI. We
found that the high-buyback group had the *lowest* median Buyback
ROI, Buyback Strategy, and Buyback Effectiveness. This, of course,
was very bad news for investors who advocate heavy use of buybacks.
As we have learned already, too much is no good.

We developed Buyback ROI during a bull market and, as of this
writing, the bull is still charging ahead. This has served as wind at
the back of the massive corporate buyback programs. But how will
these enormous buyback programs that were executed in 2018 look
through the Buyback ROI lens after the next market downturn? People
sometimes quip that there are two certainties in life, death and taxes.
But they should add a third certainty: cycles. Ever since there has
been an economy, it has gone through cycles, and the stock markets
also go through cycles. After every upturn in the past, a downturn
has always followed, then after that another upturn (and so on, into
infinity). Everyone knows this, but few behave accordingly.

As discussed above, perhaps the worst part of this buyback mania
may be how buybacks have crowded out good investment in operations, thereby depleting the potential future value of growth. At first, I
was somewhat apprehensive about my hypothesis that buybacks were
impeding good investments. Though the numbers seemed to support
that view, I couldn't envision any meaningful number of executives
deliberately underinvesting so that they could pursue more buybacks
and elevate short-term EPS. Then a series of corporate experiences
provided the confirmation I had been seeking.

My former partner, John Cryan, and I were looking for a way to bridge the gap between the notions that "Buybacks lead to worse TSR" and "Buybacks increase EPS." John began testing changes in PE multiples for companies that did or did not do buybacks. While it was his idea, we worked together on the research and published our findings that, on average, PE multiples declined relative to those of the overall market for companies doing heavy buybacks.[8] The more that EPS increased from repurchasing shares, the less valuable each dollar of incremental EPS became. Our study showed that each increment of EPS growth from buybacks was worth about half as much as EPS growth from profitable revenue growth together with operational improvements.

This was significant to us because, as former investment bankers, we had participated in many client meetings where the industry bankers and financial strategy experts expressed some variant of the following: "If your EPS rises by 15%, *and if we assume the PE multiple stays the same*, then your share price should also rise by 15%." It seemed to management like a pretty easy way to boost the share price. Back at the office, we often wondered why they would assume the PE multiple would stay the same. When we would ask them, the response was "why not?" Now we had evidence that the PE multiple declines, on average. But we are quite sure few bankers have changed their story.

OK, so I get a little intense when it comes to buybacks. At least that's what I was told by friends who read my debate with Whitney Tilson that was published as "The Pros and Cons of Stock Buybacks" in *The Wall Street Journal.*[9] But who *wouldn't* be intense if they discovered that companies were deploying an average of half a trillion dollars each year to do something that often hurts investors?

This is not to say that companies should avoid distributing cash to investors when they have a surplus and foresee few promising investment opportunities. But by doing this through buybacks, they are imposing price risk on their remaining shareholders. Given the preponderance of poorly timed buyback programs, a less risky way for them to distribute cash to investors is a special dividend, through which all shareholders receive the same treatment. Unfortunately, two major obstacles stand in the way. First, the special dividend imposes a tax event on the investor, whereas buybacks allow the investor to choose whether they want to sell and trigger a tax event. Either they get the cash if they sell into the buyback, or they get the potential benefit of a reduced share count if they don't.

The second problem is much larger, and it is the main reason we seldom see special dividends. Long-term incentives in the form of restricted stock, performance shares, and stock options are rarely insulated from special dividends. For example, consider stock options. Standard dividends reduce the valuation of stock options since the likelihood of share-price appreciation is reduced by the payment of dividends. Since each option is worth less, managers tend to be given more stock options when the company pays dividends. So, the present value of what is delivered to them is unaffected by the dividend. There is no easy way to factor in potential (future) special dividends at the time of granting, so when special dividends are paid, the value of all long-term incentives declines.

Imagine a share price of $20 and a special dividend of $2. Typically, the share price declines all or most of the way on the ex-dividend day—that is, the day the dividend is locked in even if the stock is sold. If management holds stock options with an exercise price of $16, the day the special dividend is paid they forfeit half of the *in-the-money* value. Management wouldn't want that, so they prefer stock buybacks. It shouldn't be hard to change the language in long-term incentive contracts to prevent these distorted incentives, yet few companies have done so.

The process for capital deployment decision-making includes making estimates of all sources of capital, including operating cash flow, cash expected from transactions, cash in the bank, and potential borrowings—and then determining the best way to deploy this capital across the company's opportunities for organic investment, acquisitions, buyback, dividends, and debt repayment. Many companies get this process wrong every year.

Key Capital Deployment Principles

The golden rule of capital deployment, whether we are considering capital expenditures, acquisitions, or buying back our own shares, is that value is created only when we buy something that turns out to be worth more than what we paid. If we are interested in long-term sustainable value creation, what matters is what it's worth over the long haul, not the day after we buy it.

There seem to be many more executives who can recite this simple NPV rule than can actually follow it. Few deliberately ignore it. But executives are human and face all sorts of real-world pressures and obstacles. So, while they all mean to do the right thing, they often can't help themselves.

As discussed in chapter 1, the field of behavioral finance can help explain why investor and managerial behavior often deviates from maximizing NPV or even self-interest. Remember that recency bias suggests that we often extrapolate recent events into the future. From a capital deployment perspective, this leads to investing too much, both organically and in acquisitions, at the top of the cycle (when assets are most expensive). Other behavioral biases, such as "loss aversion," exacerbate this tendency by causing procrastination and "analysis paralysis," rather than decisive action. Leverage, too, can play a part by amplifying the effects of this loss aversion and thus further slowing down the decision process.

Another critical behavior bias is "herding," in which executives find it easier to follow what others are doing, or seem to be doing. This bias leads to poorly thought-out capital deployment strategies that mimic the behavior of others in the industry. Few executives feel comfortable standing out from the pack, which also of course has to do with loss aversion. Many managers are so loss-averse and concerned with self-preservation that they appear to be content to just hand money back to investors. This may seem like a conservative and prudent decision, but it often leads to underinvestment. And managers' incentives may be, or at least are perceived to be, asymmetric with more downside than upside. Many executives have observed early in their careers that even small failures are punished more than successes are rewarded, and the result is a conditioned reluctance to pursue any growth investment with an expected outcome that is less than certain.

In addition to these biases, organizations experience all sorts of office politics, power struggles, and bureaucratic restraints that also lead to "groupthink," maintenance of the status quo, and the stifling of alternative or dissenting ideas. These effects can all severely restrict the creativity and innovation that should fuel growth.

Most of us, at least at times, fall prey to the likes of recency bias, loss aversion, herding, and poor understanding of business cycles.

Luckily, we can develop fact-based capital deployment policies and processes that help overcome these natural biases and steer us toward doing what is right for investors.

It was shown earlier in figure 33 that buybacks tend to happen when prices are high, despite the fact that most managers understand they can buy back more and deliver more benefit to their shareholders if they're patient and avoid buybacks around the peaks.

As shown in figure 35, a similar relationship exists for acquisitions; that is, companies commit more capital to acquiring other companies when they're expensive than when they're cheap. This would indicate that companies are either not considering or unable to perceive macro price and market trends when making acquisitions. In certain years, companies have overpaid by billions of dollars by ignoring this principle of "buy low, sell high." Of course, in the middle of a sharp downturn, such as the 2009 financial crisis, it is difficult to summon the confidence to make a large, acquisitive bet—unless your name is Warren Buffett. But why was almost twice as much invested in acquisitions in 2007 than in 2005, or in 2016 than in 2013?

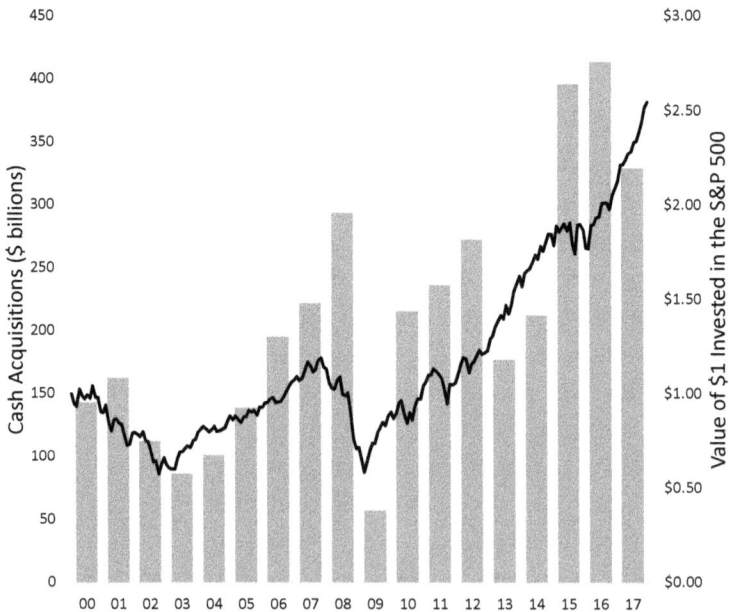

Figure 35—Cash Acquisitions for the S&P 500

If we care about the difference between the value of what we get versus what we pay, then buybacks and acquisitions shouldn't be concentrated at the top of the market cycle when prices are the highest. At a minimum, they should be spread somewhat evenly over the cycle. To achieve this requires capital deployment processes that are explicitly designed to overcome our natural human biases when they would lead us to suboptimal choices.

It is easy to be overwhelmed by the complexity of capital deployment. There is a certain amount of cash available from operations, and the company can borrow more, sell stock, or divest existing businesses to generate more for allocation. This capital can be used to invest organically or in acquisitions, to pay dividends or buy back stock, or to adjust the capital structure by accumulating cash or paying down debt. As shown in figure 36, two important decisions drive the process. First, we must assess whether there are current desirable investment opportunities; second, if there are no such opportunities, we must assess whether future ones can be expected.

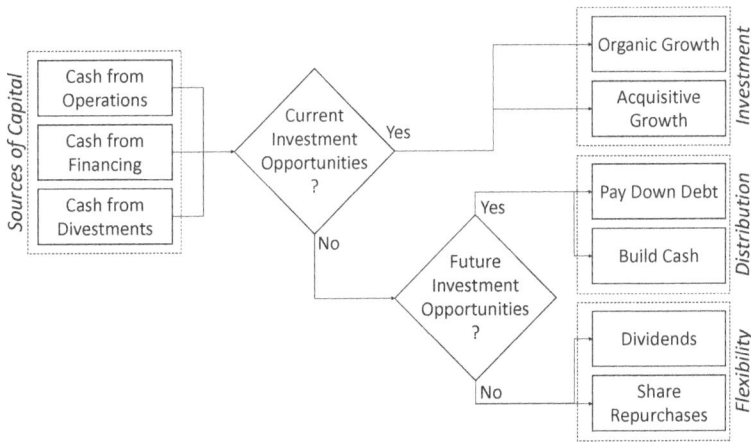

Figure 36—The Sources and Uses of Capital

The process seems simple—just two straightforward questions to answer. But every source and use of capital is as dynamic and subject to change as the critical internal and external factors that tend to drive such decisions. And to further complicate the matter, many of these factors interact. Perhaps a consumer staples business has suffered a 15% decline in its share price due to a negative market reaction to a recently announced acquisition. At this lower valuation, buybacks may look attractive; but as a result of the financing commitment to fund the announced acquisition, the company would need to borrow to fund the buyback, which may push credit stats below the desired range. Management decides against a buyback. Would the answer be different if the share price fell 25% and thus created more upside for the buybacks? What if the share price fell by half, or more?

Or consider a hot retail business that has readily found and invested in new store opportunities that have delivered consistent 25%–30% cash returns. The company is innovative and successful at marketing, so the returns are expected to be sustainable. These returns are on the order of three times the required return of 8%–10%, and an NPV analysis shows that each dollar the company invests in new stores turns into three dollars of present value. The store footprint is still rather small, so there appears to be a lot of runway to keep opening value-creating stores for years to come.

A competitor becomes available for sale, and management considers acquiring it since it is convinced it can run that brand better. But to complete the acquisition would absorb so much human and financial capital that it would slow the expansion of the existing brand. The question in this case is not whether the NPV from the acquisition is positive; it is whether the NPV is sufficiently positive to make up for the lost NPV from slowing the growth rate of the existing business. This type of analysis can be performed to evaluate alternative investment decisions and the opportunity costs associated with them—in this case weighing organic versus acquisitive growth. Consider how the decision would differ if the base business were mature and had few growth opportunities. Then there is a much lower threshold before the acquisition creates value.

Ten Key Principles for Effective Capital Deployment

Complexity is best dealt with by establishing principles to guide management and designing processes to rigorously follow those principles. The following 10 key principles for effective capital deployment provide the foundation for establishing an enduring capital deployment process to drive long-term value creation.

Principle 1—The Top Priority Is Survival: In order to have the opportunity to achieve success, company leadership must first circumvent complete failure by ensuring business survival. Management must avoid excessive risk-taking, provide adequate financing capacity and liquidity, and protect important tangible and intangible assets, including key personnel, brands, technologies, and other essential differentiators. Many business failures are avoidable with adequate forethought and planning, but most truly difficult challenges come from underestimating change. For example, companies producing record albums when CDs were introduced in 1984 probably expected a more gradual transition, but what they got was an abrupt upheaval. By 1990, most music was purchased in the form of CDs. And then CDs were replaced by electronic content ownership, which has now been replaced by streaming. What's next?

Survival is the top priority, for obvious reasons, but most managements don't pay enough attention to change. Management must devote resources to identifying potential threats to survival and then act to get ahead of change and turn these potential threats into opportunities. The biggest obstacle, of course, is *short-termism*, which is reinforced by overconfidence, procrastination, and a distaste for cannibalizing existing products or services. It also doesn't help that many managers feel they can readily influence their own short-term compensation but often view long-term incentives as a bit of a lottery. Management processes and incentive compensation must be structured to explicitly address and reduce the impact of each of these obstacles.

Principle 2—Buy Low and Sell High, *Really*: To emphasize NPV in capital deployment requires a mindset of always buying low and selling high. In the movie *Caddyshack*, Rodney Dangerfield bellowed into his golf bag phone, "What's that? Then sell! Oh, they're selling? Then buy!" Audiences laughed because of the absurdity, but also because of the cliché. Still, clichés are clichés for a reason, and the value of selling when others are buying, and vice versa, is obvious to the vast majority of investors. But we know from the previous discussions of buybacks and acquisitions that corporate executives tend to do the opposite of Rodney's maxim. It can sometimes be difficult to tell when prices are too high or low, so executives must pay careful attention to cycles and rely on thoughtful analysis to actually buy or sell assets when prices are favorable.

One important way to do this is to explicitly factor the expectation of operational, financial, and other cycles into planning and decision-making. One oil and gas CFO explained how he uses the same midrange oil price when considering the acquisition of new oil and gas reserves, regardless of where the industry is in the commodity price cycle. This way, he tends to buy more reserves when they are cheap and fewer when they are expensive. For companies in industries that don't experience much cyclicality in financial performance, it is still important to pay attention to market cycles. From the 2007 peak to the trough of the market in the 2009 financial crisis, the median utility company suffered TSR of −41%. Utilities are not viewed as being cyclical. Indeed, the median utility, Exelon, saw its EPS increase slightly from $4.03 to $4.09 from 2007 to 2009, a period when its EBITDA increased 9.5%. So why was its TSR −41%? Market fear. Exelon acquired no competitors that year, but perhaps it could have improved its long-run performance by buying a very stable competitor that would have essentially been on sale.

Principle 3—Don't Follow the Crowd: Make it a strong policy to never select capital deployment choices because some loud shareholders ask you to do it, or because bankers say everyone is doing it, or because you overheard on the golf course or at the yacht club that your rival is doing it. Did Warren Buffett see everyone buying railroads in 2009 when he announced the investment of $34 billion to buy the Burlington and Northern Santa Fe railroad? Doubtful. In fact, it was that everyone lost interest in railroads that created the opportunity. Did he care what the immediate investor reaction would be, or did he focus exclusively on whether he could buy an asset for anything less than his assessment of its long-term intrinsic value? We seek to make capital deployment choices that create value whether or not they are perceived as "trending." And indeed the best investments are often *not* trending; good—that is, value-creating—ideas that everyone is pursuing aren't value-creating for long.

This contrarian mindset is not new. In 1841, Charles Mackay published *Extraordinary Popular Delusions and the Madness of Crowds*, which discusses Dutch tulip-mania, the South Sea Company bubble, and numerous other examples where the crowd, or the market for our purposes, got it wrong. Market bubbles are an unbelievably interesting deviation from long-run market efficiency, and Mackay's book offers one of the earliest commentaries on the subject. What's most useful for corporate managers is to understand the innate desire to follow the crowd. This type of "herding" can be seen today by both companies and investors in the market. For those who were old enough at the time, look back at the Internet bubble and think about the typical business news commentary in those days. The repetitive buzzing of "profits don't matter anymore, it's about clicks and eyeballs" fueled an emotional response of not wanting to miss out. This fear of missing out feeling, or *FOMO*, afflicted even the well-schooled in finance, valuation, and basic economics, among other less sophisticated investors. Capital deployment processes must explicitly contemplate emotional bubbles and their effect on the likely trends and opportunities to be managed.

Principle 4—Investment Usually Outperforms Financial Engineering: Much more long-term value comes from investment and execution than from financial engineering. In the very same study and article behind figure 31, we showed the positive relationship between investment in the business and TSR, as shown in figure 37.

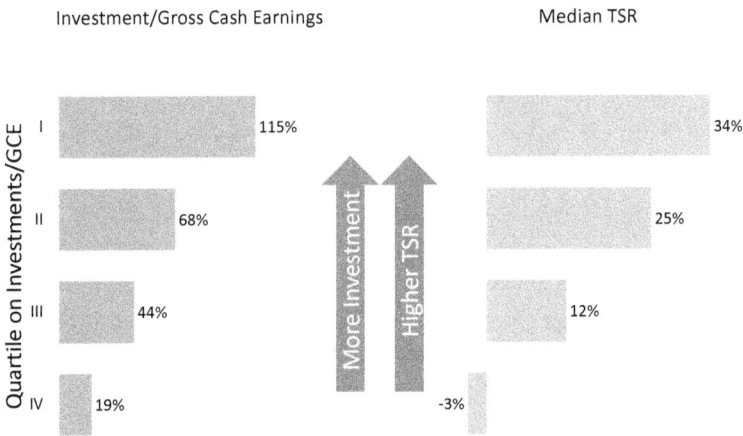

Investment/Gross Cash Earnings   Median TSR

Quartile on Investments/GCE	Investment/Gross Cash Earnings	Median TSR
I	115%	34%
II	68%	25%
III	44%	12%
IV	19%	-3%

More Investment   *Higher TSR*

Figure 37—Reinvestment Rate Positively Related to TSR

Investment creates value, on average, because it's *not* a zero-sum game; and companies, on average, deliver returns well above the required return demanded by investors. Managers need to be disciplined, since it's easy to make bad investments, but this should only lead them to be extra careful rather than leading them to avoid making investments altogether. As long as the incremental return is above the required return, managers should drive the reinvestment rate as high as possible.

Principle 5—Prioritize Organic Investment: Virtually all great business success stories began with some form of organic investment, especially investments that increase differentiation through innovation and branding. So organic investments should always be given priority over acquisitive investments. The range of organic investment opportunities is wide. It includes projects that are familiar, have reasonable risk exposures, and are expected to produce decent, but not extreme, upside potential, such as expanding production capacity, improving efficiency and productivity, and updating the look and feel of retail stores, restaurants, and hotels. These can be classified as either doing more of what we already do or doing what we do better.

Opportunities also exist to invest in less familiar areas, sometimes taking on greater risks and potentially realizing extremely substantial returns. This can include the development of new products and services, the marketing launch of totally new or significantly rejuvenated brands, or the expansion of delivering products and services to new geographies. For example, consider a pharmaceutical company that contemplates investing for many years in expensive scientific research with the hope of developing a new drug that then requires tremendous research and marketing to ensure efficacy, navigate regulatory approval, and bring the treatment to market. Every company should dedicate at least a reasonable portion of its investment budget to higher risk-reward areas; and for those with existing commercial products and services, there will usually be plenty of opportunity to make lower risk-reward investments to drive the existing business forward. But both the low- and high-risk organic investments should be prioritized over acquisitive investment.

Principle 6—Be Willing to Grow Carefully by Acquisition and Shrink Through Divestitures or Spinoffs: It has become a bit of a business cliché to say that "most acquisitions destroy value." Fortunately, this is not true, generally. The vast majority of our capital market research across industries and varying time periods shows that those investing more in acquisitions do, on average, deliver higher average TSR. We all know of spectacular acquisition failures, such as the 1998 acquisition of Chrysler by Daimler and the 2010 acquisition of Palm by HP—both deals that turned out terribly for the acquirer in rapid fashion. These, and other such disasters, make for eye-catching news headlines but are truly a small minority of cases.

Although acquisitions should be a second priority behind organic investment, it is quite possible to build a successful acquisition track record. Like learning all other skills, acquisition expertise requires development and practice. This is why serial acquirers tend to perform better than occasional acquirers. It is also critical to align acquisition strategy with business strategy, as will be discussed in chapter 11. Companies should actively monitor a list of potential targets and constantly grade them on fit and desirability, as indicated by the value expected to be received in relation to the price. Success is much less likely with such a deliberate process versus when deals originate with a banker stopping by with a pitch book of ideas, or an offering memorandum on a company that wasn't otherwise contemplated by the acquirer. It's like having a real estate agent regularly show you and your family houses that are available—you may end up moving to a bigger and more expensive house that you weren't even thinking about beforehand.

Principle 7—Leverage Tends to Stifle Investment: Maintaining high debt leverage can be a bigger problem than buybacks in some companies. In good times, leverage seems good. If our business is growing strongly with nice profit margins and decent rates of return, having more leverage will amplify the EPS growth rate, and TSR will often follow it, to at least some degree. But if, or frankly when, the economy falters, the industry loses momentum, or our company suffers a competitive setback, perhaps due to a new competitive product that leapfrogs our own, then the leverage will amplify the downside just as it did the upside. From the S&P 500 peak on October 9, 2007, through the trough on March 9, 2009, the S&P 500 fell 57%. In most sectors, the companies that had higher total debt as a percentage of EBITDA at the start of the market downturn had worse TSR over the 17-month period than their less-levered peers. The most notable exception to this was healthcare, which is one of the least cyclical of industries.

What's worse is that the amount of debt leverage seems to also have a negative impact on the willingness to invest in growth. This is unbelievably important, yet generally goes unrecognized. Many corporate finance experts claim that having more debt creates value by causing a reduction in the weighted average cost of capital and showing how the present value of free cash flow rises; but they fail to incorporate the effect the debt has on the amount of long-term free cash flow. Companies faced with the financial risk associated with high debt levels tend to invest less in the business, and this behavioral effect can make the company value drop even though the company has reduced the weighted average cost of capital.

Principle 8—Implement Buyback Execution Rules: The goal of buybacks should be to create value for the remaining shareholders by buying back shares that management believes are worth more than what must be paid to repurchase them. It's no different from buying stock in another company.

To combat the tendency of companies to buy back more stock when it's expensive than when it's cheap, as discussed above, companies should implement rules-based processes for executing stock buybacks, as will be discussed in chapter 12. It's important to recognize that companies pursuing buybacks tend to suffer declines in their price-to-earnings valuation multiple; so perhaps companies should mandate that the words "buyback" and "EPS" never be mentioned in the same meeting—whoever breaks this rule has to put $20 in the holiday luncheon fund. At least for the first year of this policy, this should provide a tidy sum for some joyous celebrating at year-end.

Principle 9—Dividends Are Value Neutral: Potentially the most misunderstood use of capital is the dividend, which is only a means of giving shareholders access to money they already own. Nothing more, nothing less. By definition, dividend policy cannot create long-term value. There is a theory that dividends communicate confidence in the business, and sometimes this is true. But, frankly, a faltering dividend trend is more likely to convey a *lack* of confidence. As will be discussed in chapter 12, dividends are more an outcome of capital deployment strategy than they are a strategy in and of themselves.

One potentially beneficial, but rarely tapped, use of dividends is as a better alternative to stock buybacks when a company wants to distribute excess capital while its share price is above the midpoint of the market cycle. This still isn't true value creation; it's the avoidance of the value destruction that would come from buying back what will later seem to have been overpriced shares.

Principle 10—Value Creation Is Hard Work: Recognize that there are no tricks, easy paths, or quick fixes. For example, if the company's earnings have been growing for a few years, but now the economy is peaking and earnings growth is slowing, a quick fix to boost next quarter's EPS by repurchasing a boatload of stock may give the share price a pop on the date of announcement. But over the ensuing cycle, management and shareholders alike will probably regret the move and wish management had held the cash to be used when assets, including the company's own share price, were more attractively priced.

A Dynamic and Integrated Capital Deployment Process

Capital should be earmarked for areas where it can provide the most benefit, rather than being smeared indiscriminately across a broad range of opportunities. To this end, the foundation for a successful capital deployment process requires insights into the company's sources of success and failure. Such insights entail an understanding of performance both across the company and in comparison to competitors, customers, and suppliers. In which business areas do we have strong strategic positions in attractive markets where we can earn high sustainable returns—and more important, why? Do we have the most sought-after product features, the most ardently desired brand, the most comprehensive distribution network, or some other source of competitive advantage that allows us to price at a premium in relation to costs, including our cost of capital? With a broad understanding of the sources of value-creation success and failure, we are better equipped to allocate resources to their best possible uses.

The market environment, the industry, and indeed everything inside the company is dynamic. The pace of disruption has accelerated in recent decades and is likely to continue to do so in the future. It is not enough to look backward when formulating capital deployment strategy; we must also constantly monitor changes and new developments, and be ready to adjust the capital deployment plan in real time. A contemplated acquisition could suddenly be more attractively priced, which could crowd out other capital uses or draw down on available debt capacity. Or a competitor may launch an unexpected, new and improved offering in direct competition with our strongest product, requiring us to accelerate our own innovation projects, step up marketing, and compete more aggressively on price until our own superior products are available. Some sectors and industries are more dynamic than others and require greater financial flexibility as well as a more active real-time capital deployment process to be able to seize opportunities and react to threats.

Far too many companies view the various areas of capital deployment as separate processes, without recognizing and dealing with their interrelationships. How much we invest organically affects what we have available to invest acquisitively, while our total investment commitment affects cash and debt balances along with the ability to devote capital to buybacks and dividends. But we often see operations managers handling a share of the organic investment, with the rest being managed by marketing and product research departments, all independently, while acquisitions are contemplated by a corporate development group. Often the treasury group manages capital structure and liquidity, and leads the discussion of stock buybacks and dividend increases, with the investor relations group having a say in the latter. Surely the people leading these groups talk to each other and share information, in most cases. Yet many companies lack a truly integrated and dynamic capital deployment process that captures and prioritizes all the possibilities and that simultaneously determines the best combination of sources and uses of capital to maximize the future value of the company.

As with much of what has been discussed so far, capital deployment is often considered over too short a period, as well. Sure, there are 10- or 20-year free cash flow forecasts with NPV calculations for new production facilities, but the overall capital deployment plan rarely seems to be considered in the context of a full cyclical view. For example, say our team is a little short on new investment ideas to fund right now, but over the last decade we have generally had plenty of opportunity to make good investments. So, perhaps we should reduce the investment budget for the time being, but hold the excess in reserve either as cash in the bank or as unutilized debt capacity. The next time opportunities present themselves, possibly when our team comes up with better organic investment ideas or when competitors are cheaper to acquire during an industry or market downturn, we will have the financing capacity to seize the day.

This may seem a difficult practice to follow, given the threat that an activist investor might come in and demand that the company lever up to buy back stock. For companies that have consistently earned well above the cost of capital, have grown, and have delivered strong TSR, such a strategy might well be defended successfully against the most ardent opposition. Yet for companies that have routinely underperformed, the activist is likely to have a point. Maybe the value of maintaining financial firepower is limited and perhaps even value-destroying, since there is a high risk of bad investments in the future. Or maybe management simply needs to earn the right to grow.

The good old net-present-value rule should guide all decisions and should be applied by determining the amount of NPV per dollar of capital being deployed, which is the RCE Profitability Index (discussed in the next chapter). For anyone with finance experience, the application of NPV to organic and acquisitive investments is straightforward. Dividends have zero net present value unless they trigger taxes that could have been deferred. And, much like acquisitions, buybacks deliver a positive or a negative NPV to the remaining shareholders, based on the difference between the price of the shares and their cyclically adjusted intrinsic value. When the share price is unusually low, the potential value creation from buybacks might be greater than some of the otherwise desirable investments in the business. But when the share price is high, the opposite is true. Cash and debt levels can affect NPV, as well, since they can influence the required return and valuation. The prioritization of opportunities should be an ongoing process, and the dynamics of the market and the business will cause priorities to shift.

The process will vary somewhat by industry and even by company. But capital deployment planning should always start with a thorough understanding of where value is created and where destroyed. Corporate leaders must recognize that the world is dynamic and always be ready and willing to change their capital deployment plans in real time. The processes for managing sources and uses of capital should be integrated by a capital deployment oversight group that manages priorities and tradeoffs. At most companies, this is the executive committee. Decisions must be made in the context of both near- and longer-term expectations. In the end, however, all capital deployment decisions should be aimed at maximizing net present value.

Notes

1   "2018 Fortuna Buyback ROI Report," accessed January 14, 2019, https://fortunedotcom.files.wordpress.com/2018/04/2018-fortuna-buyback-roi-report.pdf.

Note that this study includes all companies in the S&P 500 that bought back at least $1 billion worth of stock or at least 4% of their ending market capitalization over the five-year period.

2   Gregory V. Milano, "Are Buybacks the Best We Can Do?," *Buona Fortuna,* February 16, 2010.

3   In 2018, for example, the median company in the Russell 1000 had a 52-week high that was 52% higher than the 52-week low. This figure was 41% in 2017 and 54% in 2016.

4   The concept of Buyback Effectiveness was originally suggested by my former partner at Fortuna Advisors, Steve Treadwell.

5   S. L. Mintz, "The Most and Least Effective Stock Buyback Programs," *Institutional Investor,* September 30, 2017, accessed January 15, 2019, https://www.institutionalinvestor.com/article/b14zpnbhzxyk7q/the-most-and-least-effective-stock-buyback-programs.

6   Ryan Derousseau, "4 'Buyback' Stocks Worth Buying," *Fortune,* accessed January 15, 2019, http://fortune.com/2017/04/26/best-buyback-stocks-trump-bump/.

7   Ryan Derousseau, "Why Stock Market Buybacks Should Make Investors Nervous," *Fortune,* accessed January 15, 2019, http://fortune.com/2018/04/20/stock-market-buybacks-nervous/.

8   Gregory V. Milano and John R. Cryan, "Advocates Overrating the Benefits of Buybacks," CFO.com, October 17, 2012, accessed January 15, 2019, http://ww2.cfo.com/cash-flow/2012/10/advocates-overrating-the-benefits-of-buybacks/.

9   Maxwell Murphy, "The Pros and Cons of Stock Buybacks," *Wall Street Journal,* February 27, 2012, accessed January 15, 2019, https://www.wsj.com/articles/SB10001424052970203824904577213891035614390.

NINE

Strategic Resource Allocation

HIGH-LEVEL CAPITAL deployment choices were discussed in chapter 8. This chapter will delve more deeply into how resources should be allocated to various projects within a business. In principle, Strategic Resource Allocation,[1] or SRA, is straightforward. In a nutshell, SRA is about allocating capital expenditures, R&D, marketing, and other organic investments to where current and future expected returns are projected to be highest. Despite the simplicity of this resource allocation maxim, many management teams deviate rather significantly from the ideal allocation of their resources.

The first problem is that suboptimal resource allocations often occur for "strategic" reasons, which can, at least in some cases, turn out to be very successful. Sometimes *visionary strategists* do, in fact, deploy resources on a hunch about some new opportunity that has no clear way to deliver returns—yet the project ends up being successful. (And, of course, such successes receive extraordinary attention from the business media.) Some of the biggest game-changers in history have started this way, but most vision-inspired projects and initiatives end up being a waste of resources that could have created more value elsewhere. By contrast, the appeal of being a successful visionary strategist is hard to resist. Most CEOs are impressed by how Steve Jobs, Bill Gates, or Jeff Bezos were able to invent products and services that didn't previously exist, transform or create entire industries, and dramatically affect our day-to-day lives; and many would love to be seen by the world as visionary strategists like them. The problem, however, is that most people don't realize how rare such visionary skills are, and how stacked the odds are against success.

Let me be clear: Strategic vision can be a profound source of value for many businesses. But for vision to create value it must always be grounded in both observable (and accurate) measures and well-conceived forecasts. This usually requires pressure testing the idea by thoughtfully considering the scale of the potential advantage it would create, and then carefully anticipating customers' and competitors' reactions. Said differently, anyone can have a vision, but few come up with ideas that are sufficiently grounded in economic reality to succeed.

In any case, most CEOs of large companies didn't get where they are by being visionaries. They usually were successful at executing plans and delivering results, and their exceptional results impressed their predecessor or their board nominations committee. Or maybe their success was achieved by executing at a different company, and they were brought in through an executive search process because of their track record of delivering results. This record for delivering results probably started well before they were named CEO. Whatever department they started in, they were evidently better than their peers at getting things done and getting them done right, so they leapfrogged others along the way. Sure, they would never have been appointed CEO if they didn't seem to have both leadership and managerial skills, but in addition they brought home the bacon. Managing your way to the top also requires skills in navigating what are sometimes fairly complex bureaucracies. And without a doubt, many true visionaries, frustrated by their attempts to deal with a bureaucracy, set out on their own entrepreneurial ventures well before they get close to the CEO seat.

But for many of those who brave the bureaucracy and become CEOs, the power of the office somehow goes to their head once they get to that CEO suite. Their pay jumps immensely, their office gets bigger, their responsibilities expand, and they are finally in a position to reply, if they choose, "because I say so." Top of the world, or at least the hill. No longer are they content with selling more products or services, improving quality and the customer experience so they can charge premium prices, or driving cost efficiencies and capital productivity. They "have people" to take care of these mundane tasks, just as they took care of them for their predecessor. Now that they are CEO, they suddenly have a vision for how they will transform the industry with a revolutionary product, a pioneering business model, or a reimagined...something or other. And the more revolutionary the product, the more likely it is to require investing significant sums for an extended period without profits. It's all based on having blind faith in their vision without any compelling empirical underpinning.

Please don't misunderstand—pursuing visionary goals is wonderful when it works. Despite the tone of the prior paragraphs, there is in fact considerable value potential in developing visionary ideas, experimentation, creativity, and, yes, reimagination. But there is no reason why this must be the *only* plan. In the areas where we have proven expertise, we can focus attention on maximizing value by investing and managing effectively, while at the same time pursuing blue-sky creative ideas—though these may need to be separated organizationally for both to be effective.

The second major problem with "strategic" resource allocation is the general tendency of top management or corporate headquarters to allocate capital among business units uneconomically. As we've previously discussed, this often results from a misguided attempt to be equitable to all their projects or departments, or because of their limited understanding of where their business really creates value—or often both.

The SRA Process
Getting the most out of the current businesses requires an effective SRA process. If the company has several businesses, the first step is to determine the RCE of each, based on historical and projected financial information, to see which businesses are most successful at converting precious funding into value. The SRA process must then dig deep to identify businesses with different products, services, geographies, distribution channels, and other dimensions that warrant more growth investment. The main aim in so doing is to distinguish such opportunities from the products and services that need to improve RCE margin and thereby earn the right to grow. We want to throw good money after good, not bad.

As we touched on in chapter 7, the potential for long-term value creation is usually highly concentrated. It sounds like a consulting cliché, and it is, but the 80/20 rule—that roughly 80% of value creation comes from 20% of business activities—applies to most companies.

This 20% is where we want to concentrate new resources. Beyond this all-important 20%, there are usually some modest value creators, some value-neutral activities, and a decent-sized group of value destroyers.

Often the process of understanding where value is created gets bogged down in the assignment of cost and capital, and it is true that there is no perfect answer on this topic. Sometimes companies readjust the numbers over and over, while managers with different personal interests and biases seek the answer that helps their cause. It's the ultimate analysis paralysis.

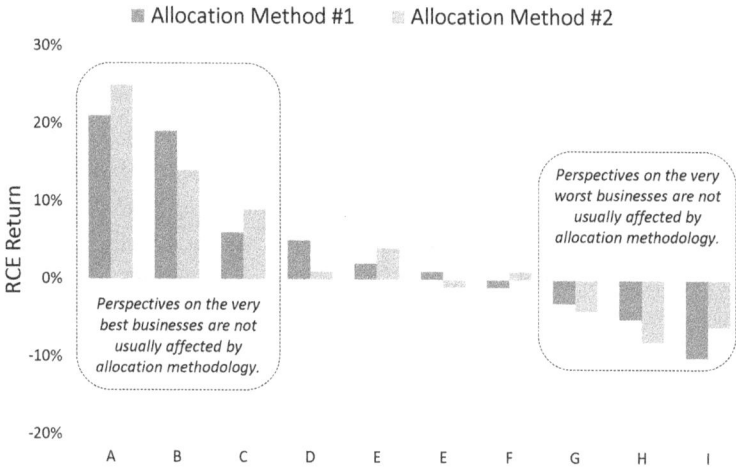

Figure 38—Perspectives on the Best and Worst Don't Change

But, as illustrated in figure 38, the reassignment of costs has little impact on one's perspectives of the best and worst businesses, and these are the ones where real value creation and destruction is happening. Once a leader has a good feel for which businesses are the strongest and weakest value creators, it's best to get about the business of investing to grow the high-RCE businesses and either fixing or disposing of the ones that are destroying value. The ones in the middle, with RCE that is slightly positive or slightly negative, depending on how costs are assigned, can be dealt with later; their strategic actions should be considered a lower priority.[2]

Knowing that one product line creates, say, five or even 10 times as much value per dollar of sales as another line invites an opportunity to redeploy resources to boost performance. However, to do this, management must know exactly where value is being created and destroyed. They must estimate RCE for product and service lines, brands, geographies, distribution channels, and customer groups to see which create significant value. Only through this process can they become confident about where they should disproportionately invest in growth.

By forecasting RCE, management can determine expected long-term value creation, which may differ significantly from current performance. Corporate finance theory and textbooks emphasize that valuation is—and should be—driven by the activities and performance of the future. But though this is right, it's important to start by examining the current level of RCE and, in cases of low or negative current RCE, to accept business-unit projections of significant increases only when such projections come with meaningful and credible proposals for improving strategy or operations. Huge sums have been wasted on businesses struggling to create meaningful value that were believed to be on a turnaround path. It's true that turnarounds can be extremely successful, but this typically comes from being effective at slashing costs, improving capital productivity, and stabilizing an otherwise poor-performing business. This can boost a negative RCE to zero (at which point, value ceases to be destroyed), though a turnaround rarely leads to meaningfully positive RCE. The exception, of course, is when the investments materially boost differentiation of products and services, as discussed below.

It's also important for executives at public companies to know that the frequency of turnaround success is far greater in private equity-owned companies than in publicly owned companies. One reason for this is that private companies often find it easier to take important, but unpleasant, actions without much publicity. They also almost always have stronger incentives that are more directly tied to value creation for the owners.

It is critical to understand why value creation and destruction occur. The basic determinants of high, sustainable RCE—or recurring negative RCE—can be traced to the good or the bad economics of the market and strategic position. Market economics refers to the growth and return of the market as a whole—is it economically attractive? When a segment of an industry is rapidly growing, and everyone is earning decent returns on capital, the more successful competitors have plenty of opportunities to drive their own growth to attractive levels by winning a greater share of the growth. This is often more feasible than growing above-market in a less attractive and slow-growing industry, where your extra revenue requires someone else to have declining revenue. Competitors don't like growing slower than the market, but this pales in comparison to their distaste for declines in revenue. Growing share in a fast-growing market is like being chased by wild animals in an open field, where there is plenty of room to maneuver. Growing share in a flat market is more like being chased by the same animals through a narrow, dead-end alleyway.

The unfortunate outcome of growing above-market in a slow-growth or flat-market segment is often a meaningful decline in profitability. As pricing, promotion, and other costs are used to juice the growth higher, usually the decrease in margin more than offsets the value of this growth. In the extreme, a price war ensues—and everybody loses. Exceptions to this can be found, but usually these only occur when the starting market share is so small that it doesn't ruffle any feathers, or when the product is so well positioned that it can achieve market share increases without excessive margin erosion.

Strategic position in a market refers to whether a business has a competitive advantage in product differentiation or costs. Perhaps the product has features not available from others, allowing an above-market price or market share gains. Or maybe the product is perceived to be of higher quality, or it sports a brand that consumers prefer to be associated with. Both real and perceived product differentiators can justify an advantaged strategic position, as can a low-cost process. The cost angle, however, will last only if the advantage can't readily be replicated. Product and service differentiation tends to be more sustainable than a cost advantage, though there are examples of companies that have sustained a cost advantage, too, such as DuPont's superior production processes for titanium dioxide—though even DuPont's advantage has been threatened by offshore theft of its important trade secrets and other intellectual property.[3]

Businesses that are advantaged in attractive markets will show high and growing RCE, while disadvantaged businesses in unattractive markets will have negative or declining RCE. Going back to our turnaround discussion, the practical limit on RCE in a turnaround often derives from a lack of differentiation. The combination of market economics and competitive position will determine how fast a business can grow and how much value the growth will create. In figure 39, some of the sources of competitive advantage that collectively drive RCE are identified.

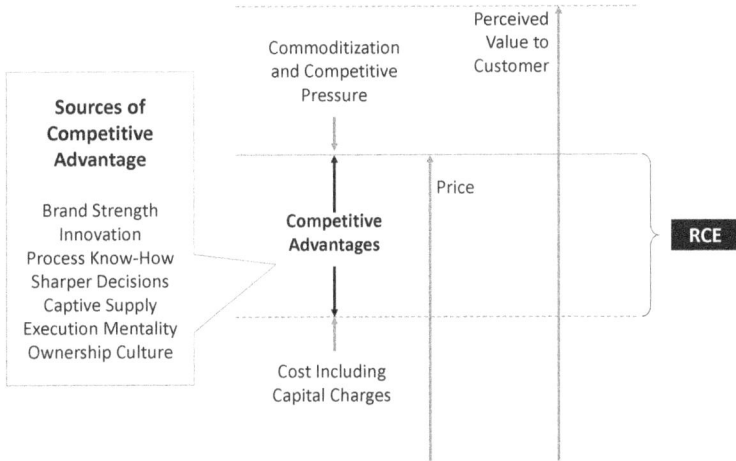

Figure 39—Competitive Advantages Drive RCE

The starting point is the perceived value to the customer. If this value is not meaningfully higher than the total cost, including capital charges, there is no hope for generating strong RCE. But simply having a product that is valuable is likely to be effective at delivering RCE only when the product has meaningful differentiation that allows the company to set prices at a level that will deliver growth and positive RCE. And this requires being able to stick with a premium pricing strategy, even when competitors compete on price, which in turn requires having meaningful competitive advantages, or differentiation.

Everyone waxes eloquent about their "competitive advantages" in investor presentations, but is your business or product truly differentiated? If so, you probably already have positive and growing RCE, because when a product is truly differentiated, management has the choice of whether either to charge a premium price or to grow faster than the market segment and thus gain market share, or some combination of the two. If your product does not sell at a premium price and is not gaining market share, then it's not differentiated. True differentiation creates value for the customer that can be monetized by the seller either via a premium price (higher RCE Margin) or by gaining share (faster growth). Be dispassionate in evaluating competitive advantages and considering investments in innovation, so you can increase the strength of your competitive advantages.

At Fortuna Advisors, we developed a strategic evaluation chart, as shown for the healthcare sector in figure 40, which can be helpful in understanding market attractiveness and strategic position. This chart is based on RCE Margin, which is a useful metric when we want to understand the value of revenue growth. But we can also recast this information into the form of an RCE Return when we want to understand the value of each element of investment. For a complete picture, we would also create a similar chart on revenue or investment growth, and the two together would provide answers about the attractiveness of our industry and whether our strategic position is advantaged or disadvantaged.

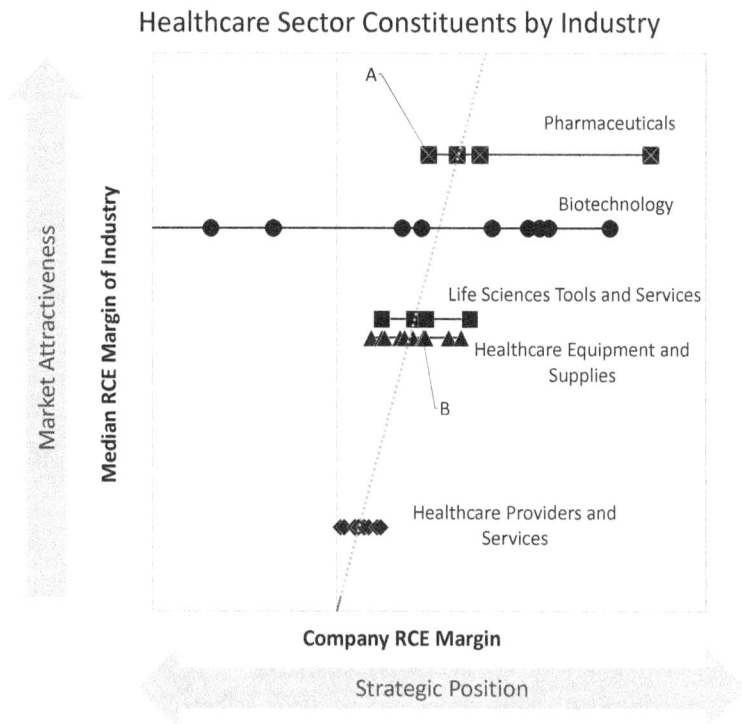

Figure 40—*Illustrative Strategic Evaluation Chart for Healthcare*

Each company or business is represented by a dot, though for visual clarity the figure only shows every third company horizontally. The horizontal dimension (x-axis) indicates the RCE margin for the company, and the vertical dimension (y-axis) indicates the median RCE margin of their industry within the sector. The pharmaceutical industry is at the top of the graph (i.e., it has the highest y-value), which means it's the most attractive in terms of RCE margin. Although healthcare providers and services make up the least attractive industry, it is still decently positive, and each individual company is positive, as well. Healthcare is a great sector for value creation.

The diagonal dotted line connects the origin and the medians of each industry. Companies to the right of this dotted line are advantaged relative to their industry because they are above the median. Those to the left of it are disadvantaged. Pharmaceutical company A is disadvantaged in the most attractive industry, while healthcare equipment and supplies company B is advantaged, though operating in an industry of only medium attractiveness. While both companies have about the same RCE Margin, the strategic import of this figure is that there is more upside for improving performance in company A because it operates in an industry with far greater proven upside potential, relative to current performance. If businesses A and B were divisions of the same company, this chart would be helpful in deciding how best to allocate resources.

Of course, there is much more information to be considered, and decisions can be complex. Business A might have been advantaged a few years ago and has perhaps slipped because a few drugs have gone off-patent while the pipeline of new pharmaceutical products wasn't adequate to replace them. Business B might have been disadvantaged, but maybe has since dramatically improved its strategic position through product innovation. The point is not that the Strategic Evaluation Charts make decisions easy, but rather that they provide useful information for judging performance, interpreting plans, and allocating resources.

Sometimes it's helpful to evaluate current and future RCE by customer or customer type, as we once were asked to do by a global oilfield service company with high asset-intensity and substantial fixed costs. Management historically had dreaded losing a project bid, for fixed-cost absorption reasons. Any unutilized capacity would effectively increase the cost of all the other capacity, since those fixed costs would be spread (and would drag down returns) across the rest of the organization. The finance and commercial teams did very sophisticated financial analysis at the time of each bid, but only high-level sales and gross profits were tracked after the fact.

We developed a line-of-sight into the RCE of each client project. In each geographic region, we allocated revenue, costs, and assets to determine customer RCE. Rolling this up globally by customer showed that many large global customers delivered negligible RCE, at best. Previously, many bids were justified based on retaining the business of these large global customers, yet there wasn't much value created. With some large customers, it was so bad that the global RCE contribution of the customer was quite negative. If we concede price on project *A* to protect projects *B* and *C*—and then use the same logic to make price concessions on *B* and *C*, too—then we end up destroying value.

The client created a small marketing group with the responsibility of overseeing global customers to ensure that their needs were properly serviced and that the regional management would accept marginal RCE projects only if meaningful positive RCE projects were found elsewhere with the same customer. One tough-negotiating customer generated such poor RCE that our client offered a contract renewal ultimatum: Either the customer had to pay more, or our client would reallocate resources. Their customer thought our client was bluffing, and the negotiations collapsed. Within months, the resources were working for a more profitable customer, and RCE improved. By understanding where they were creating value and where they were not, our client was able to materially increase the RCE run rate. Sure, for a few months RCE declined, so this also required a slightly longer-term view.

Such hard-nosed decisions are often easier for a business owner to make than for an executive who is an employee. In the short run, losing a meaningful customer can reduce RCE, as capacity utilization drops and fixed costs are concentrated against fewer activities. This makes it hard to achieve or exceed budgeted performance in the current year, which personally costs the executives, since they experience a decline in their annual incentive plan payouts. It might be great if in a few months a new, more-desirable customer is contracted, but during the current year, the new contract may not make up for the revenue loss during the uncontracted period. And the benefits of the new customer will just get folded into the budget for the following year, so there will be no benefit to annual incentive payments next year, either. This is only one of the many ways that current management practices reinforce short-term thinking, which will be expanded on in chapter 14.

For another client, we helped prepare a three-dimensional segmentation analysis by customer group, product family, and distribution channel, simultaneously, to better understand the results. The business was quite complicated and intertwined, but the client had already done a tremendous amount of good work on activity-based costing, also known as ABC. The problem was that they were long on analysis and short on useful interpretation and action. As often happens, every meeting to discuss the segmentation ended with skepticism and demands for "running the numbers again." We were brought in to help develop the logic for applying the ABC methodology to allocate capital, to help the company interpret the findings, and to identify and simulate potential changes in both pricing and the allocation of capital and marketing resources.

The idea of a three-dimensional segmentation is common, because a product may earn substantial RCE with a particular customer group that sees differentiation and values it, while a different customer group may be less sensitive to such differentiation and buy mainly on price. In some channels, such as modern online marketing, resources can be targeted to entice the valued customers without wasting resources on futile attempts to attract those that are unresponsive. Figure 41 shows how a three-dimensional allocation works. In this case, three product families exist across three customer groups, with each served by three distribution channels.

All revenues, costs, and assets must be fully allocated to the 27 (3 × 3 × 3) cubes Of course, there can be four or five dimensions, in which cases the allocations work the same, though it is harder to visualize. Or we could have, as an extreme example, seven product families across six customer groups served by 11 channels, so the number of cubes can change. Some cubes may also be empty, since some customer groups may not buy certain product families nor use some distribution channels.

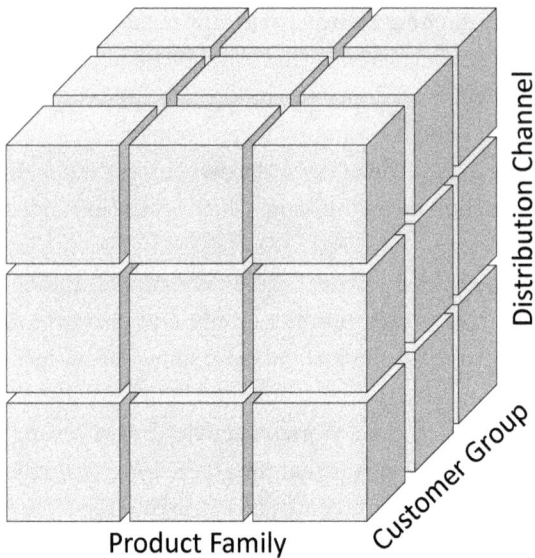

Figure 41—Segmenting RCE in Three Dimensions

When we finished creating and interpreting the three-dimensional allocation analysis, the answers were unambiguous. Certain combinations of product, customer, and channel were outstanding, with high RCE margin and, in some cases, RCE that was greater than 100% of invested assets. Back the truck up and invest as much as you can! Other segments needed to earn the right to grow, because they had meaningfully negative RCE even though they were allocated much lower costs and capital per unit of volume growth, based on their lighter-touch business model. The biggest problem, we found, was that the segments that should have been growing were shrinking, and those that should have been focused on improvements in pricing, efficiency, and productivity were rapidly growing—not good.

The problem appeared to be pricing. A high percentage of their cost structure was fixed, and the same was true of their asset base. During the 2008–2009 downturn, volumes declined and financial performance dropped significantly in the face of expanding unutilized capacity. For certain large customers, the client turned to estimates of marginal costs when setting prices, figuring, correctly, that as long as their prices surpassed these marginal costs, the incremental volume would pad its bottom line. But as capacity utilization rose, the company maintained the low-pricing policies, in some cases because of committed long-term contracts—but in others due to simple managerial inertia. The growth felt good!

Once the unutilized capacity dried up, the client began to invest considerable fresh capital on new capacity to handle the volume growth, and at that time its pricing models should have transitioned to more of a full-cost basis. But more important, even while the unutilized capacity was available, performance measurement should always have been done on a fully allocated cost basis. If our marginal cost estimates are accurate, and if we are paid prices above that level, then the new volume should increase the fully allocated results versus what would be the case without the volume. Maintaining performance measurement on fully allocated costs is an imperative, because estimating marginal costs is exceedingly tricky, especially when all sorts of shared costs and assets must be dealt with. As it turns out, many costs and assets are more variable than people want to think.

The CEO of another client once said to me, "Obviously, I don't cost any more if we sell a bit more product, so I am a fixed cost. And so is everyone else in this room. We really only want to include variable costs." I politely asked whether, if the business were to double in size, the HR department and compensation consultants would show the board that the appropriate compensation package for him and his colleagues would be higher, since they would then be managing a bigger company. He only smiled. In the long run, everything is variable, so we only ever want to use a variable-cost approach for short, tactical pricing moves to fill up an unexpected low-capacity utilization. And when we choose to do this, we have to be extremely careful, since we can inadvertently be training customers to expect lower pricing. Unless we have significant differentiation, we may never be able to raise prices back up again without meaningful market share losses.

Once we know the performance of different business areas, we need to scrutinize how well this aligns with resource allocation. The basic rule is, the better the RCE improvement opportunity, the more we should seek to invest in growth. Comparing resource allocations among businesses, products, and customer groups is best done using the concept of a "reinvestment rate," which we defined in chapter 4 as a percentage of Gross Cash Earnings.[4]

The resource reinvestment rate approach automatically biases management toward investing more in the more profitable businesses, as shown in figure 42. It's true, management may have increased the investment as a percentage of sales in the more profitable business, but maybe not to the level implied by the reinvestment rate. By limiting investment in the most profitable businesses, management may have been trying to avoid the appearance of playing favorites. But use of the reinvestment rate focuses the view of "fair and square" on cash profitability instead of revenue; and if business C wants a higher allocation, then it has to improve its profitability.

	Sales	GCE	RCE	Investment Allocated as a Constant Percentage of Sales			Investment Allocated as a Constant Reinvestment Rate		
				Investment	% of Sales	Reinvestment Rate	Investment	% of Sales	Reinvestment Rate
X	1,000	400	200	100	10%	25%	160	16%	40%
Y	1,000	250	125	100	10%	40%	100	10%	40%
Z	1,000	100	50	100	10%	100%	40	4%	40%

Figure 42—Benefits of Using a Reinvestment Rate

Of course, it's not only about moving resource numbers around. We need viable investment strategies and projects, which requires an effective process for creatively developing and rigorously evaluating resource allocation options. Don't simply consider incremental improvements on the status quo. Once good line-of-sight is available, we must search far and wide for ideas that may help us invest more resources and create value. For high-RCE businesses, look for all possible ways to accelerate growth without significantly damaging returns. For chronically negative RCE businesses, come up with options to drive RCE higher, often by shrinking or harvesting and by focusing on the parts of the business that are profitable. This is an exercise in creative thinking grounded in market economics, competitive position, and RCE. Frequently, the best ideas come from customer dialogues, so take every opportunity to learn from them.

It's also important to assess the incremental RCE for each viable option after contemplating how customers and competitors will respond. Compare the options, based on ease of implementation as well as the likelihood of success and scale, which is the amount of expected RCE and value. The best options can then be selected and converted into a strategic plan. This comprehensive evaluation, project selection, and planning process requires open-minded creativity, candor, transparency, thoroughness, and discipline, along with pace and decisiveness, to drive action and results.

A Case Example

Consider a hypothetical company, based on a former client of mine, holding a portfolio of products that is quite profitable but unable to grow much faster than GDP. The biggest resource commitment it makes each year is capital spending, which averages about 10% of sales. Traditionally, capital has been allocated proportional to sales, with slight variations across the product portfolio, mostly based on differences in EBITDA margin and, occasionally, on other strategic factors as well. Management feels they are doing well, since so many companies only use gross margin or contribution margin to evaluate product profitability; and they have taken the extra step of allocating G&A and other costs to get to an EBITDA estimate by product.

In figure 43, we see the four products, the size of each addressable market and market share, as well as the estimated EBITDA and EBITDA margins. The figure also shows the existing plan for capital expenditures and the percentage of sales for each business. Management is clearly biasing their investment toward product *A,* which is the largest product and has the highest EBITDA margin. Product *C* also has a high EBITDA margin and receives the next-highest allocation as a percentage of sales. But as we will see, since this is a less asset-intensive business, management has effectively reduced the allocation as a percentage of sales. More-asset-intensive businesses tend to require more maintenance capital, and it tends to take more capital for them to grow capacity, volume, and revenue. Products *B* and *D* both receive allocations that are a lower percentages of sales; and, again, the difference between the allocations to *B* and *D* are due to differences in asset intensity and maintenance capital requirements.

Product	A	B	C	D
Market Size	10,000	4,400	18,000	5,000
Market Share	*30.0%*	*50.0%*	*8.3%*	*14.0%*
Sales	**3,000**	**2,200**	**1,500**	**700**
EBITDA	**1,050**	**330**	**450**	**140**
EBITDA Margin	*35.0%*	*15.0%*	*30.0%*	*20.0%*
CapEx (Existing Plan)	**425**	**145**	**135**	**35**
% of Sales	*14.2%*	*6.6%*	*9.0%*	*5.0%*

Figure 43—Case: Product Portfolio Characteristics

One other consideration is market share and its implications for the potential runway for future growth. Products *C* and *D* have meaningfully lower market shares, and therefore may have more opportunity to grow at above-market rates by increasing market share. This doesn't seem to have been considered by management.

Next we will fill in some additional information on taxes, assets, and RCE, as shown in Figure 44.

Product	A	B	C	D
Tax	(100)	(30)	(45)	(15)
Gross Cash Earnings	**950**	**300**	**405**	**125**
GCE Margin	*31.7%*	*13.6%*	*27.0%*	*17.9%*
Gross Operating Assets	**6,000**	**3,300**	**1,200**	**350**
Asset Intensity	*2.00x*	*1.50x*	*0.80x*	*0.50x*
Capital Charge (@10%)	(600)	(330)	(120)	(35)
Residual Cash Earnings	**350**	**(30)**	**285**	**90**
RCE Margin	*11.7%*	*-1.4%*	*19.0%*	*12.9%*
RCE Return	*5.8%*	*-0.9%*	*23.8%*	*25.7%*

Figure 44—Case: Product RCE Calculations

Once we know the estimated taxes, which are determined after considering the depreciation each product is allocated based on production and other property, plant, and equipment, we can calculate Gross Cash Earnings, or GCE. We also estimate Gross Operating Assets, or GOA, including both net operating working capital and gross property, plant, and equipment, so we can then calculate Residual Cash Earnings. The tax rates don't vary much for this company, so the GCE margins are directionally similar to the EBITDA margins above. But once we bring the assets into the picture, the story completely changes. Products *A* and *B* are vertically integrated, with all parts manufactured and assembled in their Western European and Canadian plants. This production strategy, when compared to outsourcing, maintains control and keeps operating costs down; but it is very asset-intensive, which means higher capital costs.

Once detailed line-of-sight information is available, the first important observation is that products *C* and *D* are both delivering RCE that is over 20% of their Gross Operating Assets, which we call RCE Return—and remember that RCE already reflects the charge for capital, so these performances are absolutely outstanding. This is particularly noteworthy for product *D*, whose low EBITDA margin is more than made up for by its efficient use of assets. Several years earlier, when their aging production facility was causing production delays and quality problems, they were faced with a decision to either build a new replacement production facility or find suppliers to do their production for them. Due to their lack of scale, they found the overall economics to be better by outsourcing. It may be that once they have scale, performance would be better with in-house production.

These two businesses also have the lowest market share. So now that we know that they have both the most value-adding growth (high RCE margin) and the biggest potential for more growth, we can see that *C* and *D* should be the strategic priorities. Finding creative ways to invest in and grow these products will have the largest impact on the success of the overall company.

Many financial managers reading this will be surprised that the emphasis is first and foremost on products *C* and *D*. Their eyes are finely tuned from years of hard work examining financial reports, and they are unconsciously drawn to any negative numbers in a table. They may even have been frustrated while reading the previous three paragraphs, waiting for an emphasis to be placed on the negative RCE being delivered by product *B*. "DON'T THEY SEE THAT IT'S

NEGATIVE!" Yes, of course it's negative, and addressing that is important. But as discussed in chapter 7, more value is usually created by nurturing and driving success in the best businesses than by fixing the worst businesses. We therefore want to reduce the rate of investment in product *B* and encourage the product management team to find ways to improve price, reduce cost, and become more productive in utilizing assets, so they can earn the right to grow. But fight the urge to spend so much time trying to fix problem businesses that you pay too little attention to the successful ones.

In the upper portion of figure 45, we see the existing CapEx allocation again, with some additional statistics, including the reinvestment rate, which shows the percentages of Gross Cash Earnings that are reinvested back into the business as capital expenditures.

Product	A	B	C	D
CapEx (Existing Plan)	425	145	135	35
% of Sales	*14.2%*	*6.6%*	*9.0%*	*5.0%*
% of Assets	*7.1%*	*4.4%*	*11.3%*	*10.0%*
Reinvestment Rate	*44.7%*	*48.3%*	*33.3%*	*28.0%*
CapEx (Reallocation Plan)	300	75	275	90
% of Sales	*10.0%*	*3.4%*	*18.3%*	*12.9%*
% of Assets	*5.0%*	*2.3%*	*22.9%*	*25.7%*
Reinvestment Rate	*31.6%*	*25.0%*	*67.9%*	*72.0%*

Figure 45—Case: Product CapEx Reallocation

The existing plan has a higher reinvestment rate in the two more-asset-intensive businesses, which is exactly the opposite of the priority we determined when we examined RCE return, above. The lower portion of the figure shows an illustrative reallocation of the same total capital expenditure budget with the priority on products *C* and *D*, so they have the resources they need to grow. How do we go about deciding on such reallocations of resources?

To improve value creation and the likely TSR going forward, various strategic resource allocation options should be considered. Of course, the first priority is to shift the capital expenditure allocations to increase the reinvestment rate in the business delivering more RCE improvement per unit of investment. To make this work often involves both investing significantly more in innovation to extend and grow the higher RCE products and developing paths for growth through capital expenditure. These products are highly valuable, so if we can create new product extensions and applications, we may be able to amplify the total amount of potential value-creating investment and hence the amount of RCE we can generate.

Finally, we need to reduce the cost and capital intensity of the big products, especially B, to drive RCE higher so that they earn the right to grow. Consider all possible cost cutting, process streamlining, and improvements in asset productivity via improved inventory management and capacity utilization. Also, given the success of product C, which has outsourced all production and assembly, it would be worth considering partial or complete outsourcing for products A and B, as well. Perhaps production is not our core competency. Maybe we can sell the production facilities to someone with strong manufacturing expertise and buy finished products under contract. In some cases, we can improve quality and reduce cost at the same time. Keep in mind throughout this process, though, that the goal is to create value, not to minimize costs. So be active in eliminating unnecessary costs and assets, but avoid a slash-and-burn mindset that can sometimes lead to cutting as much muscle as fat.

Though it may start as a one-time special project, strategic resource allocation needs to become an ongoing way of life if the benefits are going to be significant. At a minimum, it should be repeated before every important strategic discussion at the front end of the annual planning process. And for companies that truly embrace the ownership culture, it should become a central feature in every strategic and tactical resource allocation decision, in performance evaluation, and in post-investment reviews.

Investors Care About Strategic Resource Allocation

Where and how a management team allocates its capital, R&D, and marketing resources tells investors a lot about its priorities. Investors and analysts ask questions at investor presentations and on earnings calls, and, even though details may not be published, the answers that management provides help build a picture of where they earn decent returns and how well their resource allocation is aligned.

For companies that report segment information, investors can patch together a quick and revealing image of how well management invests its resources. Consider IBM, with primary operating segments reported as Cognitive Solutions, Global Business Services, Technology Services & Cloud Platforms, and Systems. IBM also reports a financing segment, and there are line items for eliminations and unallocated other items.

If we focus on the four primary operating segments, it is fairly simple to estimate returns and reinvestment rates. The company reports segment revenue, operating profit, and depreciation and amortization, which collectively get us to an approximate EBITDA and EBITDA margin. It does not provide tax information, so we can do our segment analysis on a pretax basis to get a general idea of where it earns better returns. It is quite possible that the company's performance and earnings power would be reflected more accurately if R&D were treated as an investment (instead of an expense), since it invests more than $5 billion a year in R&D. But since it's not disclosed in the segment data, we will ignore it. Actual investors can ask questions during earnings calls and conference presentations to get a sense of such things, and a careful review of investor communication transcripts may reveal answers.

We can determine a simple estimate of EBITDA and of EBITDA margin by segment, as shown in figure 46.

The stock market has not been kind to IBM over the period, and it is easy to see why. Every segment has had declining revenue, declining net profit before tax, and declining estimated EBITDA. Three of the four segments have had declining estimated EBITDA margin, too, and the one with an increase in estimated EBITDA margin suffered the largest percentage decline in revenue.

Next we turn to the assets, shown in figure 47, where we have much less information. Most companies, IBM included, provide only one total number for assets, which makes it hard to really know what's included and what is operating or not. To keep it simple, we are relying exclusively on the reported segment information. But investors and analysts who follow the company can delve more deeply into published information and can ask questions to try to build out a more detailed model of IBM's segments.

Revenues

	2014	2015	2016	2017	CAGR
Cognitive Solutions	21,906	20,055	20,817	21,100	-1.2%
Global Business Services	20,055	17,664	17,109	16,711	-5.9%
Technology Services & Cloud Platforms	39,729	35,840	36,052	34,934	-4.2%
Systems	13,300	10,325	8,464	8,945	-12.4%

Net Profit Before Tax

	2014	2015	2016	2017	CAGR
Cognitive Solutions	8,215	7,245	6,352	6,817	-6.0%
Global Business Services	3,347	2,602	1,732	1,401	-25.2%
Technology Services & Cloud Platforms	7,084	5,669	4,707	4,344	-15.0%
Systems	1,384	1,722	933	1,135	-6.4%

Depreciation & Amortization

	2014	2015	2016	2017
Cognitive Solutions	1,040	921	1,228	1,121
Global Business Services	98	81	104	101
Technology Services & Cloud Platforms	1,982	1,944	2,224	2,359
Systems	734	321	375	341

Estimated EBITDA (Net Profit Before Tax Plus Depreciation & Amortization)

	2014	2015	2016	2017	CAGR
Cognitive Solutions	9,255	8,166	7,580	7,938	-5.0%
Global Business Services	3,445	2,683	1,836	1,502	-24.2%
Technology Services & Cloud Platforms	9,066	7,613	6,931	6,703	-9.6%
Systems	2,118	2,043	1,308	1,476	-11.3%

Estimated EBITDA Margin

	2014	2015	2016	2017	Average	% Change
Cognitive Solutions	42.2%	40.7%	36.4%	37.6%	39.3%	-11%
Global Business Services	17.2%	15.2%	10.7%	9.0%	13.0%	-48%
Technology Services & Cloud Platforms	22.8%	21.2%	19.2%	19.2%	20.6%	-16%
Systems	15.9%	19.8%	15.5%	16.5%	16.9%	4%

Note: CAGR is compound annual growth rate

Figure 46—Estimated EBITDA Margin for IBM Segments

With the assets given, we can calculate a simple cash return by dividing the estimated EBITDA by the reported segment assets.

This information is admittedly incomplete, since it depends on the modest disclosures required by accounting rules. So, we tend only to compare returns, rather than to make absolute judgments about what is good or bad. It's beyond the scope of this book, but in the more elaborate segment models my colleagues and I have built to understand the segments of client competitors, we allocate every element of the consolidated company's GCE and GOA to the segments, using logical allocations like accounts receivable as a percentage of revenue and accumulated depreciation as a percent of assets. This would give us a picture that is likely to be more accurate, but the quick estimated approach depicted here provides directionally correct insights in most cases.

Estimated EBITDA (Net Profit Before Tax Plus Depreciation & Amortization)

	2014	2015	2016	2017	CAGR
Cognitive Solutions	9,255	8,166	7,580	7,938	-5.0%
Global Business Services	3,445	2,683	1,836	1,502	-24.2%
Technology Services & Cloud Platforms	9,066	7,613	6,931	6,703	-9.6%
Systems	2,118	2,043	1,308	1,476	-11.3%

Assets

	2014	2015	2016	2017	CAGR
Cognitive Solutions	19,525	20,017	25,517	24,829	27.2%
Global Business Services	8,831	8,327	8,628	8,713	-1.3%
Technology Services & Cloud Platforms	22,512	23,530	24,085	24,619	9.4%
Systems	4,219	3,967	3,812	3,898	-7.6%

Asset Intensity (ASSETS / Revenue)

	2014	2015	2016	2017	Change
Cognitive Solutions	0.89x	1.00x	1.23x	1.18x	0.29x
Global Business Services	0.44x	0.47x	0.50x	0.52x	0.08x
Technology Services & Cloud Platforms	0.57x	0.66x	0.67x	0.70x	0.14x
Systems	0.32x	0.38x	0.45x	0.44x	0.12x

Quick Cash Return (Estimated EBITDA / Assets)

	2014	2015	2016	2017	Average	% Change
Cognitive Solutions	47.4%	40.8%	29.7%	32.0%	37.5%	-32.6%
Global Business Services	39.0%	32.2%	21.3%	17.2%	27.4%	-55.8%
Technology Services & Cloud Platforms	40.3%	32.4%	28.8%	27.2%	32.2%	-32.4%
Systems	50.2%	51.5%	34.3%	37.9%	43.5%	-24.6%

Note: CAGR is compound annual growth rate

Figure 47—Quick Cash Return for IBM Segments

Each segment had higher asset intensity in 2017 than in 2014. So, since revenue and EBITDA have been sliding, each segment has also increased assets per dollar of revenue over the three-year period. This contributed to the decline in quick cash returns experienced by all four segments. Although all four have fading returns, it's clear that Global Business Services has the lowest and sharpest-fading quick cash returns, while Systems has the highest and least-fading returns. It's also notable that Systems had the largest decline in assets, despite apparently having the highest and most sustained quick cash returns.

Because IBM also provides Capital Expenditure information by segment, we can estimate a reinvestment rate as CapEx divided by estimated EBITDA, as shown in figure 48.

Quick Cash Return (Estimated EBITDA / Assets)

	2014	2015	2016	2017	Average	% Change
Cognitive Solutions	47.4%	40.8%	29.7%	32.0%	37.5%	-32.6%
Global Business Services	39.0%	32.2%	21.3%	17.2%	27.4%	-55.8%
Technology Services & Cloud Platforms	40.3%	32.4%	28.8%	27.2%	32.2%	-32.4%
Systems	50.2%	51.5%	34.3%	37.9%	43.5%	-24.6%

Capital Expenditure

	2014	2015	2016	2017	CAGR	% Total
Cognitive Solutions	413	448	495	373	-3.3%	12.9%
Global Business Services	79	86	55	50	-14.1%	1.7%
Technology Services & Cloud Platforms	2,321	2,619	2,382	2,290	-0.4%	78.9%
Systems	627	321	453	189	-33.0%	6.5%

Note: Percentage of Total applies to 2017.

Quick Reinvestment Rate (Capital Expenditure / Estimated EBITDA)

	2014	2015	2016	2017	Average	% Change
Cognitive Solutions	4.5%	5.5%	6.5%	4.7%	5.3%	5.3%
Global Business Services	2.3%	3.2%	3.0%	3.3%	3.0%	45.2%
Technology Services & Cloud Platforms	25.6%	34.4%	34.4%	34.2%	32.1%	33.4%
Systems	29.6%	15.7%	34.6%	12.8%	23.2%	-56.7%

Note: CAGR is compound annual growth rate

Figure 48—Quick Reinvestment Rate for IBM Segments

During this period, IBM invested heavily in R&D, so a more suitable reinvestment rate would include both capital expenditures and R&D. But because the published segment data doesn't include the R&D information, we use only capital expenditures in the example. Our goal, after all, is to illustrate the technique.

Capital expenditures in the Systems segment, which has the highest and most sustained quick cash returns, have declined by 33% per year, on average, and its quick reinvestment rate has been cut by more than half. Technology Services & Cloud Platforms, by contrast, received 78.9% of the 2017 total segment capital expenditures and has a quick reinvestment rate that is well above the rest—and indeed well above the rate of reinvestment in 2014. This is undoubtedly the area IBM is focused on growing, but it is somewhat concerning that at least on the dimensions studied here, the company doesn't seem to be driving stronger or increasing returns; and its corporate revenue, estimated EBITDA, and estimated EBITDA margins are all heading meaningfully down. If it is increasing R&D in this segment, could that be influencing the apparent decline in margins? This would be a good question for investors to ask management.

Companies should do this analysis on their own segments and make sure that the signals investors receive are accurate and as intended. There are, of course, limitations to this type of analysis. Since good and bad businesses can be mixed in the same segments, the segment performance details may be quite different from our quick estimates, based on segment reporting; and the numbers could even be clouded if management is trying to influence the interpretation. For example, in some cases it seems that management may be trying to make some segments look better through allocations and transfer pricing, of course within the constraints of what is legitimate, given the accounting rules. Perhaps it would like a segment that normally attracts a higher multiple to show a bit more profit. This, of course, is spin.

Regardless of these shortcomings, it's important to be aware that investors can do this analysis themselves and will form judgments on whether they believe management understands and embraces the idea that they should be investing more where returns are higher. To avoid any potential confusion, the message here is that companies should have better resource allocation—not that they should improve their presentation tactics.

Notes

1   A good portion of this chapter was derived from an article I coauthored with Jim McTaggart that was published by *FEI Daily*. Gregory V. Milano and Jim McTaggart, "Overcoming 3 Roadblocks to Strategic Resource Allocation," *FEI Daily*, accessed January 15, 2019, https://www.financialexecutives.org/FEI-Daily/February-2018/Strategic-Resource-Allocation.aspx.

2   Joseph Theriault, "How to Allocate Less Time to Allocations," *FEI Daily*, January 9, 2019, accessed June 25, 2019, http://fortuna-advisors.com/2019/01/15/how-to-allocate-less-time-to-allocations/.

3   Del Quentin Wilber, "How a Corporate Spy Swiped Plans for DuPont's Billion-Dollar Color Formula," *Bloomberg Businessweek*, accessed January 14, 2019, http://www.advancedsecurityprotection.com/files/stealing_white.pdf.

4   Many wonder why the reinvestment rate isn't defined as a percentage of RCE. Determining it as a percentage of Gross Cash Earnings works better because RCE, being a residual income amount, is more often negative, making the outputs meaningless.

TEN

Investment
Decision-Making

WHEN GOLDILOCKS TESTED the beds of the Three Bears, she found Papa Bear's bed to be too firm, Momma Bear's bed to be too soft, and Baby Bear's bed to be just right. So it is with the propensity to invest exhibited by different companies. Some companies invest too much and make several value-destroying investments; some don't invest enough and miss a number of value-creating investments; and some get it just right by accepting all value-creating investments and turning down all value-destroying ones.

In principle, this may seem obvious. But certain companies put such an emphasis on the *quantity* of growth that managements at times will pursue investments that grow the revenue line of the company without delivering enough cash to sustain worthwhile profits. This was common a few decades ago. But since then, more emphasis has been placed on delivering profit margins and returns on capital. These companies that emphasize the *quality* of growth, as measured by margins and returns, often experience a stagnated growth profile because their executives have become so conservative that they pass on many investments that would create value and instead prioritize only the cream of the crop. Investing too much and investing too little are, of course, both suboptimal strategies. Like Goldilocks, we want our investment strategies to be *just right*.

Consider a company that makes too many investments and, on top of all its good investments, management includes an investment of $25 million with a net present value of negative $10 million. This company has decreased its value creation by $10 million. Another company acts very conservatively to avoid precisely such a bad investment outcome. But perhaps it's *too* conservative, which leads it to also leave out a few value-adding investments that collectively would have added $10 million of net present value. Just like the overinvesting company, this underinvesting company has underdelivered on its value creation potential by $10 million. In a sense, forgoing the opportunity to make an investment that would have created $10 million of net present value destroys as much value as pursuing the opportunities that wipe out $10 million of value.

What motivates some companies to make too many investments, while others make too few? It all comes down to the behaviors that are encouraged by the culture, the management processes in place, and the incentives available. Is the culture aggressive and entrepreneurial, or is it careful and conservative? Are growth rates emphasized more in operating reviews, or is the emphasis on percentage margins and rates of return on capital? And, importantly, what drives the incentive plan—how is performance being measured?

Historically, back in the 1970s and early 1980s, companies commonly overemphasized growth and economies of scale. This led to a "growth at any cost" mindset and, though some companies managed to grow in a profitable fashion, many did not. One client's CEO told us in the early 1990s that he felt that he had "fallen behind," because one of his former colleagues who became CEO of a public company around the same time had grown revenue nearly twice as much as he had. We sought to convince him that his counterpart had, in fact, likely destroyed substantial value. Still, it was clear that growth and sheer size were extremely important to our client.

Twenty-five years later, many companies still would benefit from shifting their focus to growing profits, not merely revenue. Yet in the intervening decades, many management teams have adopted more discipline about increasing or maintaining margins and rates of return. Unfortunately, the pendulum has swung too far in countless cases, and many companies are now so focused on maximizing rates of return that they have refused to consider all but the very highest-return investments.

Why *has* the pendulum swung too far? At least in many cases, the emphasis on holding managers accountable for delivering high and improving rates of return has stifled investments in the best businesses where growth is the most valuable. The answer is not to ignore rates of return, but instead to use a measurement and investment analysis framework that does a better job of motivating good investment, while at the same time holding management accountable for delivering a sufficient return.

As discussed extensively in chapter 3, the cash-flow-based economic profit measure known as Residual Cash Earnings (RCE) does a better job than other measures at spreading the recognition of value over the life of the investment. Most traditional measures of rate of return and economic profit show front-load costs and reflect most of the benefits later in the asset's life—at a time when it's mostly depreciated! With these types of measures, even a reasonable forecast often looks like a hockey stick.

As an example, consider a retail business that over decades has successfully opened some 1,000 stores that have been quite profitable. The enterprise value of the business is at a 25% premium to its asset value. The chain invested in attractive local markets and achieved a competitive advantage in merchandise selection and customer service, including a thriving e-commerce platform. Management is confident that it can identity perhaps another 150 locations that will duplicate the advantages of the existing stores, so it develops a plan to open these stores over the next three years. From a strategic standpoint, the expansion looks like a clear winner, though management needs to confirm this by evaluating the profitability of the growth strategy.

Let's assume the average capital commitment per store is $2 million. In total, the company will invest $100 million of capital expenditures per year, and, for simplicity, we assume that the company forecasts that the revenue run rate will be flat after each store is opened. Once all the stores are open, they are expected to deliver $300 million in new revenue with a 20% EBITDA margin, to have a 21% corporate tax rate, and to use net working capital (mostly inventory) equal to 25% of annual sales. All investments have a 10-year depreciation life, and the operations are expected to continue for two years after the assets fully depreciate on the accounting books, with no terminal value in the net present value calculation.

The net present value of free cash flow for this investment program is quite positive, equaling 24% of the peak investment of free cash flow. So, by most measures, these are truly desirable investments. It's like investing $100 each year in order to buy something worth $124.

But the cumulative free cash flow breakeven point does not occur until year nine, as shown in figure 49, which may serve as a deterrent to management's pursuing the investment program.

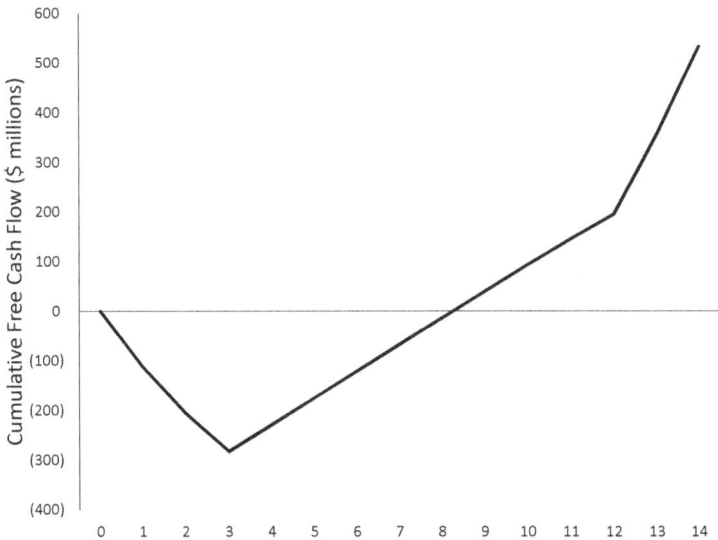

Figure 49—Cumulative Free Cash Flow from Three-Year Expansion

On an annual basis, free cash flow doesn't turn positive until year four, as shown in figure 50. This is really not a problem, but these days many investors, analysts, and journalists often misuse the concept of "free cash flow," treating it as a suitable period measure when it clearly should not be. Some even talk about free cash flow yield, as if that were a meaningful measure. The lower a company's growth prospects, the lower the valuation multiple; and the less it invests, the higher the free cash flow. So, this maxim goes, if you don't invest and therefore you don't grow, you can achieve a high free cash flow yield (high free cash flow divided by a low share price).[1] It's hard to think of a measure with more potential for misleading investors! The point is that if a company is determined to tell its investors that it is improving annual free cash flow, this investment would definitely be shelved, since it would reduce annual free cash flow for three full years and cumulative free cash flow for nine years. Figure 50 shows the annual cash flows from this three-year investment program.

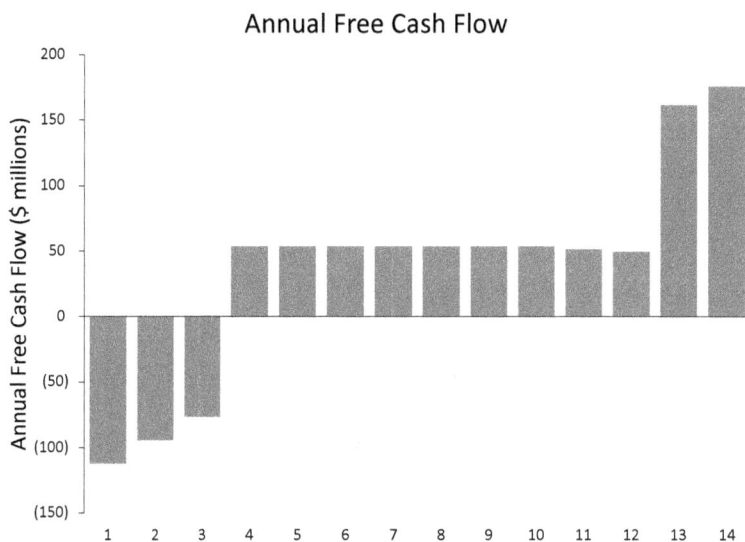

Figure 50—*Annual Free Cash Flow from Three-Year Expansion*

In fairness, far more companies examine the rate of return on the invested capital profile for new investments than they consider free cash flow profiles. And this is good, since rate-of-return measures are designed to indicate capital productivity by dividing a measure of current profits (or cash flow) by the cumulative amount of net (or gross) investment that is used to deliver those profits (or cash flow). This is a proper comparison, but in the three-year new store investment case we have been examining, the rate of return on invested capital does not rise above the 8% cost of capital until year five, when the return on invested capital reaches 8.8%. So, if management seeks to deliver returns above the cost of capital, they have to wait for the results. This is viewed as a long-term investment that takes time to pay off. And this is so, despite the simplifying assumption that each store delivers full run-rate revenue in year one of the investment. In reality, the revenues may ramp up more gradually and the rate of return may not exceed the cost of capital until much later in the duration of this investment program. Figure 51 shows the rate-of-return profile.

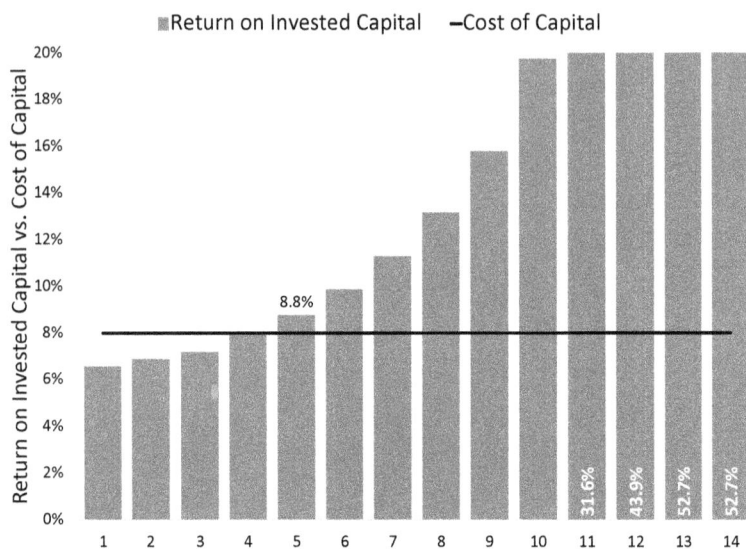

Figure 51—ROIC from Three-Year Expansion

In addition to the delay in achieving a rate of return on capital above the cost of capital until year five, the rapidly depreciating asset base provides its own bias, and the returns keep increasing aggressively after surpassing the cost of capital and are above 30% for the final four years of the forecast. Note, too, that the revenue and EBITDA in this example are absolutely flat from year three through year 12, and yet the depreciating asset base drives rising returns that give the illusion of tremendous ongoing value creation in those years. With any kind of ongoing EBITDA growth, even from inflation, this artificial upward drift in rates of return would become far more dramatic. It is easy, then, to see how a rate-of-return focus using traditional rates of return can encourage managers to (1) milk old, depreciated assets since the returns look great and (2) avoid making new investments, because it takes so long for them to drive returns above the cost of capital.

This conventional accounting treatment is a big reason that many companies are underinvesting. Management teams are right to care about earning adequate returns on capital but are using an approach that makes new investments look bad and old investments look good, which leads to demonstrably lower investment.

In one extreme case, a large consumer products company seemed to be underinvesting in its businesses with the highest rates of return on capital. When prodded to consider allocating more to these businesses, executives said they would "love to," but the business-unit management had been unable to identify any additional desirable investments. That was attributed to a lack of market growth coupled with a reasonably high market share, though other business units in similar situations *were* able to find desirable investments in brand extensions and permutations. Further discussions uncovered the real problem: The business-unit management teams were paid incentives based on the percentage improvement in return on capital. In some businesses, the existing return was 3% or 4%, so finding investments that earned a higher return, and would therefore bring up the average, was relatively easy. But for the very highest-return businesses, which were earning cash-on-cash rates of return of 30% to 50%, it was harder to find new investments earning returns above the current return. And any investments earning less than the current return would result in lower bonuses for management, since they would drag down the average return. The emphasis on rates of return seemed careful and wise—yet it led to substantially less-than-optimal investment in the best businesses. And in an odd paradox, one part of the business was encouraged and financially rewarded for investing in projects earning 6%, while others were discouraged and financially penalized for investing in projects earning 30% (five times the return!).

EVA, as well as all traditional economic profit measures, in fact, was intended to improve the balance of growth and return by determining the dollars of profit above a minimum acceptable return, or capital charge, on the investment base. Though this is better, EVA suffers from the same depreciation distortion as traditional return on capital; it takes five years for EVA to turn positive in our example, as shown in figure 52.

Much like return on capital, the strong EVA doesn't show up until the assets are more than halfway depreciated—again reinforcing the milking of old assets and underinvestment in new assets. EVA is better than a percentage return on capital measure, but it is still flawed.

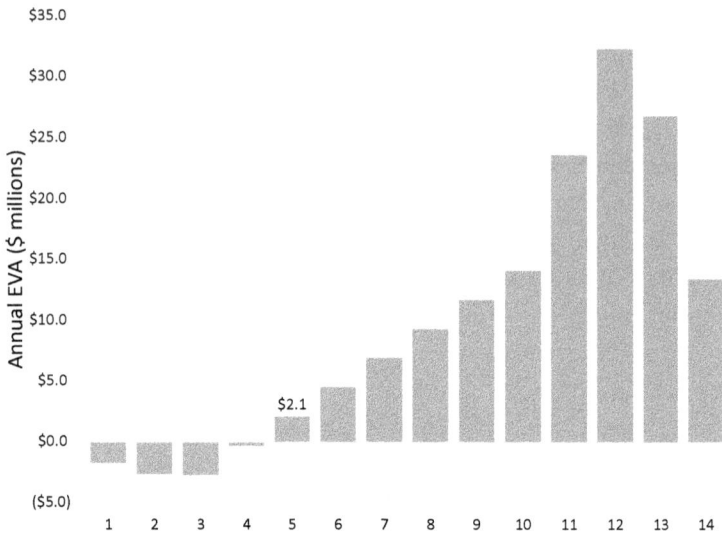

Figure 52—EVA from Three-Year Expansion

Some may wonder, "Why the heavy emphasis on how long it takes the results to show up?" If we are telling managers to think long-term, shouldn't NPV settle the question? Simply take all positive-NPV projects and reject all that are negative. Unfortunately, we live in a world where there are annual performance measures, and even quarterly metrics matter a whole lot to managers. Therefore, finding a measure that provides a similar NPV signal but that spreads the benefits out more evenly over the life of an asset will encourage more good investment, since managers won't have to wait for results due to depreciation distortions while still they're being held accountable for delivering returns.

Residual Cash Earnings properly balances growth, margin, and asset intensity while also spreading the benefits over the life of the investment, as figure 53 demonstrates.

Through the RCE lens, the results appear desirable sooner and are spread out more evenly over the life of the investment. We won't get to incentive design until chapter 14, but it's easy to see that if we pay managers to improve performance compared to the prior year, then measures such as free-cash-flow, rate-of-return, and EVA would likely lead to this investment proposal's being turned down. RCE, however, *encourages* such investment.

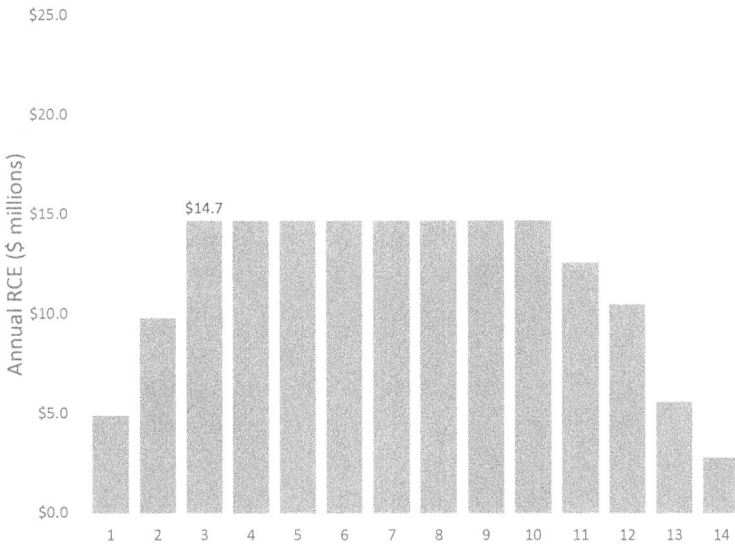

Figure 53—RCE for Three-Year Expansion

In the context of this chapter, the important point of all this is that the primary analytical framework for investment evaluation and approval should be the very same RCE framework that is best for evaluating the ongoing performance of the overall business. Much like when using discounted cash flow analysis, a forecast is prepared; from it we calculate Gross Cash Earnings, Gross Operating Assets, and RCE year by year. Then we calculate the net present value of the forecasted RCE. Because of the way RCE works, these NPVs tend to be a bit higher than traditional NPV, which in practice means that managers don't need to create unrealistic hockey-stick forecasts to get their projects approved.

In addition to applying RCE to individual investments, managements require a methodology for comparing investments, prioritizing them, and ultimately making investment decisions. As mentioned before, corporate finance theory states that companies maximize value when they accept all projects with a positive NPV. But, in practice, managements should establish minimum criteria for what is "enough NPV to be worth it." This can be established based on an RCE Profitability Index (RPI), which is simply the NPV of RCE as a percentage of the peak investment, or in other words the amount of value created per dollar of investment. Using such an index, projects can then be ranked and prioritized based on this profitability index. This way, the portfolio of investments selected for implementation will maximize the value-creation potential, given the size of the total investment budget. If other limitations are in play, such as having a minimal number of project managers for implementing investments, the best NPV strategy will be the one that delivers the most NPV while fitting within the constraint.

The typical approach to prioritizing investments is to use the internal rate of return, or IRR, but four major flaws affect this approach. The first is that, if a project has cash flows that flip direction more than once, there will be multiple IRR solutions. Which one do you use? The marketing team likely emphasizes the higher IRR, while the finance folks care about the lower IRR. The second flaw is that projects with different durations can have the same IRR and yet very different net present values, which can lead to poor prioritizations and underperformance. Third, IRR also assumes that cash in-flows are reinvested at the IRR, while NPV doesn't. Finally, IRR doesn't indicate the dollars of value creation, whereas NPV does. This is important when thinking about prioritization under constraints, such as a limited number of managers or a fixed capital budget, because only NPV can be used to optimize value optimization.

The project duration limitation on IRR came into play recently when the CEO of an oil and gas exploration and production company was considering rates of return from wells with varying reserve lives and production capacities. In some regions, the annual returns were high, but the reserves didn't last very long—sometimes only two to three years before production faded. In other areas, natural geological formation created reserves that produced at a slower rate, but for a longer period. So, the peak returns in these reserves were not as high, but they lasted much longer. The IRR framework is particularly poor at properly comparing these different investment options. Instead, we recommend using the RPI, which indicates the amount of value created, per dollar of investment, regardless of the combination of IRR and duration expected, and can therefore be better used for prioritization.

The RPI is a highly intuitive metric. For just a moment, forget everything but three pieces of information about an investment. We know the expected NPV, the amount of investment, and the ratio of the two (which is the RPI percentage). Consider an investment of $50 million with an NPV of $25 million—the RPI is 50%. Essentially you are paying $50 million to buy something worth $75 million, giving you a net profit, or net present value, of $25 million. Let's imagine this is an acquisition and these numbers are based on your review of the company before any discussions. Let's assume we need to pay a 20% premium to get the deal closed. Now the purchase price rises to $60 million, the NPV is $15 million, and the RPI drops from 50% to 25%. Half the benefit is gone.

Let's further assume that, after discussions begin—and then become public through the loose-lipped investment banker you mistakenly chose to use—other potential buyers show up. After some public bidding, the market price rises to $68.2 million, and it looks like the RPI will be 10% ($6.8 million divided by $68.2 million). We are rapidly losing ground as the purchase price rises and the value received stays the same. In many deals this is where the buyer "finds new synergies" to somehow convince itself the value is over $75 million. Lesson learned: Try to avoid justifying higher prices by changing the numbers that drive your estimate of the value you are getting. Except in rare cases, people do this to make themselves feel better. Most often, they feel much worse later.

Now, say the deal arouses the interest of a few private equity firms that realize the target company is in play and can support a lot of debt, so they make a bid. You stick with your plan and are determined to buy this company. After all, you told your board it's "strategic." A few rounds of posturing and bidding go by, and the price reaches $71.4 million. It continues to rise, and ultimately you pay $73.5 million, which makes for a 2% RPI. Of the initial $25 million of NPV, 94% of it was yielded to the selling shareholders during negotiations.

This could *still* turn out to be a good deal, but after the acquisition closes and you begin to integrate, you would have a fairly small margin of safety before the NPV drops to zero and then turns negative. If, in the end, the synergies are a bit less than expected and additional investment is needed to achieve them, the value you get could be much less than the originally estimated $75 million. Let's assume it is only $70 million. Unfortunately, you paid $73.5 million, so the negative NPV of $3.5 million results in an RPI of –4.8%. Bottom line: It's worth less than what you paid.

Note that, if the deal went through at the original $60 million, which was a 20% premium to what the company traded for before any deal discussions, there would have been enough margin of safety to more than absorb the unexpected synergy shortfall. The positive NPV would have been $10 million ($70 million minus $60 million), which, when divided by $60 million, would result in an RPI of 16.7%. Despite all the due diligence we may do, we can never know for sure what will happen both inside the company we acquire and across the industry and the economy. We are always better off with a greater margin of safety, which, fortunately for us, can be quantified by the RPI.

The most interesting and useful applications of the RPI become evident when we apply it to a portfolio of investments as a means of prioritizing them and making strategic choices. This could have been done in real time for each of the negotiation rounds in the deal above. As things unfolded, where did the acquisition stack up? This process can provide managers with a good, continuous feel for their "opportunity set," which can help them know when to walk away and when to come back to the table.

At the start of the planning process, a company or business unit should evaluate major potential investments to come up with a high-level RCE and RPI analysis. Then these investments can be prioritized from highest to lowest RPI. In figure 54, we show a group of 12 investments prioritized by RPI. The first seven are shaded darker, indicating they have an RPI with a desirable margin of safety. The next three are shaded lighter since, though they have a positive expected NPV, it's not high enough to provide an adequate margin of safety against unexpected differences between the projection and the actual results. Put more simply, these investments aren't expected to deliver enough NPV to be worth the effort and risk.

The final two investments have negative NPV. Whereas we might be willing to make an investment with a slim RPI if it's strategic, we should always avoid negative-NPV investments.

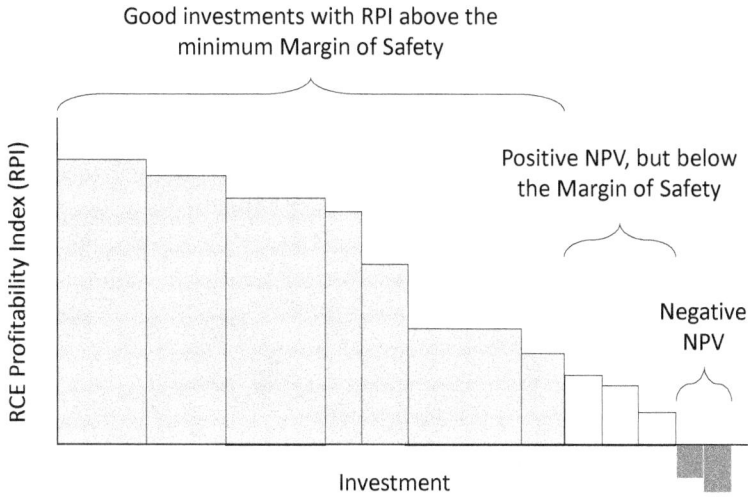

Figure 54—Project Prioritization with the RCE Profitability Index

Project Look-Backs

Most companies lack a rigorous process for evaluating how their investments turned out after the fact, and those that do usually fail to apply it very consistently or effectively. To have an effective look-back process requires work at the time of the original investment evaluation. Before giving a go-ahead to authorize capital spending, the project managers should be required to establish how often and how a look-back will be done to validate the effectiveness of the investment. Measurable financial and nonfinancial criteria, including specific metrics, data items, and minimum acceptable readings, should all be established in advance to ensure that the data is captured and reviewed as needed. Deciding to do a look-back two years after the investment takes more effort, time, and cost than making it part of the process from the start.

Since many companies develop discounted free cash flow models of net present value at the time of the investment, this is often the financial basis for a look-back. But beware—this approach can confuse good *and* bad progress by mixing investment and operating cash flows. Consider the cumulative free cash flow graph in figure 55. From a cumulative free cash flow perspective, this look-back seems to be better than was projected, since we are ahead of where we were expected to be. Unfortunately, this is not because the investments are turning out better than expected; it's because the investment results showed lower revenue, revealed thinner margins, and were altogether so bad that the investment program was discontinued after only 40% of the capital had been invested. What we see here is a shortfall of investment, not a surplus of profits. We could construct another case that looks exactly like this, where all the investment happened but the profits were way higher than expected. From the cumulative or annual free cash flow alone, we can't tell if this is a good or bad outcome.

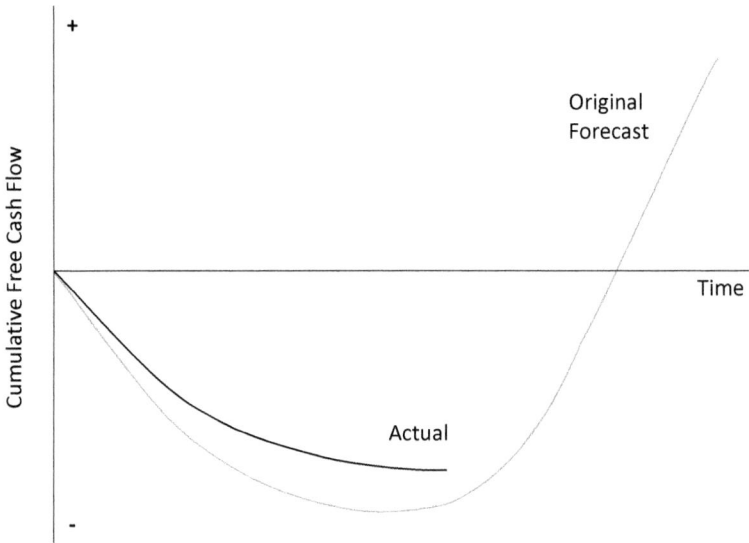

Figure 55—Project Look-Back Cumulative Free Cash Flow

Since RCE always compares the actual Gross Cash Earnings during a given period to the capital charge on the actual cumulative investment in Gross Operating Assets, there are no mixed messages. If RCE is higher, the investment project is doing better than planned, and vice versa. Figure 56 clearly shows that this look-back is for a project that is simply not good, which we would expect with lower revenue, tighter margins, and a discontinuation of the investment program after only 40% of the capital had been spent.

The frequency and nature of look-backs tend to have an important impact on both the propensity to invest and the accountability after the investment. Companies that rarely do look-backs—or do them with a process that is fragmented, ad hoc, or inconclusive—often consider capital to be *free* and thus can be inadvertently supporting a culture of overinvestment. To avoid this, many managements clamp down on the investment budget at the center, which can shift the pendulum too far toward underinvestment. In addition, when the process is governed by control rather than economics, midlevel managers won't feel accountable, and as a result it's more likely that investments won't be prioritized where they can do the most good but instead will be focused on the proverbial squeaky wheel.

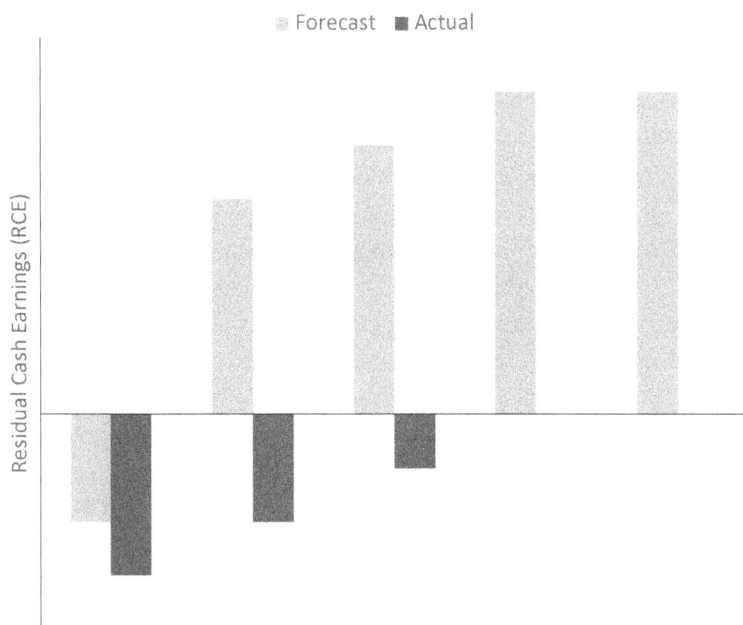

Figure 56—Project Look-Back RCE

Look-backs can also be used to improve capabilities and recalibrate forecasts by analyzing and adjusting the assumptions that were originally made in projections. For example, did customers and competitors respond as we initially expected them to? In any case, be wary of focusing too much on differences between the forecast and the actual results. Some companies spend far too much time and money analyzing these variances to an updated forecast, as if they really mattered. One of the worst comments ever uttered in my presence, and my good friend John Ballow remembers it well, was "That was very profitable *after the write-off.*"

Of most importance, though, is whether the investment in fact created value. If a project's RCE contribution is positive, that's good. If it's large and positive, that's even better. If after three years we calculate that project *A* has delivered cumulative RCE of $125 million but was originally projected to deliver $150 million, I might discuss the reasons why it fell short of the original forecast. Still, I'm going to be much happier with project *A* than with project *B*, which employed a similar amount of investment but produced only $25 million in RCE, even if that's way ahead of the $15 million that was originally planned for project *B*. Results matter—not variances.

Two important behavioral problems can arise from emphasizing variances rather than focusing on absolute RCE. First, too much focus on variances can lead people to sandbag their forecasts to be barely above the allowable margin of safety, so that they get their project approved and their performance looks better when the results come in. This degrades the information available to those making investment decisions. Second, criticizing the managers responsible for project *A* may cause them to think twice before proposing more high-RCE investments, and this may inadvertently prod those with the best investment opportunities to reduce their reinvestment rate.

Notes

1 In some cases, the definition of "free cash flow" is adjusted to only subtract ongoing and maintenance investments, and not to charge growth investments against the free cash flow measure. This makes the measure less bad, but it still is a poor period measure.

ELEVEN

Loose Ends in Investment Decision-Making

A LITTLE OVER a decade ago, I attended a seminar run by New York University Professor of Finance Aswath Damodaran, which he called the "loose ends in valuation." It was highly informative, practical, and entertaining, too. As you probably noticed, it was also the inspiration for the title of this chapter, which discusses special applications of the investment analysis and decision principles discussed in chapter 10, each of which requires us to alter our approach and, in some cases, also to incorporate additional information.

Investments in innovation and marketing are, in principle, similar to investments in machinery and equipment, but in practice these investments are expensed for accounting purposes and must, therefore, be treated differently. Acquisitions are also different from capital expenditures; it's a specific core competency to be skilled at tracking acquisition ideas, vetting them, negotiating deals, and, most important, running the acquired companies after the deal closes. One last special situation addressed in this chapter is "investments that don't earn a return"—as, for example, replacing the roof on a production facility or doing repairs after a major flood. In other words, these are investments that are hard to justify by using financial criteria alone.

Premium (Discount) Valuations

Just 15 years ago, a young Harvard University student named Mark Zuckerberg launched the "FaceMash" website to allow visitors to compare and comment on student pictures. But the site was shut down by the Harvard administration and Zuckerberg was almost expelled. In 2004 he launched "TheFacebook," and certainly few, if any, corporate strategy departments knew or cared. This seemingly trivial idea was the seed from which grew the now globally dominant relationship-based social media site and ad platform called Facebook. Over the 12 months through mid-2018, Facebook delivered revenue of $48 billion and net income of $19 billion, while attaining a market capitalization that surpassed *half a trillion dollars* that summer—talk about Jack (or Mark) and the beanstalk, with his magic seeds! To allocate capital effectively requires forward thinking, awareness of what's happening in adjacent markets, and an organizational desire to place enough bets on the future to be reasonably sure of not being left behind, like Facebook's predecessor Myspace.

Who could have seen this coming? I certainly didn't, and I'm not sure Zuckerberg did either, at least not while inventing the future in his college dorm room. I don't believe that aiming to match Facebook's miraculous track record is a realistic goal for anybody's corporate innovation processes, but it's helpful to understand that such a story is possible.

Using straight accounting figures, the net book value of all tangible assets owned by the companies of the S&P 500 totaled $4.7 trillion at the end of 2017. This sounds like a humongous figure, but it actually represents a mere 18% of the total enterprise value of these organizations. When they complete acquisitions for prices that are above the attributable net assets, the price paid is recognized either as goodwill or as "other intangibles" in the accounting books. This adds another $5.0 trillion, making the value of all tangible and intangible assets on the books of the S&P 500 companies much larger—$9.7 trillion, to be more precise. But even this number represents only 37% of total enterprise value.

As shown in figure 57, the total enterprise value of these companies also includes another $16.8 trillion worth of what I call the "value premium." It's simply the difference between the actual enterprise value and the total net book value of both the tangible and the intangible assets. This value premium is worth 173% of the total net book value of the tangible and intangible assets! Where does it come from?

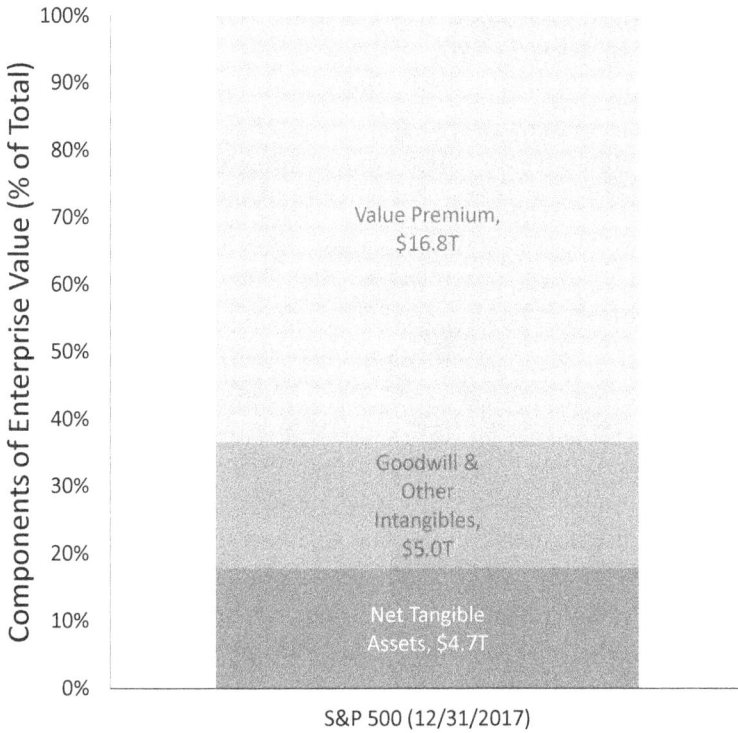

Figure 57—Importance of Intangibles

Of course, one important source of value premium is innovation, as in the Facebook example discussed above. Yet brand strength is also important, since differentiated brands can support premium pricing, market share growth, or some combination of the two.

Occasionally, a company controls a captive supply of some commodity or an intermediate product that offers a sustainable edge over the competition, such as a plastics plant built adjacent to a sustainable natural gas production field. Premium value can also derive from proprietary process know-how, sharper decision-making capabilities, and both an execution mentality and a focus on results. And even the ownership culture that this book aims to help management create, as we show in chapter 13, can itself be a competitive advantage, especially in large organizations.

Managing Innovation and R&D Investments

Executives should be sure to manage R&D and other forms of innovation and development with a sharp focus on value creation. We can't actually force innovation to happen with financial measures and controls, but we can certainly stifle it by using the wrong measures. Our resource allocations for planning and innovation, therefore, should be focused on areas where strong economics have been achieved or where we believe the numbers are desirable. Innovation funding should be freely available to fund good (or potentially good) ideas, but this must go hand-in-hand with ongoing accountability for both nonfinancial milestones and, eventually, financial results.

Managers sometimes seem to worry more about how much they invest in innovation than about the result. As long as their expensive benchmarking studies show that their spending on R&D as a percentage of sales is reasonable, then all is fine, or so they assume. If poor innovations result, they claim they have a bad R&D head or team. They fire, they hire; but the results may never get any better. They spend excessive time justifying expenditures and not enough making sure that their investments generate a return. In many entrepreneurial companies, the founder has a passion for innovation that inspires everyone else to reach for the stars. Their collective excitement about results reinforces the idea that it's not the research itself that matters, but instead the fruits of the research.

Many think the greatest virtue of Silicon Valley is its ability to identify and fund good investments. But an even greater contributor to the success of venture capital is the speed and decisiveness with which firms in that innovative place often cut funding for bad ideas or pivot to a more tenable strategy. This is also one of the biggest differences between the corporate world, where R&D is frequently allocated on the basis of arbitrary qualitative factors with ineffective monitoring and infrequent spending reallocations, and the world of venture capital, where the emphasis is on results. Many corporate projects continue to be carried out for many years after their lack of potential has already been identified. They place very little emphasis on true accountability and delivering results. What's missing is any urgency about commercial viability—a criterion for investment that is often subject to the whims of the head of the R&D department, who may simply "have a feeling this is going to work."

In an ideal world, the allocation, performance monitoring, and portfolio management of a corporate R&D effort would function like a micro-economy of angel investors, venture capitalists, startup businesses, mature companies, and capital markets. The champion of an R&D idea would secure funding by submitting a plan laying out resource requirements, milestones, activities, projections, and payoffs. If a sponsor approved it, our champion would then gradually be given funding, as the projections deem appropriate, and as long as periodic milestones are met. If the milestones are not reasonably achieved, the sponsor would have the opportunity to pull the plug and reallocate the financial and human resources. There would be ongoing monitoring, coupled with resource reallocations as needed to divert resources away from bad ideas and toward good ones.

From the outside, investors don't know the exact state of affairs in corporate R&D—and for the purpose of protecting trade secrets, this is likely as things should be. But corporate management must have a firm grasp of what the innovation investments aim to accomplish, the status of development programs, and the expectations for the magnitude and timing of results. This is *not* a delegated function. Did Steve Jobs sit back and let innovation magically happen at Apple? No, he led the process. This is one of the biggest obstacles to success for conglomerates, since the CEO may well be responsible for overseeing businesses in five different industries (as opposed to just the one where he cut his teeth). How would Steve Jobs have overseen innovation at Ford? I know, I know: He would have done pretty well for sure, though most "normal" corporate people have a hard time understanding customer needs and problems as well as the innovation paths, technical drivers, and performance tradeoffs in an industry they are less familiar with. So, they delegate with inadequate accountability and the result, in the vast majority of cases, is that the conglomerate business units are less innovative than their stand-alone peers. They spend the money. They have nice, shiny "innovation centers." They reimagine everything reimaginable. But they just don't get the innovation bit.

Both in form and in function, the corporate innovation process, which normally falls within an R&D functional mandate, should try to adopt as many elements of American venture capital practice as are found workable. A process is needed for midlevel and business-unit managers to propose new R&D ideas to the corporate heads of the innovation process and perhaps, depending on the size and scope of the proposed investments requested, even to senior management. There should be well-established project selection criteria, again ones that simulate the approach of venture capitalists and investors alike. Each proposal must include a description of the project, the expected outcomes, impact on the business, milestones, resources, and projections. Clear opportunities for go/no-go decisions must be specified in advance, including the metrics, data collection methods, and boundaries for continuation.

A formal and regular periodic review process can be developed and streamlined to focus exclusively on results and go/no-go decisions, with reassessments of the future when appropriate. The management process must be as fact-based and objective as possible, to ensure that projects are delivering at or above planned minimum milestones, otherwise resources should be properly reallocated. To be sure there is adequate discipline, as in the venture capital setting, the default should be that, when previously approved funding runs out, the project ends unless it can secure additional funding. There should be forced rankings, portfolio pruning, and maybe even forced ramp-ups for especially attractive projects. We don't want to be content with a "steady as she goes" mindset for the best ideas; we want them to always be backed with funding—funding that may well end up coming from defunding the projects that didn't turn out as well as originally expected (though this should generally not be a requirement).

This innovation process should then directly feed the overall business-planning process. This, after all, is not just a sandbox for adult playtime—it's *work*, often the most important work. Once these R&D ideas begin to take shape, they should be assigned probability-weighted projections that feed the revenue and RCE growth of the plan as a separate line item. The R&D pipeline should be discussed in the planning reviews to the extent that the various initiatives are expected to affect the five tools of value creation. Particular attention should be given to reinvestment effectiveness, which, again, is a measure of revenue growth per dollar of investment over a three- or five-year period. When managers are asked to commit to the revenue they need to deliver with R&D, they are more likely to prune ideas that are not delivering according to expectations so they can focus on ones more likely to make the R&D payoff.

The method of financial measurement is often an obstacle in and of itself. Unfortunately, management teams are influenced by the differences in accounting treatment between various types of investments, and this affects how they prioritize investment opportunities. Investments in R&D and marketing are expensed immediately as period expenses, while investments in property, plant, and equipment are typically capitalized and treated as having a longer life. These differences can lead executives to invest far too much in one form of investment, such as capital expenditures to build a new manufacturing plant, and not enough on other types, such as R&D spending for product development or brand-building marketing expenditures.

The Special Case of Acquisitions and Goodwill Accounting

Perhaps the most challenging of the rules for investment accounting are the complexities and issues arising from acquisition goodwill. If a company pays more for another company than a reasonable amount that can be ascribed to tangible and intangible assets, the accounts need to show an asset somewhere that is being purchased—hence the creation of what's called "goodwill." Let's say there is a $100 million acquisition and, even after marking up some of the assets to reasonable levels, we have $60 million of property, plant, and equipment and $15 million of intangible assets like customer lists and brands. The $25 million difference between the $100 million paid and the $75 million of acquired assets is attributed to the somewhat mysterious goodwill, which reflects the purchase price premium over the book value of the assets received.

Why would a company pay a premium over asset value? Perhaps it has desirable products, brands, technologies, or customer satisfaction that are capable of driving higher revenues and cash flows, possibly through synergies. As we saw earlier in figure 57, across the entire spectrum of U.S. publicly traded companies, well over half of their current market value resides in this premium. When the acquired company invested in its products, brands, technologies, or customer satisfaction, this investment was expensed. But when someone else acquires the company, then the new owner gets to treat these items as investments in assets. Of course, after the acquisition, all new R&D and marketing expenditures will once again be expensed as period costs. To be sure, there is no logical problem with the notion of goodwill—the problem is that at all other times accounting treats these investments in products, brands, technologies, and customer satisfaction as period costs rather than longer-term investments.

In principle, accounting treatment shouldn't matter. If we invest $100 million and it is reasonably expected to earn an adequate annualized return over the next five or 10 years, that should be sufficient for management to decide that the investment is worthwhile. For an investment in a new plant, this is straightforward. But for investments in R&D and marketing, many managements hesitate, because of the treatment of these investments as period expenses in the accounting books. Again, in principle, few executives will honestly claim they're driven by short-term profit and loss accounting. But in practice, as management prepares for the never-ending stream of quarterly earnings calls, investments that are expensed are often given a lower prioritization than investments that can be capitalized and recorded against earnings on a gradual basis over time, if at all.

If investments such as R&D and marketing are important to *your* business, your process for evaluating these expenditures should be the same as that for evaluating capital expenditures. Using the methodology set out below, such investments should be considered and prioritized simultaneously. All investments should be subject to a similar test of worthiness, and the main question should thus be whether the investment creates enough value to be included in the company's investment plans.

Managements tend to seek smoothly growing earnings and, since R&D and marketing are expensed immediately against earnings, they have an incentive to smooth out these expenditures, too, to avoid making earnings unnecessarily volatile. But because opportunities for good investment are often not so predictable, in years when fewer prospects loom on the horizon, the company may tend to invest more than the optimal amount in these expensed investments—while in other years it invests less than it should.

Marketing Resource Allocation

Though the principles are the same, the typical impediments to effective marketing investment are different from those that tend to stifle innovation. Ask finance officers how much to invest in marketing for a given brand, and they often seem at a loss.[1] When it comes to allocating marketing resources across a range of products and geographies, the value-maximizing solution can be even more of a mystery. What impact will this spending have on volumes, the ability to raise prices, and long-term brand value? If marketing dollars are reallocated from product *A* in region 1 to product *B* in region 2, what is the likely impact on aggregate sales and profits? And what effect do these decisions have on the stock price?

For the last 25 years or so, the standard approach to allocating marketing resources has been through "marketing-mix modeling," which involves statistical analysis of periodic marketing and sales data to estimate the near-term volume impact of raising, lowering, or shifting marketing resources and also adjusting promotion and pricing policies. Advocates use such modeling to enhance the effectiveness of marketing allocations, even though the analysis ignores most of the cost structure, the balance sheet, and changes to the strength and differentiation of the brand itself. At most companies, the real focus of such modeling is actually on maximizing sales alone.

While the mix-modeling approach seems somewhat logical, critics claim that it is too short-term focused and doesn't help build long-term brand value. They contend that mix modeling emphasizes current sales through promotion and price discounts, while largely ignoring the value of innovation and brand-building investments, such as advertising. True, mix modeling helps meet quarterly sales and earnings guidance, but in many cases it will do little to drive the valuation multiple and share price over the next few years.

For those who don't think long-term brand value is an investor priority, consider the case of the activist investor Trian Group and the H. J. Heinz Company. The asset management group condemned Heinz's management for putting too much money into trade allowances and promotion to drive short-term profits, while neglecting the advertising and product innovation that would nurture differentiation, long-term brand value, and stock price. After a failed proxy fight and acceptance of some new board members, Heinz acquiesced and increased its advertising budget. With such a strong emphasis on making investments that provide long-term brand benefits, potentially at the expense of sacrificing near-term results, this was certainly not the old story of shortsighted activists pillaging a venerable company for immediate gain that has become so common in business news.

So, what can be done to avoid the "sales-at-all-costs" trap of mix modeling while ensuring that managements allocate marketing resources in ways that will drive long-term value? Are there metrics and decision tools available that can improve the balance between delivering current performance and building long-term value?

As mentioned in chapter 7, in 2017 my colleagues and I began working with a firm called BERA Brand Management, where Ryan Barker and his team developed one of the largest brand-equity assessment platforms in the world to explain and quantify how brands grow. The framework and database they created not only explains how brand growth translates to financial performance, but also takes things a step further by explaining differences in market valuations.

As my colleague Joe Theriault and I reviewed some of Barker's original research on the linkage between BERA metrics and valuation, a few lightbulbs went on. Managers constantly face a tradeoff between driving current performance and managing for the long term. The problem is that, from a purely financial perspective, they have fact-based measures of current performance, but only forecasts and opinions about the future. Most executives talk a good long-term game, but when push comes to shove they make sure they hit their near-term numbers, even if it means giving up some long-term opportunity. It's simply the present-day business version of "a bird in the hand is worth two in the bush." But now, thanks to BERA, we have a fact-based way to measure, and not just guess at, the drivers of valuation multiples that represent future expectations. Managers can balance fact-based current performance and fact-based objective measures of future performance. Having done what I've done for over 25 years, I regard this as a true epiphany—and by far the most outstanding breakthrough I have been part of.

But I am getting ahead of myself. BERA, which stands for Brand Equity Relationship Assessment, is built around a battery of 100+ metrics that are rooted in behavioral science and market research. While traditional marketing wisdom emphasizes awareness and preference for a brand, BERA has found that these two qualities—plus the metrics associated with each—offer an incomplete and unreliable picture of the complex, often irrational dynamics of consumer choice. Awareness and funnel metrics, like consideration and preference, are informative but tend to be lagging indicators that tell you more about what has happened than about what *will* happen. They follow sales or, at best, provide contemporaneous indications. These metrics don't capture the underlying drivers of customer intent or consideration, which makes them a far less reliable basis for driving brand optimization or for validating, predicting, and orienting investment in the brand.

With the aim of addressing these shortcomings, BERA has developed a multidimensional brand model that consists both of lagging indicators, which explain how brand characteristics contribute to a brand's market share or revenue today, and of leading indicators that explain and predict how a brand contributes to tomorrow's sales volume and pricing power. It is this combination of leading and lagging indicators that makes the BERA framework ideal for bridging the analytical gap between marketing and finance.

Fortuna Advisors completed a capital markets research study that found strong relationships between the BERA metrics and a variety of measures of stock price performance, financial performance, and valuation. We studied a list of over 160 publicly owned monobrand companies in the BERA database. ("Monobrand" refers to companies whose majority of revenue comes from a single brand, such as Coca-Cola, Delta Air Lines, or Facebook.) The study spanned an eight-quarter period from the third quarter of 2015 through the second quarter of 2017.

The first step was to verify that these brand metrics correspond to the ultimate goal of driving higher TSR, or total shareholder return, which includes dividends and share price appreciation. The monobrand companies were sorted into high, medium, and low groups based on their *Today* score, and the median TSR was calculated for each group. The companies that scored highly on *Today* delivered median TSR that was 0.7% higher per year than the median for companies with low *Today* scores. This is a slightly positive relationship, but *Tomorrow's* impact on TSR was considerably stronger, with the median TSR for the high *Tomorrow* companies being a significant 7.3% higher than for the low *Tomorrow* companies.

Next, the *Today* and *Tomorrow* metrics were related to periodic financial metrics like sales growth and rates of return, as well as to valuation multiples, which indicate the collective view of investors with regard to a company's long-term trends in performance and value creation.

The monobrand companies in the top *Today* group had 2.1% more median revenue growth than the low group, and the top *Tomorrow* group delivered an extra 2.3% revenue growth. Since revenue growth is an important driver of TSR, it's reassuring to note these findings that the *Today* and *Tomorrow* brand scores correlate so strongly with growth.

Yet growth for growth's sake isn't very valuable, so we tested the relationships to return on assets (ROA), return on capital (ROC), and return on equity (ROE). In all cases, scoring high on both *Today* and *Tomorrow* were associated with higher returns and more improvement in returns than the low *Today* and *Tomorrow* groups. The strongest results were associated with ROE, whereas the median company in the high *Today* group delivered 8.4% more ROE and 4.6% more improvement in ROE than the low *Today* group. The high *Tomorrow* group delivered 5.0% more ROE and 3.5% more improvement in ROE than the low *Tomorrow* group.

It is encouraging, then, that higher *Today* and *Tomorrow* scores correspond to higher sales growth; higher rates of return using ROA, ROC, and ROE; and positive improvements in these return measures. To complete the study, we examined the relationship of these brand scores to valuation multiples, since high and increasing multiples can be interpreted as signals of increasing brand value. The relationships were tested for *Today* and *Tomorrow* versus the price-to-earnings (PE) ratios and the enterprise-value-to-EBITDA ratios using both trailing and forward (analyst consensus) figures. The analysis also included price-to-forward-revenue and price-to-book-value ratios. For every one of these valuation metrics, the companies with high *Today* or *Tomorrow* scores were valued higher than companies with low *Today* or *Tomorrow* scores. And in each case, *Tomorrow* showed a more meaningful impact than *Today*. Since multiples tell us about the value of the future in relation to today, perhaps it is no surprise that *Tomorrow* seems to be a more powerful indicator than *Today*.

In sum, our research confirms that these metrics are highly related to growth, profitability, and valuation multiples; and as such, the metrics provide comprehensive indicators of both short- and long-term performance that can significantly improve the typical mix modeling signals. Integrating the insights provided by detailed brand metrics with value-based financial analysis can materially enhance the allocation of marketing investments, as well as boost innovation, CapEx, and acquisition investments, by enabling optimization of short-term versus long-term performance. We can improve strategic allocations at a high level, as well as strengthen tactical allocations deep within the organization, by consistently focusing resources where they create the most value.

Chief financial officers tend to prefer better financial performance to a vague expectation of future benefits, so when they hear marketing folks wax on about brand attributes, their eyes may begin to glaze over. Chief marketing officers, on the other hand, probably view long-term brand stewardship as critical to long-term success, and may see the excessively short-term profit focus of their financial executive counterparts as a sacrilege. Sometimes the marketing and finance subordinates form teams to collaborate, but that's a bit like asking cats to collaborate with dogs. It takes more than the idea of collaboration; it requires a strategic framework that bridges the two functions in a way that encourages the evaluation of tradeoffs with consistent, analytical rigor.

The first step in evaluating marketing investments is similar to that taken for almost any other investment—we determine how much revenue growth we can expect the investment to deliver. It is common to rely on traditional marketing mix modeling to forecast revenue, but the incorporation of brand-trait information substantially improves the accuracy of sales forecasts (a common complaint of the finance team, of course). This is because changes in scores can be used to accurately predict changes in sales over both the near and the long term. The other benefit of understanding these brand characteristics and their changes over time is that it informs the best strategy to maximize brand value—but more on that soon.

The second step is to estimate changes in RCE, which requires an understanding of expected costs and investments involved with sustaining and expanding capacity. Using our estimated RCE, we can develop our first estimate of value, which is simply based on Gross Operating Assets plus capitalized RCE (which reflects the present value of the future performance if we expect RCE to remain flat.) Some companies trade at a premium to this valuation, which means investors are pricing in future RCE improvements based on new value-creating investments that have not yet been made. Other companies trade at a discount, which implies an expectation that RCE will fade.

The third step is to gather and analyze the BERA insights. When the BERA scores are high and rising, especially the *Tomorrow* score, we expect a premium valuation, and vice versa. When we combine the second and third steps, we get a value estimate, which we can divide by current sales to ascribe a value-to-sales ratio to each brand or subbrand.

In our article "Bridging the Gap Between Marketing and Finance," Ryan Barker and I demonstrated this process by building a case study based on a hypothetical apparel company with four business units, each represented by a real public company. The businesses chosen were the following: Columbia Sportswear, designer and marketer of outdoor and active apparel; Urban Outfitters, a retailer and wholesaler of women's and men's apparel, home goods, electronics, and beauty products; Chico's FAS, a specialty retailer of women's casual-to-dressy clothing and accessories; and, last but not least, Lululemon Athletica, designer and distributer of athletic and "athleisure" apparel. Several of these companies operate multiple brands, but for the purpose of simplicity we only included brand information on each company's primary brand.

Based on BERA's data, Columbia Sportswear scored the highest on both *Today* and *Tomorrow*, while Lululemon Athletica had the highest Ratio of *Tomorrow* to *Today*, followed, in order, by Columbia Sportswear, Urban Outfitters, and Chico's. The ratio of *Tomorrow* to *Today* appears to be a telling indicator of financial performance, as suggested by the fact that it ranks these four brands in the same order as when they are ranked in terms of four key financial metrics: five-year revenue growth, current RCE margin, EBITDA multiple, and value to sales. As can be seen in figure 58, neither the brand nor the financial information is alone sufficient to explain the differences in value to sales for these four companies. The Ratio of *Tomorrow* to *Today* is quite similar for Urban Outfitters and Chico's, but the difference in RCE Margin is why the difference in value to sales is material. Similarly, Columbia Sportswear and Urban Outfitters have similar RCE Margins, but the difference in the Ratio of *Tomorrow* to *Today* explains the difference in value to sales.

Of course, it may seem that we want to maximize either RCE, which the chief financial officer may prefer, or BERA brand scores, as the chief marketing officer may favor. It is likely, though, that neither of these extreme choices is the value-maximizing decision. Maybe the ideal marketing mix of TV, radio, and print advertising, when coupled with selective social media, packaging, and in-store promotions, will deliver a bit less than maximum RCE, but will do more to drive BERA brand scores, which in turn drives the valuation multiple higher. This combination of the financial and brand improvements could thus deliver a better total return for shareholders.

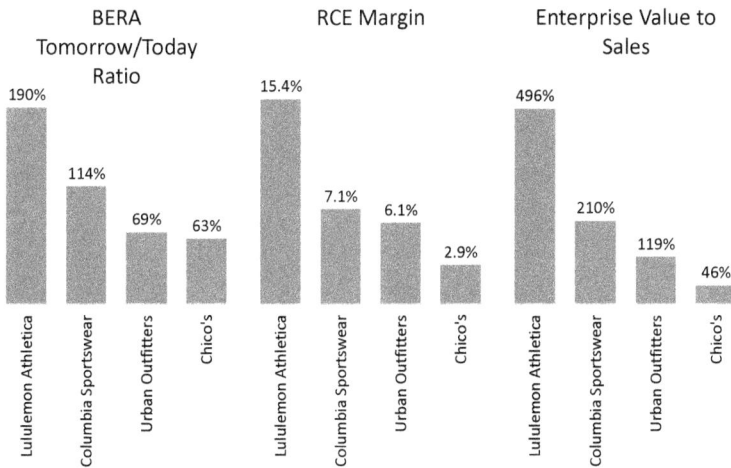

Figure 58—Value to Sales Driven by RCE and the Tomorrow/Today Ratio

Some have asked why the value-to-sales ratio is so important. One investor friend reminded me that such ratios were often used during the Internet bubble to describe companies that had sales but no profits or cash flow. Just the thought of such abuse of metrics makes the hair stand up on the back of my head...or it would if there were any left.

The value-to-sales ratio is the key to transforming marketing mix models from sales optimization to value maximization. Look back at figure 58—and no, that's not a typo—and note that the enterprise value of Lululemon Athletica really was almost five times the company's sales, while the same metric for Chico's was less than half of sales. In effect, each dollar of Lulu's sales was worth over 10 times as much as a dollar of Chico's sales. If these were truly business units of a single multi-business corporation and the company had managed marketing resources to maximize sales growth, as most companies' marketing departments do, then it is certain that this corporation would drive too much low-value sales growth in Chico's and not enough high-value sales growth at Lulu.

Figure 59 illustrates the importance of the value-to-sales ratio. First, let's consider a baseline situation with two brands, A and B, each of which is allocated $25 million of marketing spend. Once the funds are optimized across multiple media, the brands deliver the sales volumes shown in the figure.

Brand	Baseline Marketing Spend	Baseline Sales	Baseline Sales/ Marketing
A	$25	$500	20.0x
B	$25	$250	10.0x
Total	$50	$750	15.0x

Figure 59—Baseline for Illustration of Value to Sales

Notice that brand A delivers twice the sales with the same marketing spend, so the marketing department decides to allocate $5 million that's currently being spent on brand B to brand A while keeping the total budget fixed. This is oversimplified, yet decisions like this happen all the time as marketing-mix models are employed for optimizing marketing spend both across media supporting a specific brand and across brands, to optimize the overall growth rate.

Brand	Baseline Marketing Spend	Baseline Sales	Baseline Sales/ Marketing	Modified Marketing Spend	Modified Sales	Modified Sales/ Marketing
A	$25	$500	20.0x	$30	$600	20.0x
B	$25	$250	10.0x	$20	$200	10.0x
Total	$50	$750	15.0x	$50	$800	16.0x
%Δ				0.0%	6.7%	

Figure 60—Sales Growth Optimization by Reallocating Marketing Resources

As shown in figure 60, the marketing management team accomplishes 6.7% revenue growth through its sales-growth optimization process, and with no incremental marketing budget. When one brand has a different elasticity of sales to marketing spend, these sorts of opportunities will always be available. If our goal were to maximize sales, we would be celebrating. But our goal is to maximize *value*, so we need to know how valuable these sales are in each brand. And that's where the value-to-sales ratio fits in.

To make the example interesting, let's assume brand *B* has a value-to-sales ratio of 500%, as does Lulu in the case above, and brand *A* has a value-to-sales ratio of 50%, which is similar to Chico's. Now if we examine the value implications of the sales growth optimization strategy, shown in figure 61, the celebrations quickly halt as we realize that this reallocation of marketing spend is actually a value-destroying catastrophe.

Brand	Baseline Marketing Spend	Baseline Sales	Baseline Business Value	Baseline Value to Sales	Modified Marketing Spend	Modified Sales	Modified Business Value	Modified Value to Sales
					Sales Optimization			
A	$25	$500	$250	**50%**	$30	$600	$300	50%
B	$25	$250	$1,250	**500%**	$20	$200	$1,000	500%
Total	$50	$750	$1,500	200%	$50	$800	$1,300	163%
%Δ					0.0%	6.7%	-13.3%	

Figure 61—Introducing the Value to Sales Ratio

The marketing reallocations may have driven sales growth, but they do so by increasing growth in the brand that contributes much less value per dollar of sales. Why are the value-to-sales ratios so different? Perhaps brand *B* is so sought after by consumers that market share is generally rising, even though it is priced at a premium to the competition, while brand *A* has the opposite situation: It is losing share even though it's constantly being discounted and promoted. Brand *B* probably has more revenue growth and higher RCE margin, and its *Tomorrow* score stands well above its *Today* score, indicating a bright future and a higher valuation multiple.

Unfortunately, most marketing departments have zero idea what the value to sales is for their brands, so in their minds the sales-growth optimization plan seems ideal. What would they do if they had the value-to-sales information? Perhaps they would reallocate resources in the opposite direction—from brand A to brand B. In figure 62, we see that sales actually decline with this reallocation, though the value of the company significantly increases.

Brand	Baseline Marketing Spend	Baseline Sales	Baseline Business Value	Baseline Value to Sales	Value Optimization			
					Modified Marketing Spend	Modified Sales	Modified Business Value	Modified Value to Sales
A	$25	$500	$250	50%	$20	$400	$200	50%
B	$25	$250	$1,250	500%	$30	$300	$1,500	500%
Total	$50	$750	$1,500	200%	$50	$700	$1,700	243%
%Δ					0.0%	-6.7%	13.3%	

Figure 62—Using Value to Sales to Maximize Value

This is only an illustration, of course, but the optimal plan may be to increase the marketing spend on brand B, as illustrated, and at the same time to hold or increase the spending on brand A, as well. As already intimated, the goal of this spending is not to maximize near-term sales, but rather to improve differentiation *and* the *Tomorrow* score, so that the value to sales rises. The *Tomorrow* score is composed of two metrics: *Uniqueness* and *Meaningfulness*. While these are useful constructs for quantifying a brand's overall health across all sectors, what it means to be *Meaningful* or *Unique* is particular to each brand and sector. To address this, BERA has developed an array of emotional and image-based traits whose associations with each brand can be both measured and benchmarked so as to define *Uniqueness* and *Meaningfulness* for each brand. These traits can be thought of as a brand's DNA, or the building blocks that form our impression of that brand. Put simply, to move the needle on *Meaningfulness* or *Uniqueness*, we must change what people associate with the brand. And the BERA approach guides the way.

In practice, defining and using the value-to-sales ratio is a bit more involved, yet it's not too complex for most managers to understand. Even the basic notion of multiplying the sales output of the marketing mix models by the value-to-sales ratio to maximize value would be a huge process improvement for most branded companies.

Making Acquisitions that Create Value

It's in vogue to say, "Most acquisitions destroy value"—but, however fashionable, it's simply not true. As previously discussed, companies that invest more to acquire other businesses deliver average long-term TSR that is higher than in companies investing less in acquisitions. For example, in our article "Improving the Health of Healthcare Companies,"[2] we showed that highly acquisitive healthcare companies delivered median annual TSR that was 3.3% higher than their less acquisitive peers. We find directionally similar results in most industries. Some acquisitions fail spectacularly, to be sure, but on average acquisitions create value for the acquirer's shareholders.

The necessary steps for success with acquisitions are clear, but achieving them can be challenging and requires discipline to overcome natural human tendencies that can stand in the way of success. To be successful, an acquirer must first select a target company that would genuinely be worth more as part of its organization than as a stand-alone company or business unit of another company. Perhaps there are production or distribution synergies, or maybe there is the ability to scale marketing to new levels and achieve a level of revenue growth the stand-alone company could never hope to achieve.

Often these benefits result from poor resource allocation—especially at the tails, in big-value creators and destroyers. Some companies simply tolerate waste in costs and assets, hold excess cash, or underuse their debt capacity. These are the types of inefficiencies that tend to attract PE firms. But "strategic" acquirers, which tend to be competitors, or are at least operating in an adjacent market, rely more on synergies to create value. Synergies are produced when an increase in sales or reduction in costs or assets results from the two firms' being integrated. For example, consider a large firm with global distribution that buys a small, regional firm with differentiated products. Both businesses benefit from the other's core competencies.

An acquirer can seek a deal in three areas: in-market, in adjacent markets, or in an unrelated market. For the reasons mentioned above, private acquirers can be less discriminating, but strategic acquirers should rely foremost on companies in the same market or in adjacent markets to achieve synergies. This all may seem obvious, but it's important to have a clear acquisition agenda so that those seeking and sourcing the deal don't waste time and resources considering uneconomic acquisitions.

Next, the acquirer must negotiate a reasonable price for the purchase—one that's above the stand-alone value of the target, to entice them to sell, but below the value of the target company to the acquirer, with all synergies included. Finally, the acquirer must effectively manage, and in many situations also integrate, the acquired business and finally execute the plan successfully. Each step is fraught with obstacles, so success isn't likely to happen by chance. It takes careful planning, shrewd decision-making, hard work, and leadership.

The worst method for finding good acquisition deals, though, is to sit back and wait for investment bankers to come by shopping their ideas. Occasionally, gems can be found this way; but first ask: "If this business is so valuable, why does it have to be shopped?" Investigate whether management has taken actions to inflate results before "considering strategic options." Look out for future performance cliffs looming from possible patent expirations, fading brands, or leapfrogged technologies. Try to spot any active short-termism by current management designed to temporarily drive up prices and revenue—and therefore the company's valuation—while potentially creating headwinds for future growth. Or maybe the company is excessively sweating tangible and intangible assets by underspending to maintain and support them. Inquire about the process to see if you will be bidding against every strategic buyer and financial sponsor out there, and always consider the odds of getting a good price.

Though good deals do sometimes drop in your lap, if you want to be a successful acquirer, it's best to set up an ongoing process to track companies that could become acquisition targets. These are not fully vetted targets; they're just reasonable ideas that appear to make strategic sense and can be tracked over time. All available information on products, services, investments, and financials should be gathered and evaluated to continuously update the status of each opportunity. It's useful to meet with management occasionally, perhaps even informally at industry conferences or through interaction of midlevel employees. Most newly gathered information will merely be collected, but at times fresh insights, such as the launch of a new, innovative product or the cheap disposal of an unattractive business, will make an opportunity more desirable. At other times, new information that comes your way will make the target *less* desirable. It is best to have a scoring system to quickly convey the status of what may be a dozen or more tracked targets; and as targets reach a sufficiently high score, they should be thoroughly reviewed as a potential acquisition. This acquisition-tracking and -planning process helps your company find deals that aren't being shopped on the market; it helps provide context for comparison when a likely deal does appear; and it enables you to act quickly and decisively when a transaction becomes more attractive—or less.

Often, corporate development groups have a short list of businesses they think their company can make more valuable on acquisition, even though the purchase price is currently prohibitive. As is often the case in business, patience is a virtue in such situations. In a similar fashion to equity investors who, looking for desirable entry prices, follow attractive companies, corporate acquirers should establish share price guidelines and track their best targets while waiting for their number to be hit. Be sure to set the price low enough that it will still be acceptable after adding a reasonable acquisition premium.

When discussing the monitoring of acquisition-target prices, an executive for one client asked us whether this patience was really going to matter, given the efficiency of the stock market. True, markets are relatively efficient over time, but new information is always emerging, and expected long-term trends get whipsawed back and forth, so prices can and do deviate from "perfect efficiency." As mentioned previously, during 2018, the median premium of the 52-week high over the 52-week low for the Russell 1000 was 52%. If a company acquires another when the share price is close to its low, the price can become much more attractive, even after an acquisition premium that may be a bit higher to compensate for the cheap price. Therefore, waiting around for a good price can pay off, simply due to general volatility in the market.

It is critical that the acquisition planning process actually facilitate deals, and not just create some "for show." Corporate development executives sometimes express frustration with all their effort that goes into tracking and evaluating opportunities, only to see that deals actually get done when bankers visit the CEO with "hot ideas." A properly designed planning process instills discipline, yet that discipline can only be effective if the process is relied on for the majority of acquisitions.

Once a deal becomes live, regardless of how it originates, the real fun begins. Always start by understanding the stand-alone business before considering the acquisition plan. Learn the products and services, the customers and distribution channels, the production capabilities and capacities, and, of course, the expectations for growth, profitability, and investment. It is worthwhile to forecast and value the stand-alone case to see how it stacks up on its own. For public companies, this can be very useful as a comparison to the pre-deal public valuation. It's hard to make a deal work well when the starting point is a public share price that overvalues the stand-alone business, though there are always a few exceptions.

One example of an exception is a large pharmaceutical company with a broad, deep, global distribution network. Such a company may be able to create so much value when it acquires a fledgling biotechnology company with a solid drug pipeline that it can still create value when the acquisition price is several times what the biotech target would be worth on a stand-alone basis. Some of this tremendous potential upside will likely reside in viewing the target's share price as an ongoing premium to recognize the potential of an acquisition, even well before any announcement of an actual transaction. But as long as the value created is sufficiently above the preexisting value plus this premium, the deal can still be successful. In "Improving the Health of Healthcare Companies," we found that highly acquisitive pharmaceutical companies were much more successful acquirers than the typical healthcare company, generating almost 6% more TSR per year than less-acquisitive pharmaceutical companies.

Once you understand the stand-alone business, you'll need to measure and then build a case for potential synergies, including revenue synergies as well as all investments needed to generate them. For some reason, many management teams emphasize cost synergies more than revenue growth, which is unfortunate for both their decision processes and their acquisition integration plans. For example, sometimes the acquirer has a global footprint, as Becton Dickinson did when it bought CareFusion. Considerable value can result from the growth associated with global expansion of the target company. So, be sure to explore and to include revenue-growth synergies, otherwise good deals may be either missed completely or suboptimally executed.

Some corporate development teams do extensive sensitivity analysis, in which they test major assumptions in sensitivity tables or cubes. This can be informative, though an even more useful approach is to prepare a few thoughtful, comprehensive cases, both upside and downside, for review. Mechanical sensitivities tend to miss the interaction between external assumptions and the ensuing internal reactions and choices. For example, consider a retail acquisition in which the acquirer decided to pursue the more-expensive of two store refurbishment strategies. Only probing same-store sales growth would miss the fact that, if sales fell short of expectations, management would have the early option to scale back to the less-expensive refurbishment strategy for all remaining stores. By evaluating meaningful cases, then, we gain a better sense of the true upside and the downside, and we are encouraged to build flexibility into our integration strategies so that we can adapt them when things turn out better or worse than expected. Flexibility often costs money, so the baseline case may suffer a bit. But by protecting against severe downside situations, the average NPV across a realistic set of high, medium, and low cases will likely be higher, at least over a long-enough period.

Once the baseline and acquisition forecasts have been developed, we are ready to consider the maximum desirable acquisition price. Again, RCE provides an exceptional framework because we can compare the forecasted capital charges—a function of the purchase price and expected investments after the deal—to the expected GCE, both with and without synergies, as shown in figure 63.

The stacked bar chart shows the projected GCE both as stand-alone and with synergies. The dashed box in year 1 reflects a reduction in GCE, based on the costs associated with achieving synergies. The solid line shows the expected capital charges, based on the expected initial purchase price and the planned CapEx after the deal closes. At that price, RCE is neutral in year 2 and positive from year 3 on. But when negotiations get intense and either the seller demands a higher price or another bidder jacks up the price, this type of RCE graph can be quickly consulted. At the higher price, the capital charge solid line rises to the dotted line, and the acquirer would have to wait until year 4 for RCE to break even and would give up half the year-5 RCE. This is a *great* tool both for providing insights and for maintaining discipline during negotiations.

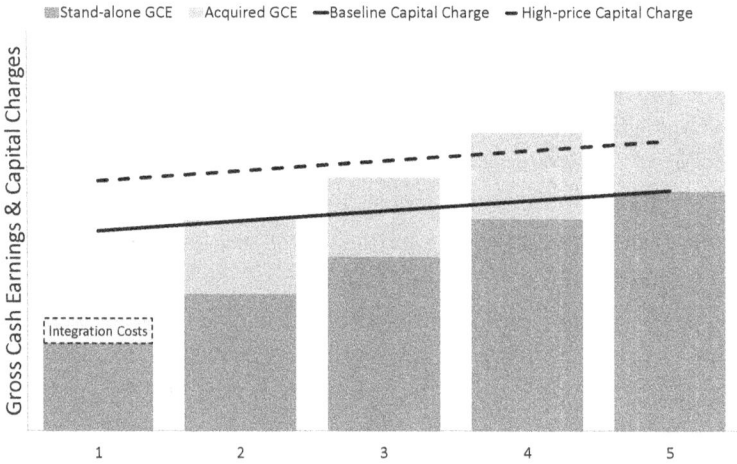

Figure 63—Purchase Price Sets the GCE Targets

Some acquisitions take a long time to pay off, even with the smoother recognition of performance made possible by using RCE versus traditional rates of return and EVA. One important consideration in such deals is that the longer a deal takes to show positive RCE, the higher the minimum acceptable RCE Profitability Index should be, both to compensate for the added risk and to be sure that the value creation is truly worth the wait, in comparison to other deals that show positive RCE sooner.

The final key element for acquisition success is execution. Topics surrounding acquisition execution— including how goals are set, plans developed, decisions made, incentives introduced, and newly acquired managers trained—will be discussed in the remaining chapters of the book.

Projects with Zero or Negative NPV

The NPV rule is considered the golden rule of corporate finance and is featured in virtually every corporate finance class in business schools. After decades of working in the shareholder value field, I have come to firmly believe that the NPV rule is an accurate and comprehensive way to evaluate decisions, as well as an extremely useful way to value prospective companies.

Despite the general acceptance and validity of NPV, however, every single company makes investments that appear to have zero or negative NPV.[3] This is not bad per se, as long as it is done for the right reasons and properly managed. Unfortunately, many corporate executives pursue negative NPV projects for the wrong reasons, and fail to manage the process well.

Executives often, oddly, describe a decision as "strategic" when it can't be justified financially. It's true that sometimes the benefits of an investment are hard to quantify or are expected to take an unusually long time to materialize. Yet if the financial benefits never arrive, the investment probably wasn't all that "strategic" after all! Don't rationalize a forecast that amounts to throwing darts at a wall; just recognize that the benefits do exist—or will likely come to exist—but may simply be hard to quantify or to predict.

In many companies, the problem begins at the start of the process. Often, the capital investment approval process launches with a request form indicating at the top whether this investment is for growth, for improved efficiency, or for some other strategic reason. This latter category can include investments to improve safety, comply with environmental regulation, or maintain assets (recall our example of the aging roof or catastrophically flooded plant).

Too frequently, when the "other" box is checked, it is just assumed that the investment is required, so the approval process moves along with little or no financial analysis. After all, if we know the NPV will be negative, why do the analysis? It won't affect the decision, *right*? Herein lies a catch.

We can realize many benefits by preparing forecasts and evaluating NPV, even when we know in advance that the results will yield zero or negative NPV. We can still consider different investment alternatives, to try to find the least-negative NPV solution. Perhaps we are installing a scrubber designed to reduce emissions from a chemical or industrial process. Our facilities engineering team has identified a scrubber capable of handling the job, but it recommends a scrubber twice the size that right now costs only 20% more. Purchasing the larger scrubber will significantly delay the point at which the next one must be added. Over a life cycle, this larger scrubber may be a choice that has a less-negative NPV. Or maybe the smaller scrubber is better. Who really knows, unless we do the analysis? Without it, it's almost certain that the smaller scrubber will be selected, as it consumes less of the capital budget. And, after all (we assure ourselves), we will have a new capital budget when a new scrubber will be needed!

Often, the problem isn't that the investment has a negative NPV but that the benefits are hard to quantify. Instead of throwing up one's arms and saying it can't be analyzed, it is far better in some cases to at least back into the NPV-breakeven forecast and to qualitatively assess whether management believes the investment will be above or below the NPV breakeven line. For example, we might think that if we install a new research information storage system, and if the researchers will access it on average 100 times per week, the system will pay for itself (versus the manual retrieval process currently in use). Will the new system be used enough to justify the new investment? Corporate decision-makers are often more willing to indicate whether a breakeven level of an activity can be achieved than they are to submit a forecast of what might in fact happen.

Also important, we can then use the breakeven assumptions to establish minimum milestones, financial and otherwise, that can be tracked after the investment. We can monitor how many people access the system each day and at least see if the expected benefits are being achieved. This will also be useful information the next time an investment of this type is considered.

Sometimes projects seem to have negative NPV because the investment doesn't make anything better; instead, it keeps something from getting worse. If the roof isn't replaced, it will leak and eventually we will need to close the facility—or worse, it could collapse, resulting in liabilities and safety hazards. Keeping a bad (or potentially catastrophic) outcome from happening can save a company huge sums, but whether the facility is running or not isn't material to the NPV analysis. So, we calculate the negative NPV of roof replacement costs and investments, and still try to find the least-negative NPV solution.

In other cases, though, some companies go to great lengths to execute strategic investments that appear to have negative NPV, but nevertheless are believed to eventually provide some long-term, nonquantified benefit. In some cases, managements deliberately tweak transfer prices and misallocate costs and assets in ways that penalize more-profitable projects to make these strategic investments appear more attractive. These cross subsidies are intended to keep a results-oriented organization from terminating strategic initiatives before they have a chance to stand on their own. Unfortunately, this propping up of strategic investments masks their true level of performance; this often endures for unconscionably long periods because of organizational inertia and political posturing, resulting in bad decisions where truly profitable projects are rejected for being saddled with costs wrongly allocated to them.

Picture a private equity investor overseeing a portfolio company that is making strategic investments that may cause losses for quite some time, but where both management and the investor believe the eventual scale and profitability will justify the early investments. The investor plans to inject equity funds to support the burn rate during the early stages, but, to manage risk and ensure accountability, the investor may provide the funding in stages to be sure that everything is on track before each tranche of funding is released.

Now imagine an unlikely scenario where the investor would prefer *not* to see the burn rate in their strategic portfolio company, so instead they provide excess funding to their other, more-profitable portfolio companies, with instructions for one to provide seconded employees at half their all-in cost; for another to provide raw materials at a steep discount to market; and for a third to buy product from the strategic business at a significantly marked-up price. Each of these other businesses would suffer losses, which would distort their strategic decision-making, their performance, their exit strategies, and their compensation for the portfolio company managements. The resulting mess would prevent any reliable analysis of the performance and potential of all four companies. It's no different with cross subsidies within multi-business public companies.

When corporations rely on cross subsidies, eventually the misaligned costs and assets run the risk of being treated as *real*. This distorts operational processes, such as pricing, as well as strategic decisions such as how much money to invest in growing both the subsidized and the subsidizing business. It is better by far to face the negative NPV, support the initiative anyway (if truly warranted), and set clear financial as well as nonfinancial milestones that will signal that the activity should either continue to grow (into positive NPV) or be shut down.

To summarize, doing financial analysis on zero and negative NPV investments is every bit as important as doing analysis for positive ones. This will help both in evaluating alternatives to find the least-negative NPV solution and in setting up minimum milestones that can be used to track performance after the investment. When forecasts are hard to create, consider using NPV breakeven analysis. And always avoid subsidizing activities to make them look better; facing reality consistently leads to wiser decisions.

Notes

1   Some of these opening paragraphs, slightly modified, come from "Brand Value Drives Corporate Value," by Gregory V. Milano and Joseph Theriault, and "Bridging the Gap Between Marketing and Finance," by Gregory V. Milano and Ryan Barker. Gregory V. Milano and Joseph Theriault, "Brand Value Drives Corporate Value," CFO.com, August 21, 2018, accessed January 15, 2019, http://ww2.cfo.com/budgeting/2018/01/brand-value-drives-corporate-value/. Gregory V. Milano and Ryan Barker, "Bridging the Gap Between Marketing and Finance," *Journal of Applied Corporate Finance* 30, no. 2 (Spring/Summer 2017).

2   Gregory V. Milano, Marwaan R. Karame, and Joseph G. Theriault, "Improving the Health of Healthcare Companies," *Journal of Applied Corporate Finance* 29, no. 3 (Summer 2017): 18–29.

3   Gregory V. Milano, "When Projects Have a Zero or Negative NPV," CFO.com, August 8, 2017, accessed January 15, 2019, http://ww2.cfo.com/cashflow/2017/08/projects-zero-negative-npv/.

TWELVE

Financial Policies that Support Business Strategy

THE PRIMARY EMPHASIS in this book is on business strategy and operational execution, but financial policies are important, too, and can help or hinder value creation. In most cases, financial policy should be subordinated to business strategy. With that in mind, this chapter provides insights on capital structure, operating leases, dividends, and cash balances that are part of an integrated, overall view of corporate finance.

Capital Structure Policies

Ever since the wave of leveraged buyouts in the 1980s, it has been commonplace for investors, academics, and commentators alike to suggest that "levering up" the balance sheet can be beneficial for shareholders. As we first argued in "Is Financial Leverage Good for Shareholders?"[1] on CFO.com, our capital market research suggests otherwise.

Most people generally try to be careful with how much debt they take on in their personal lives, so why do many corporate finance experts believe that high levels of corporate debt and leverage are a *good* thing? And why doesn't it seem to work out as well as these experts tell us it should?

The appeal of debt originates in academic corporate finance classes, where students are taught that reducing the weighted average cost of capital (WACC) by operating with the optimal proportion of debt and equity can be a major contributor to shareholder value.

Because the U.S. tax code allows a deduction for corporate interest payments, WACC tends to be lower for companies that are able to support more leverage, as long as the risk of financial default doesn't become excessive. A lower WACC increases the calculated present value of anticipated future cash flow, which is expected to increase the share price.

In addition to the argument that debt reduces WACC through tax savings, corporate finance scholars provided another explanation for how the heavy use of debt increases efficiency and value—namely, by disciplining the otherwise free-spending ways of managements running companies in mature industries with limited growth. When formulating this argument in *The American Economic Review* in 1986,[2] Michael Jensen wrote, "Thus debt reduces the agency costs of free cash flow by reducing the cash flow available for spending at the discretion of managers." The presumption here is that management would squander capital on value-destroying projects, so leverage is needed to rein in capital spending, improve cost efficiency, and drive superior performance. Many investors, analysts, and bankers encourage companies to increase leverage to reduce their WACC, and further to communicate their leverage policy to investors, with the expectation that such steps will increase both the efficiency and the long-run value of these companies.

But is this really what happens? With the aim of shedding some light on this question, we undertook a study in which we started with the 1,000 largest nonfinancial U.S. companies and eliminated those without full financial and market data for 2001 through 2010, which left us with 512 companies. We separately explored two subsets of time—pre-crisis (2001–2007) and mid-crisis (2008–2010)—to see if we could distinguish the effects of higher leverage during different points in the economic and credit cycle. Simply sorting companies based on leverage seemed to produce industry distortions, since some industries tend to use significantly more debt than others. In fact, some of the industries that delivered the highest TSR over the study period, including food retailing, pharmaceuticals and biotechnology, software, and technology hardware, also happen to be those that use less debt.

To avoid industry distortions, we compared companies within each industry that carried above- and below-industry average leverage, using three different measures, and then averaged the results.

The leverage measures were: (1) debt to debt plus the book value of equity, (2) debt to debt plus the market value of equity, and (3) debt to EBITDA. Over the full 10-year period, the companies with above-average leverage within their industry delivered 0.6% lower annualized TSR. We repeated the analysis for 2008 through 2010, when credit was less available, credit spreads were generally higher, and the heavy use of debt was more punished by investors. As expected, we found that highly leveraged companies performed even *worse* during this tighter credit period by delivering annual TSR 1.7% lower than their less-leveraged peers. As also expected, during the credit boom from 2004 through 2006, highly leveraged companies performed better, with 1.2% higher TSR per year.

Over the full 10 years, then, leverage had a negative impact. Thus, our findings may appear to contradict the common wisdom that "leverage is beneficial for shareholders." Does this imply that the theory behind WACC and its impact on valuation is wrong? I do not believe so, but there are reasons to believe that corporate managers behave differently when carrying higher debt levels. For example, those companies with higher debt delivered 3% lower median revenue growth per year than the less-leveraged companies in the same industry. One possible interpretation is that the growth opportunities of the more highly leveraged companies are less profitable than the opportunities faced by their less-leveraged counterparts. Perhaps that's why they have taken on more leverage, or possibly it's the debt that leads to management's making fewer growth investments.

As discussed throughout this book, our capital market studies have demonstrated a strong link between revenue growth and TSR both for the market as a whole and for many specific industries—so at least *some* of the more-leveraged companies in a given industry may well be forgoing investments in profitable sales growth in order to service their heavier debt. These companies and their shareholders clearly would have been better off with less debt.

In other words, the association of higher leverage with lower TSR has nothing to do with the effects of leverage on valuation per se—but likely everything to do with how leverage affects the managers who have to service that debt. For mature businesses with few opportunities for profitable growth, heavy debt, as Jensen told us, is likely to add value by putting the firm on a diet; that was a big part of the success of the first wave of LBOs. But for the vast majority of companies that have at least a decent array of promising growth opportunities, the use of high leverage is quite likely to reduce value by forcing managements to think twice about making even clearly value-adding investments.

In fairness to Jensen, in the middle of the 1980s LBO boom, it seemed really obvious that many, if not most, companies were inefficient and unproductive. In that environment, the discipline of debt may have been more valuable than the drag of reduced growth. But over the last few decades, the pendulum has swung, and now we see many companies with extremely high rates of return that have underperformed on growth—and leverage, as I suggested, seems to have been part of this problem. For example, toward the end of 2018, almost nine out of 10 of the largest 1,000 nonfinancial companies had positive RCE, so with only about 10% of companies delivering negative RCE, there are fewer companies today, as compared to the past, that struggle to beat the cost of capital and would therefore benefit from the discipline of debt.

Should companies increase leverage as a means of driving shareholder value? We believe this only works in a limited number of cases in which profitable reinvestment in the future is not readily available. Sure, such temporarily higher debt levels to facilitate investment in desirable growth opportunities *can* be beneficial, as long as there is a clear plan plus a commitment to paying down that debt. But for most companies, increasing leverage tends to make management more conservative, which in turn tends to reduce the propensity to be strategically opportunistic—something that is often required to deliver valuable revenue growth. Leverage constricts revenue growth, which leads to worse share-price performance, on average. So, notwithstanding the potential benefits of leveraging up the balance sheet for very mature companies, most companies would deliver better share-price performance over time if they acted more prudently with the amount of leverage they take on.

Putting Financial Policy into Practice

To operationalize these principles and research findings into actual financial policies requires insights on a variety of business characteristics. The starting point is always that financial policy should be subordinated to business strategy and should be designed to help get the most out of the available business opportunities.

Of course, less debt should be used in industries with highly variable performance, due to either cyclicality or volatility. Companies using business models that carry more fixed costs and have greater capital requirements than their industry competitors should also use less debt. But this prescription is often ignored when a company replaces a more expensive outsourced service with an in-house capability that, though providing cost and capital savings on average, may also limit the firm's ability to respond to downturns or other changes in conditions.

As a general rule, the most important determinant of a company's capital structure should be the size and nature of its investment opportunities. Of course, it may be difficult to quantify the size and frequency of unexpected valuable investment opportunities, but it's important to recognize them, at least qualitatively. We don't ever want to have to turn down a significant value-creating opportunity because we had too much debt at the time. For companies that come across such unexpected opportunities more frequently, there is a higher value to financial flexibility, and debt levels should be kept lower. By contrast, in many commodity businesses where returns are rarely sustained well above the required return, the opportunities that do materialize will tend to carry lower NPVs, so there is less risk that high debt will lead to missing out. Tech, in particular, is an industry where the ability to deliver high returns is common, where new organic and acquisitive investment prospects come along all the time, and, therefore, where carrying less debt is desirable. More will be said on this in the final section of this chapter.

Strategic Leasing

Some say that operating leases are really just a form of financing and thus are not "strategic." But leases *can* be strategic by virtue of the option value they create; and when they *are* strategic, we want the use of these business structures to be encouraged and, to reinforce this, to be reflected in RCE.

Some CFOs and company treasurers avoid operating leases as a matter of course. They claim that leases dilute EPS and EBITDA and are merely expensive forms of financing that other companies employ to artificially push assets off their balance sheets. Further, they correctly point out that rating agencies and creditors recognize this off-balance-sheet financing by determining the capital obligation associated with minimum lease commitments.

Nevertheless, operating leases can be a more-efficient use of capital and provide greater operating flexibility in many businesses. In an uncertain business world, operating leases enable a company to commit to only a portion of the life of an asset. They pay a "financing premium" to do this; but if a portfolio of leases is managed properly, with staggered expirations, the leases allow companies to dial up and down the capital they employ in order to mitigate risk at the bottom of a cycle. When times are tough, it's much easier to decide not to renew leases than to sell assets just when demand for them has collapsed.

What's more, many successful companies follow a strategy of constantly refreshing their assets with newer versions. Having updated assets can help companies maintain reliability while improving customer experience and perception. Indeed, leases create an automatic prompt for companies to consider upgrades on every renewal. This can be an important consideration when leasing retail space, automobiles, trucks, aircraft, and other assets.

To be sure, employing operating leases more aggressively tends to reduce EBITDA. That's clear in an industry like retail, where the use of operating leases is substantial. In a study whose findings we reported in "Can Leases Be Strategic,"[3] we separated the 84 largest retailers into high- and low-lease groups, based on the size of their latest annual rent payment as a percentage of net property, plant, and equipment. The median EBITDA of the high-lease group was 43% lower than it would be before rent (also known as EBITDAR, which is earnings before interest, taxes, depreciation, amortization, and rent). That's a much larger reduction in EBITDA than the 23% median decline of the low-lease group.

However, this hit to EBITDA was largely offset by how these companies were valued. For the high-lease group, the median ratio of enterprise value (market capitalization plus net debt) to EBITDA was 7.4x over the period, which was about 20% higher than the median of 6.1x for the low-lease group. The lower EBITDA didn't seem to penalize valuation at all.

Several important considerations must be noted when a company develops an effective operating-lease strategy. But first, it can forget about the distinction between "on-balance-sheet" and "off-balance-sheet." Indeed, accounting rules are likely to change soon, and all leases with multiyear commitments will be put on the actual GAAP balance sheet. Admittedly, this accounting change has been expected for years, but it *will* happen at some point. Before and after such a change to generally accepted accounting principles may occur, your focus should be on comparing the capital commitment of a lease to the purchase price of the asset. Signing a multiyear lease with minimum required payments is scarcely different from borrowing money to buy the asset and therefore committing to payments of interest and principal. The operating lease is merely of a shorter duration, so it's like borrowing less money to buy a portion of the asset's useful life and only a portion of its benefits. Of course, in some situations with scarce assets, it can be better to sign longer leases to ensure access to the asset, but the approach makes these costs clear when comparing tradeoffs.

To improve the comparability of companies that lease with those that buy, Standard & Poor's adjusts a company's debt to include the debt-equivalent value of its lease contracts by calculating the present value of its lease commitments. This is a useful general approach for companies to employ. For example, consider a company that leases assets with a 30-year life and an underlying value of $10 million for five years at a rate of 10% of the original underlying asset value per year. Assuming the company has a marginal cost of debt of about 6%, the present value of the five-year lease commitment is $4.2 million at the outset. That is about 42% of the purchase commitment. And this amount declines over the life of the lease as the remaining commitment gets shorter.

This is strategically significant. The company could buy more than *twice* as many assets for the same amount by committing to a shorter period of use than the full life of the asset. For some companies, such moves can help propel a growth strategy.

When confronted with this math in the 1990s, a retail client in London told me, "If that's how you will determine my capital base, I will sign one-year leases with 24 one-year-renewal options" rather than the standard 25-year leases that prevailed at the time in London retail. Of course, if he could convince a lessor to agree to such an arrangement, he would have full use of a store with the right but not the obligation to walk away every year, which would provide strategic flexibility and risk protection in downturns. Imagine never having unused or underperforming capacity! Of course, the lessor will want to charge a higher rent when giving away such flexibility, and that's where the tradeoff comes in. Luckily, RCE treats the present value of lease commitments as an investment, so it's the perfect tool to measure this tradeoff and thereby make an informed decision.

To make the best use of the strategic flexibility and maximize the value created by leases, you need to structure a portfolio of leases to expire gradually over time, rather than all at once. For example, if 20% of the assets under five-year leases come up for renewal each year, evenly spread over the quarters, you have an ongoing opportunity to reduce capital by not replacing expiring leases when unexpected tough times arrive. This tends to salvage more value than selling assets in such tough times, since the resale values often decline then, as well.

Most operating leases last more than one year. But they can often be structured so that the company must commit to only a portion of the asset life, which is why the capital commitment is lower. The implied interest rate embedded in leases often seems high compared to borrowing rates, but this is simply the cost of the flexibility that leases provide.

Yet, as we have learned, too much is no good. Like most things in life, leases can be a problem if taken to an extreme. The annual cash fixed charges are usually higher for leases than for owned assets. Companies thus must be careful to limit the proportion of their assets under lease to ensure that, through good times and bad, they haven't taken on excessive financial risk. Traditional debt and the implied debt equivalents of leases must be considered together in setting the right financial policies. When determining how far to push a lease strategy, be sure to prepare robust scenario analyses to test the downside and see how the leases help or hinder the situation when an unexpected crisis hits.

Are leases right for your company? Consider the types of assets, the uniqueness, and the specialization of those assets and the frequency with which you may want to replace or upgrade them. Also consider industry cyclicality and volatility, because the optionality afforded by leases has greater value when more peaks and valleys are likely to occur in the business. Then think about this in the context of the lease rates, durations, and covenants available, to determine whether leases would be likely to provide significant strategic or financial benefits. Many companies are likely to find that they should be leasing somewhat more than they do now.

Dividend Policy

When do dividends truly matter?[4] They have a positive effect on valuation during a financial downturn and a negative effect when markets are booming—but under normal circumstances, and on average, they have little effect at all on shareholder returns.

Throughout the 2008–2009 financial crisis, there were substantially fewer dividend increases and an abnormally large number of dividend cuts. These generally stingy dividend policies were often in response to a true liquidity crunch. But for many companies, dividend prudence merely reflected general conservatism. As economic fears subsided, managements evaluated whether reinstating or boosting dividends would help their share price.

The dividend decision is difficult in the face of an abundance of divergent views. In his celebrated paper "Do Dividends Really Matter?"[5] the renowned Nobel Laureate Merton Miller argued that "the seeming evidence that dividends do matter…is not to be trusted. It's an optical illusion." He claimed that the apparent effect of dividends on share prices is not caused by the dividends per se, but is merely the market's recognition of what the dividends communicate about investment policy and future earnings trends. Given this, it would seem an open-and-shut case that dividends *don't* matter.

Then why the fuss? Many investors pester managements by demanding new or increasing dividends. The investors cite studies showing that high-dividend-yield stocks are better than low and nondividend stocks at delivering TSR. A flurry of such recent studies has attracted attention in the media and the boardroom. What should management do?

It depends. Our capital market research on the dividend policies of the largest 1,000 nonfinancial companies, excluding those that were not public for the full decade of the 2000s, indicates that there is no one-size-fits-all answer.

Our research shows that dividends *do* have a positive effect on valuation during downturns, when economic confidence is low and investors fear the worst, and thus prefer the cash in hand. But in boom times investors have more confidence that companies will invest their money wisely, so dividend hikes (or initiations) may actually be interpreted as signs that investment opportunities are drying up. We determined this by looking at valuation in terms of enterprise value to gross operating assets and then compared this to the cash-on-cash return on capital. We found a strong correlation between these measures of valuation and return, as documented in the article "Postmodern Corporate Finance." Some companies were valued higher or lower than their returns alone would imply, so we tested whether dividends influenced this premium or discount. From 2004 through 2007, a majority of companies trading at a premium were nondividend payers. This flipped from the first quarter of 2008 through 2009, when a majority of companies trading at a premium *were* dividend payers.

Do some companies' share prices benefit more from dividends? If so, when do dividends really matter? In principle, investors should prefer higher dividends from companies with few desirable investment opportunities, so that the investors can redeploy the capital elsewhere. And companies with an abundance of desirable growth opportunities can probably create more value than the investors can, so logically they should maintain low or no dividends. From the outside, however, we can't assess the quality of investment opportunities, so we characterize companies by the returns and revenue growth they have generated historically.

We evaluated average cash-on-cash returns over the 2000s to separate companies into high-, medium-, and low-return groups. We then divided each of these groups, based on whether a company experienced revenue growth above or below the 8.1% median annualized revenue growth for the full sample. Each company was classified as a nondividend payer, a low payer, or a high payer, depending on whether it was below or above the median dividend as a percentage of after-tax operating cash flow.

Regardless of return, the companies with low revenue growth delivered higher TSR if they paid a dividend. The size of the dividend did not matter much, but paying a dividend was better than not. This effect was most significant for the group that was low on both growth and return, where both low- and high-dividend payers delivered median TSR that was a whopping 13.7% higher than the nondividend payers. For the medium-return group, the high-dividend payers delivered 6.9% more TSR per year than nondividend payers, and for those with high returns this difference was 3.5%. In sum, dividends seem to help the share prices of all low-growth companies, but the benefit is larger for low-return companies than for those with high returns.

This pattern reverses for high-revenue-growth companies. Comparing the high payers to the nondividend payers, the TSR gaps for the high-, medium-, and low-return groups were –0.7%, –3.6%, and –0.5%, respectively. For high-growth companies there seems to be a drag on TSR from paying dividends, though the data is more scattered since company-specific circumstances vary more.

So, what are the implications for managements contemplating dividend policy? First, recognize that changes to dividend policy will be heavily scrutinized by investors, analysts, and the media. But that's no reason to avoid desirable changes. Also, remember that your reinvestment rate and future earnings stream will influence your share price more over time than your dividends, so keep your capital deployment priorities straight. Given the research, here are some guidelines:

- If your company doesn't earn the required return, and you expect growth to be lower than 8% per year, then your company should absolutely pay a dividend.
- Even if your company does earn a high return, if you are not growing rapidly, then your TSR would probably benefit from paying a dividend.
- If you expect to grow rapidly, dividends may constrain your TSR, particularly if they consume cash you could have invested in profitable growth. This is even true, though less so, if your returns are currently below the required return.

Consider your prospects for deploying capital in high-return investments over the next few years. If the amount of expected investment is a large percentage of the cash you generate, you should be less inclined to initiate or increase dividends. But recognize that, if you have had returns that have fallen persistently below the required return, your share price may be penalized if you don't pay a large-enough dividend.

For companies with fewer desirable future investments, dividends should be more attractive. But if you have been aggressively investing in growth and have delivered returns well in excess of the required return, a dividend increase may hurt the share price. That's because investors may conclude that you have run out of desirable investments.

If you are on the fence, then more-modest dividend policies may be warranted, since this will leave more cash available for reinvestment in future growth.

Cash Balances

With the backdrop of record-setting repatriation of international cash balances in the wake of the Tax Cuts and Jobs Act of 2017, shareholders, analysts, and pundits are all up in arms about corporate America's ballooning cash balances, and are demanding share repurchases to make productive use of the cash. Oddly, managements sometimes get more questions from investors about what they plan to do with idle cash balances than about strategy and operating performance. Should managements listen to their shareholders and distribute cash balances? Should they disgorge the financial slack, or is the flexibility it provides more valuable than any drag on performance of holding the cash?

A number of strong arguments can be made in favor of cash distributions. Often, having a surplus of cash can take the pressure off and make executives less forceful in driving cost efficiency and capital productivity. Reducing the financial cushion can heighten the urgency for them to streamline operations and management processes in order to purge waste and eliminate unneeded activities. We have all witnessed this in our personal lives. When times are good, we spend on things that are not necessities; when times are tight, we avoid such purchases. That's fine when we're doing it with our own money and realizing the benefits for ourselves. But when working with other people's money, we should have zero incentive to spend wastefully, whether it's deliberate or inadvertent.

The more financial slack a company has, the more investors worry about how prudent management will be in making investments. When money is tight, the burden of bad investments is quickly and sharply felt. But when cash is abundant, there is less sensitivity to such outcomes. Distributing cash reduces these perceptions of the risk of inefficient reinvestment. And reducing cash imposes the need for management to go to the market to raise capital for investments, which provides a market test of the validity of their investment strategy. Can management convince outside investors of the merit of its investment plan?

The buyback is used more and more to distribute excess cash and yet, as discussed in chapter 8, the beauty of many buybacks is only skindeep. Despite surface appearances, our extensive capital market research at Fortuna Advisors has led us to conclude that a majority of repurchases are less attractive than they appear. Most companies would be better off either investing more in their business or holding the cash to wait for potential investment opportunities. If they do want to distribute cash, ordinary and special dividends tend to be more effective over the business cycle, since there is no price risk.

Integrated Financial Policy Decisions

So, what's a management team to do? They will ask themselves: Should we have more or less debt? More or less cash? How aggressively should we use leases? Should we pay dividends? And should we buy back stock?

The same financial flexibility arguments that apply to capital structure also relate to all elements of financial policy, so there is a consistent theme throughout this chapter. Corporate financial policies for target leverage, cash balances, leases, dividends, and share repurchases should *not* be the inadvertent outcome of a series of haphazard "insights," such as "the leases looked cheap" or "in the one-on-one meeting, investors told us they'd like us to increase our buybacks." Instead, financial policy should be deliberately and holistically designed to maximize value in the context of the chosen corporate business strategy as well as the desirability, size, and timing of investment opportunities.

For a stable company with limited or predictable investment opportunities, financial flexibility is not particularly valuable. So, it would be appropriate to institute more aggressive leverage, cash, and distribution policies. But too often, management puts its company in this category when in fact the company has peers that are making successful large investments in their future. If a company has sizable growth investment opportunities despite uncertain timing, more flexibility may be required. Such situations dictate lower leverage, higher cash balances, and less distribution to shareholders.

Operating leases should be used when their option value is strategically worthwhile. If a company typically buys assets in a highly regular pattern and uses them well past their depreciation life, then it probably should continue to buy them. Using debt to purchase assets is cheaper than leases in such cases. But if a company faces cyclicality and volatility such that the option to not renew leases from time to time would be valuable, then operating leases that commit to only a portion of the asset life would be better. As discussed above, it's critical that the lease expirations be staggered so that in each quarter and each year there will be some leases that can be cancelled (not renewed), thereby pushing the asset risk back on the lessor. Another important consideration is whether assets tend to be replaced before they are fully depreciated. When this is the case, it reinforces the benefits of operating leases as a meaningful part of the capital structure.

One thing is abundantly evident: *Companies need to fully integrate their capital allocation and financial policies with their corporate strategy.* This holistic view of strategy, capital allocation, and financial policy should be clearly communicated to the market, and companies should target investors who value their strategy appropriately. In the absence of a clearly defined corporate and financial strategy, investors will likely be skeptical or even fearful that the company will misuse its cash at the expense of shareholders. In such cases, the stock price is likely to fall, and investors are likely to demand their capital be returned, so that they can redeploy it elsewhere.

Notes

1   Gregory V. Milano and Joseph Theriault, "Is Financial Leverage Good for Share-holders?," CFO.com, April 13, 2012, accessed January 15, 2019, http://ww2.cfo.com/capital-markets/2012/04/is-financial-leverage-good-for-shareholders/.

2   Michael C. Jensen and Richard A. Posner, "Agency Costs of Free Cash Flow, Corporate Finance, and Takeovers," *American Economic Review*, May 1986.

3   Gregory V. Milano, "Can Operating Leases Be Strategic?," CFO.com, March 15, 2012, accessed January 15, 2019, http://ww2.cfo.com/management-accounting/2012/03/can-operating-leases-be-strategic/.

4   Gregory V. Milano, "When Do Dividends Really Matter?," CFO.com, April 1, 2011, accessed January 15, 2019, http://ww2.cfo.com/banking-capital-markets/2011/04/when-do-dividends-really-matter/.

5   Merton H. Miller, "Do Dividends Really Matter?," Selected paper No. 57, Graduate School of Business, University of Chicago.

PART IV

EMBRACING
AN
OWNERSHIP
CULTURE

THIRTEEN

Understanding and Creating an Ownership Culture

BUSINESS OWNERS, LIKE all people, are a diverse lot, and the company cultures they create vary greatly. But some common characteristics set owners apart from the typical manager or employee. They tend to be more motivated to make their businesses prosperous, because so much of their personal success and satisfaction is tied up in the business. Owners often strive to accomplish objectives that seem unrealistic to others, and they don't mind, and may even prefer, being the underdog.

Few public companies have ownership cultures. Yet over the years, it has always seemed to me that ownership cultures perform better. So, it is important for public company executives first to fully understand their company culture (and its gaps) and then to develop a plan to align it with ownership values. And this is not soft and fluffy stuff to keep up appearances; it is objective and factual. Getting the culture right is likely to be as critical to the success of the organization as anything else a CEO does.

Motivated to Succeed

For anyone who's played or watched sports, it's clear that momentum plays an important role in outcomes. When a series of plays goes well, confidence trickles down the roster and fuels a conviction that the team can—and will—win. In the same way, a leader who exudes confidence can motivate those around her or him.

This all may sound like marketing nonsense, but when these sparks ignite, they are palpable—electricity in the air, chills down your back, massive crowds animated with an ecstatic fervor. And when they occur against all odds, they are nothing short of sensational. When the New York Giants defeated the otherwise undefeated New England Patriots in Super Bowl XVII in 2008, it was a true Cinderella story. The Giants were the underdog in every round of the playoffs and somehow performed so improbably well that they were able to knock off heavyweight after heavyweight, eventually winning the championship game by three points. The Giants fed off a surge in momentum late in the game, held the "unstoppable" Patriots to only 14 points, and came back to win it all in the final minutes. Their performance was spectacular, almost surreal at times—and all this after barely making the playoffs!

Few sports analysts or Vegas casinos believed that a Giant victory over the Patriots was even remotely possible. But as was obvious to everyone watching the game, the Giants had other ideas. They may not have been the best team in the NFL that year, but they *were* the best team throughout the postseason, and certainly on the field that day.

Admittedly, I live in the New York area and am a Giants fan, so perhaps this example comes off a bit strong—my apologies to Patriots fans. To be fair to Boston-area readers, let me also recall another spectacular, perhaps even less probable, comeback. In 2004, the Boston Red Sox trailed the New York Yankees three games to none in the American League Championship Series—and then they did something no baseball team had ever done in over a century of major league baseball playoffs: They came back from a three-games-to-zero deficit to win the series by winning four games in a row (and I can still feel the pain). The Red Sox broke the alleged "curse of the bambino," which was said to plague the team since it traded away Babe Ruth soon after its (then) last World Series Championship in 1918.

The same sort of upsets occur across the pond, as well. The Union of European Football Associations (UEFA)—yes, that's soccer in "American"—conducts a Champions League competition each year that pits the best teams from each country's top league against each other. It starts with a few qualification rounds followed by a very rigorous 32-club group stage, and then a 16-club knockout-style tournament to determine a champion. The format is similar to that of the World Cup, but with twice as many fixtures, so each club can play both at home and away against each opponent. Only the final is played at a neutral stadium.

In the 2004–2005 Champions League, one of the teams to qualify for the group stage by successfully navigating the qualification rounds was Liverpool F.C. The club had finished fourth the year before in the English Premier League and was not considered a likely challenger for the Champions League title. In an unexpected run, Liverpool made it to the Champions League final against A.C. Milan but was still considered the underdog to win it all that night in Istanbul. After the kickoff, Liverpool's odds cratered when Milan scored three unanswered goals before halftime. For those who are unfamiliar with typical soccer score lines, most fans would have considered this game to be over already—the odds against coming back to win the final must have been positively enormous.

But, like the Giants in 2008 and the Sox in 2004, the Liverpool players had other ideas. In the second half the Liverpool captain, Steven Gerrard, scored first, then two more goals followed to bring the match to a tie. Liverpool and Milan held the 3–3 tie through the end of the match, including "extra time." So, it all came down to penalty kicks, and Liverpool won 3–2 after its goalie, Jerzy Dudek, saved two penalties. Liverpool had done the unthinkable. Even the Argentine legend Diego Maradona said, "The English club proved that miracles really do exist. I've now made Liverpool my English team."

Still, this wasn't enough for Liverpool F.C. In the 2018–2019 Champions League semifinal, it did it again. The club was down 3–0 on aggregate after the first leg of the semifinal, and scored four unanswered goals to beat the favorite, F.C. Barcelona, and advance to, and win, the final. What are the odds? (66:1.)[1]

How did the New York Giants, Boston Red Sox, and Liverpool F.C. pull off these improbable victories, and what lessons can be learned that apply to corporate management? Many come to mind, but perhaps the most important one is not to rely solely on what seems achievable but instead to stretch for what seems unachievable. Momentum comes from confidence and conviction, and leaders must foster these attributes in their teams, even when facing discouraging odds. While cautious incrementalism has become the norm in many of today's businesses, it's indisputable that the drive to create new products and services, pursue and conquer new and existing markets, and develop new ways of doing business remains the largest source of value creation across all industries and economies.

Indeed, the great business success stories of recent decades, including those of Bill Gates, Warren Buffett, Steve Jobs, and Jeff Bezos, among many others, did not happen by playing it safe and striving only for the achievable. Successful entrepreneurs challenge themselves and their organizations to step beyond what seems possible to redefine what can be done.

These days, though, corporate leaders are often more concerned with avoiding failure than achieving success. In the wake of a series of spectacular management catastrophes—including Enron, World-Com, Bernie Madoff's Ponzi schemes, and the 2008 subprime mortgage disaster and subsequent financial crisis—far greater attention is now being paid to risk management. The U.S. Congress has passed measures to compel companies, in particular financial institutions, to better manage risk. Shareholders have expressed outrage by the size and speed of losses in many cases and have pressed companies to be more careful. The industry of risk management experts and tacticians has grown in size and scope, and senior corporate risk management executives play a more-direct role in the management and governance of public companies. And the more recent escalation of cyber risks has added even more fuel to the risk-management fire. It will be interesting to see if this emphasis on risk management leads to fewer catastrophes.

Though it is extremely important to manage risks, many companies have taken doing so to such an extreme that, for fear of making bad investments, they have passed up on countless *good* ones. As Roberto Goizueta, a former Chairman and CEO of the Coca-Cola Company, said, "The moment avoiding failure becomes your motivation, you're down the path of inactivity. You stumble only if you're moving." He also remarked, "If you take risks, you may fail. But if you do not take risks, you will surely fail. The greatest risk of all is to do nothing."[2] This is perhaps the business-world equivalent of hockey legend Wayne Gretzky's famous line, "You miss 100 percent of the shots you don't take."

Many exceptions can be noted to this wisdom, but it seems that most people really do want to fit in and limit their errors (think "loss aversion"); many do so by avoiding potentially value-adding risks. Taking a risk and failing can result in severe punishment, including humiliation or getting fired, while maintaining the status quo typically leads to consistent, but limited, rewards. This paves the way to less investment, less growth, and overall less value creation.

Since about 2000, when the tech bubble burst, U.S. public companies have collectively invested less in growth. To prove this point, I gathered various key financial data points on a large sample of companies going back to 1996. I started with the current Russell 1000 membership, and then eliminated financial, real estate, and utility companies, because they have different investment patterns and financial metrics. Next, I eliminated any company that did not have full information for all the years studied and was left with a sample of 316 companies. To get a rough measure of growth investment, I calculated the aggregate capital expenditures each year for all 316 companies and subtracted the aggregate depreciation. The general assumption here is that when capital expenditures equal depreciation, a company is sustaining itself; and when capital expenditures are *above* depreciation, the surplus comes from growth investment. For any one company, this approximation can be off for various reasons. But when viewed in aggregate and normalized as a percentage of net income, it provides a fairly good indicator of how much managements are investing in growth.

What did I find? As can be seen in figure 64, the proportion of net income being invested in future growth was quite high in the latter half of the 1990s. But it fell in the first decade of the new millennium, and has fallen further in the current one. The graph on the right (displaying the CAGR, or compound annual growth rate) shows that when growth investment fell, growth in revenue dropped, as well.

Many companies say they don't invest because they feel concerned that the economic growth won't be there to create the demand for the products and services that their investments will seek to deliver. But isn't this merely a chicken-and-egg problem? If companies were investing more, they would employ more people, and consumers would have more money, so they would spend more—and the virtuous cycle of capitalism would prevail! But since we tend to extrapolate without considering cyclical effects, when the economy is down, or growing slowly, we act as if it will be that way forever and miss the opportunity to invest and benefit from the next upswing.

CapEx-Depreciation as
Percentage of Net Income

Revenue Growth CAGR

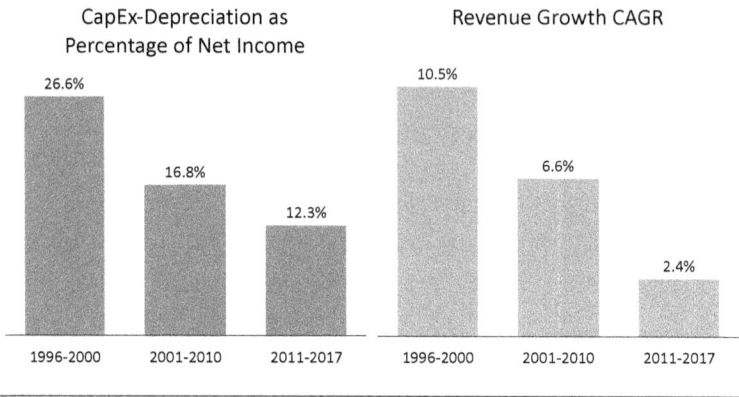

Figure 64—Growth Investment Drives Revenue Growth

On top of the behavioral impact of the heightened risk aversion discussed above, many executives have become infatuated with efficiency and productivity, as reflected in the increased prominence of percentage measures like profit margins and rates of return on capital. Sometimes, they feel so concerned about maximizing these measures that they forgo good investments that may pay off over time but that reduce their percentage measures in the short term. They become so obsessed with the quality of performance (margins and returns) that they forget to balance it with quantity (growth). In figure 65, we see that aggregate margins and returns have been relatively stable, though with a slight upward drift over time.

EBIT Margin

Rate of Return (EBIT/D+E)

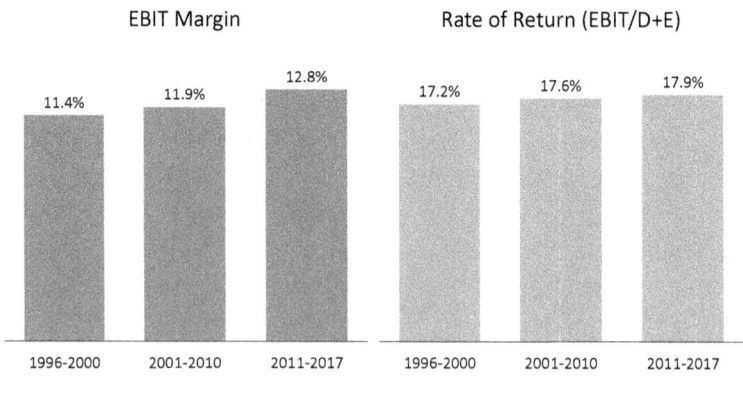

Figure 65—Margins and Returns Drifting Higher

Some may look at these last two figures and say that managements have been prudent to curtail investment and to emphasize margins and returns. Unfortunately, it hasn't worked out that way for investors. The S&P 500[3] delivered average annualized returns of 18% from 1996 through 2000, and since then we have realized a paltry 6% per year through the end of 2017.

Indeed, the idea that investing in growth would automatically drive down returns on capital doesn't always hold. Consider the retail industry. In January 2012, my then-partner Steve Treadwell and I published an article[4] on CFO.com about the capital deployment practices, financial performance, and shareholder returns of more than 100 companies in the retail sector over the prior few years. We evaluated the influence on TSR of sales growth, profitability, return on capital, reinvestment rates, and distribution policies.

We found, as some might expect, that the best returns for shareholders were delivered by the companies that grew their sales the most. These successful companies tended to achieve their higher sales growth by reinvesting a greater percentage of the cash flow they generated back into the business to fund capital expenditures, working capital, new lease obligations, and acquisitions.

Interestingly, these higher-reinvestment, high-growth companies also tended to deliver higher cash-on-cash returns on capital, which seems at odds with the common wisdom that holds that investing in growth tends to come at the expense of delivering high returns on capital. How is it that the very same companies that deliver the highest growth through heavy investment also exhibit the highest rates of return? Admittedly, some retail brands have been so well managed that strong demand is actively driving the sales growth, and so the investment is facilitating the growth more than causing it. Yet even these strong brands would not be able to grow as they do without the investments. The main point, really, is that it's not always a tradeoff between growth and return—sometimes you can achieve both simultaneously.

Perhaps we need to reflect again on the confidence and belief displayed by the victorious Giants, the Red Sox, and the Reds of Liverpool. Their managers, coaches, and players believed they could win against all odds—and they expressed it in both word and action. As corporate leaders, executives must similarly inspire their teams to excel, though this can be difficult when executives are too focused on maximizing percentage measures of margins and returns by cutting costs, slashing investment, and, in many cases, minimizing risk-taking.

Most middle managers and rank-and-file employees become discouraged in an organization that is preoccupied with cost and capital minimization, and discouraged employees don't perform any better than discouraged athletes. When seeking to maximize shareholder value, then, we must encourage as much investment in the business as possible while holding managers accountable for delivering adequate returns on those investments. To this end, embracing an ownership culture can stir managers and employees alike out of complacency and make them more accountable.

The Value of an Ownership Culture

Sam Walton famously said, "There is only one boss: the customer. And he can fire everybody in the company from the chairman on down, simply by spending his money somewhere else."[5] Owners like Walton, who founded Walmart, think differently than others because they take responsibility. Their success isn't based on how well they can negotiate their objectives or whether they can explain away performance variances as "not my fault." If a business opportunity falls through, there is no one to blame other than the person in the mirror. And missed opportunities are quickly backfilled by new opportunities, since no one is going to get the business back on track other than that same person staring back in the mirror.

In an ownership culture,[6] managers up and down the organization ranks own their decisions, results, and consequences. When all managers and employees accept their business responsibilities as if they owned them, the collective organization delivers greater success. In addition to their own sphere of influence, employees should see colleagues as partners whose mutual success or failure depends on how effectively they jointly serve the customer. There may be a managing partner (a.k.a. the CEO) who leads the group, but an ownership culture means that each employee wants to improve the customer experience and the company performance. Responsibility and accountability often become diluted below the executive level—especially as a company grows big, complex, and bureaucratic, and particularly if accountability and rewards are decoupled from individual performance. In an ownership culture, employees take more pride in their work and have greater reason to value opportunities to prove themselves.

An ownership culture doesn't require risking one's life savings like an actual entrepreneur, but it does require that results be prioritized and that they determine rewards. My partners and I have identified the five most-distinguishing owner-like traits, and each is within reach in every company.

1. Spending Like the Money Is Yours: As we learned from the noted economist Milton Friedman, people tend to spend more than necessary when they are using other people's money. Whether it's a dinner at a nicer restaurant, an upgraded airline seat, or some other item or service being expensed, managers and employees often don't treat the company's money as they would their own. Owners rarely feel shy about spending their money, and often they are more than eager to invest in growth, happier employees, and higher-quality products. But most won't waste money on anything that doesn't deliver a tangible benefit.

Many companies lack the results-oriented and accountability-minded approach required to reinforce an ownership culture. As discussed extensively in chapter 6, negotiated performance targets can insulate rewards from performance improvements. Is the business underperforming? Is there a problem with excess spending? It often doesn't matter, since managers in most companies can still be paid well if they're able to negotiate a sandbagged target.

As mentioned in other chapters, one solution can be to measure performance improvements versus the prior year, rather than against a budget. This requires a comprehensive measure of performance that balances revenue growth, cost efficiency, and capital productivity; and this is where Residual Cash Earnings (RCE) once again comes in handy. When RCE improvements determine compensation, managers are encouraged to treat the company's money like their own. If they spend wastefully, RCE will decline and the value destruction will be reflected in their compensation—and they won't be able to negotiate around it this time! If they generate wealth, by both investing in profitable growth and removing inefficiencies, they will get a definitive share of that, too.

2. Adopting Extreme Prioritization: One of the more common complaints of public company executives is that they have too little time to accomplish everything that needs to get done. Indeed, we've all been told, "sorry, but he's been bouncing from meeting to meeting all week." In such situations, prioritization is not enough, for there are simply too many initiatives and projects.

Successful owner-managers often practice extreme prioritization to make absolutely sure that all value-creating projects and practices take off, while not being distracted by mediocre, lower-return ideas and tasks. They recognize that 80% of potential success typically comes from 20% of the activities, as we've discussed, so they give these fruitful opportunities their full attention. With the lesser opportunities screened out or delegated, the executive team's full attention and resources can be applied to their most productive uses.

An intensive and comprehensive prioritization of opportunities should be based on a fact-based strategic resource allocation process, as discussed in chapter 9. Capital, marketing, and R&D should be concentrated where desirable improvement and trends in RCE appear sustainable and expandable. Of course, you should spend where it's important for the well-being of your organization and to meet regulations, but stop wasting resources on activities with mediocre returns.

One way to reinforce prioritization is to create an "agenda" of important issues facing the company. This starts with the CEO, who has created an agenda for the entire company, and cascades down the organization. Two key criteria for such agendas are the "value-at-stake," or how much value hinges on the matter's being resolved successfully, and the level of urgency—when a decision needs to be made. Extreme prioritization requires selecting the five to 10 issues with the highest values-at-stake and urgency, then devising a disciplined, fact-based process to resolve each one.

3. Embracing a Willingness to Fail: Company leaders often appear more concerned about avoiding consequences than ensuring the very best outcomes. This "loss aversion" tends to prioritize incremental improvements over what a company already does, while placing less emphasis on bold things the company *could* do. Efficiency and productivity metrics typically improve things, which benefits the quarter, but less innovation and growth restrict long-term value creation.

The same owner-managers who ruthlessly prioritize resource allocations are often willing to experiment and fail. But when they fail, they take care to fail fast, limit the damage done, and learn from it. The willingness to fund new good ideas helped make Silicon Valley successful but, as discussed earlier, the ability to swiftly defund bad ideas is potentially every bit as important.

A willingness to experiment and accept failure is necessary to create the fresh and differentiated products and services that fuel long-term growth. However, leaders must set expectations up front, so that their managers and employees have a clear sense of what success and failure look like, and how to react when the latter shows up.

4. Doing More and Talking Less: Making decisions can be really uncomfortable. "What if it goes wrong?... What if I am blamed?... What if there is information I should have had when making this decision?... This could be bad for my career, so let's study it more to be sure before we make a decision." We can never know everything about anything, so we have to make judgments even when faced with uncertainty and accept that we can't eliminate all risks.

Obviously, owners don't want to be wrong. But they know that investing $10 million in something worth $12 million creates $2 million of wealth; but spending $3 million studying it before investing consumes more than 100% of the value creation. That's why owners are decisive. They *do* carefully evaluate decisions, but there is no analysis paralysis because they care about results, not covering their butts.

Results-oriented managers spend more time doing things and less time talking about them. They consider the pros and cons of a situation and then act decisively. Before they present an idea to others, they convince themselves that they believe it will work. And if they are presented with an idea, they have more confidence in what is presented when they know the presenter is personally, and absolutely, accountable for the result.

5. Remembering that It's About the Long *and* the Short Term: It's unfortunate that many public company executives act as if next quarter's results are the goal. As first mentioned in chapter 1, John Graham of Duke University and his colleagues showed in 2005 that over three-fourths of businesses would knowingly sacrifice shareholder value to report earnings that rise smoothly year to year.[7] This logic is nauseating, and the behavior seems to have gotten even worse since then. There is a saying in sports that "You can't win them all, unless you win the first one."[8] As inspiring as that may sound, it's still terrible business advice.

At the other end of the spectrum, some executives advocate taking only a long-term strategic viewpoint. Sure, they can be commended for avoiding the typical short-termism, but often this comes at the expense of important near-term considerations. This further exacerbates the common hockey-stick forecast that shows a decline in the short run—but, if you believe the numbers, the future's so bright we'll have to wear shades. With insufficient focus on shorter-term results, the bright future we anticipated gives way to clouds far too often.

The strategic first priority of owner-managers is *always* long-term value. They pursue all investments that drive long-term growth and return higher, and they want to drive current-year performance, too. They wouldn't cut investments in advertising or R&D to meet short-term EPS objectives, but they continue to motivate the sales team to sell, the manufacturing team to stay productive, and everyone else to work as efficiently as possible. Thus, they seek profitable growth in the near term to pay for the long-term investments. It's not about the short term *or* the long term—it has to be about both.

Embracing an Ownership Culture

Public company executives and managers get most of their compensation either as fixed payments (salaries) that don't vary with performance, or from cash and equity-based rewards that are loosely related to share performance. So how can we get the employees in the lower ranks to act like owners? Even in privately owned companies, most executives and managers are not owners. This conundrum becomes especially important as private companies grow and as a greater percentage of their executive teams is composed of non-owners.

This brings us back to our recommended performance measure: RCE. Unlike traditional return on capital, economic profit, and economic value added measures, Residual Cash Earnings spreads the benefits of investments over time, which in turn encourages greater investment in the future while holding managers accountable for returns on investments over time. In other words, it encourages managers to meet short-term demands without cutting into long-term results.

It is also of unmistakable importance that companies apply a consistent framework to make high-level decisions regarding strategy, resource allocation, and investments. RCE provides this comprehensive framework and allows the comparison of seemingly incongruous alternatives in a way that other measures are simply not designed to do. By measuring resource allocation, investment alternatives, and performance through this common denominator, RCE provides a reliable map of potential and actual value creation across a company, and even within business units and down to product lines. All this makes it easy for managers at every level to make the right decisions. And when companies hold managers accountable for improvements in RCE, they ensure that these managers believe their own forecasts, thereby internalizing the ownership culture. If RCE declines, they make less; and if it rises, they make more. Period! It is a true simulation of ownership.

To embrace such a culture requires extensive communication and training about how these principles should translate into behaviors and actions. It is most effective to avoid a green-eyeshade accounting training style and instead use case-based training that simulates real decision-making, so that employees can see how their plans, actions, and results translate into success (or failure) for the company and themselves.

Executive buy-in is critical. If senior managers *talk the talk* but do not *walk the walk*, the culture will fail. Managers and employees must witness the senior executives treating the company's capital as their own, prioritizing initiatives, experimenting with innovative ideas, emphasizing results over variances from forecasts and plans, and balancing the long- and short-term. And senior executives must be seen taking concepts like "competitive advantage" and "strategy," which are often mere platitudes, and make them points of emphasis and action every day. After all, competitive advantage is the most significant driver of RCE improvements.

We must also ensure that we have an organizational structure that lends itself to clear, insightful analysis. Most structures are inherently political, so they're structured around people, or a "political map." This can be important, but more important is envisioning an "economic map" that plots where value is, and has the potential to be, created in the company. "Value Centers" that are relatively independent units should be tracked, each with a fully loaded income statement and a balance sheet. And every value center should be led by an executive who runs the business in ways that accountability and responsibility for RCE are crystal clear. All this makes it much easier and more efficient for the CEO to delegate decision authority.

To reinforce the business management processes and all the training and communication, properly designed compensation can provide owner-like upside opportunity as well as downside accountability. Why make managers choose between what's good for the company and what's good for themselves and their family? Companies that embrace an ownership culture develop better strategies, improve execution, and deliver more profit and cash flow. And this all culminates in higher total shareholder return, greater compensation, and more-secure jobs. Like most things worth doing, embracing an ownership culture requires considerable effort. Yet it provides defensible competitive advantages that are difficult to replicate.

Notes

1 Tom Bloomfield, "66/1 Liverpool Win 4–0 and Reach the Champions League Final," Oddschecker.com, May 7, 2019, accessed June 27, 2019, https://www.oddschecker.com/insight/football/20190507-66-1-liverpool-win-4-0-and-reach-the-champions-league-final.

2 "Roberto Goizueta Quotes," Goodreads, accessed January 15, 2019. https://www.goodreads.com/author/quotes/3948921.Roberto_Goizueta.

3 Returns for the S&P 500 were approximated based on total returns, including dividends, for the Standard & Poor's Depositary Receipts S&P 500 Trust Exchange-Traded Fund, or ETF, which is designed as an investable product that tracks the S&P 500 and trades under the ticker symbol "SPY."

4 Gregory V. Milano and Steven C. Treadwell, "Growing Retailers Spark High Returns," CFO.com, January 6, 2012, accessed January 15, 2019, http://ww2.cfo.com/budgeting/2012/01/growing-retailers-spark-high-returns/.

5 Sam Walton, *Made in America: My Story* (New York: Bantam Books, 1993).

6 Adapted from "Embracing an Ownership Culture," FEI, April 12, 2018, accessed January 15, 2019, https://www.financialexecutives.org/FEI-Daily/April-2018/Embracing-an-Ownership-Culture.aspx.

7 John R. Graham, Campbell R. Harvey, and Shiva Rajgopal, "The Economic Implications of Corporate Financial Reporting," Working paper, Duke University, January 11, 2005, https://faculty.fuqua.duke.edu/~charvey/Research/Working_Papers/W73_The_economic_implications.pdf.

8 While this quotation has been nebulously attributed to many, the original speaker remains unclear. In my mind, I imagine the great Joe Namath speaking it.

FOURTEEN

Designing Owner-like Compensation Plans

THERE ARE FAR better ways to motivate executives to think and act like owners than the typical corporate incentive program. But before getting to the details, the following will set the stage by identifying a few common obstacles. The first is that compensation committees, and many compensation experts as well, seem to care more about following what others do and less about whether an incentives package motivates the right behavior.

When we were young, many of us were asked by our parents whether we would follow our friends if they jumped off a bridge. Typically, this was in response to our saying, "Well, Jimmy did it!" We all responded "no," of course, but we were never really tested. My wife and I were blessed with four wonderful children who are all adults now. But as they grew up, I feared the possibility of peer pressure, and the harm it could inflict on them. Though admittedly to a lesser degree, I have felt similar anxiety talking to client executives and compensation-committee members over the years. Frequently, they justify features of their compensation design by saying, "this particular approach is common in our industry," even while conceding that it really doesn't make particular sense for their business. I always want to ask if they would jump off a bridge if their industry counterparts had done so. The few times I couldn't help myself, and did ask, they simply laughed—and we moved on. (Probably better that way....)

To be clear, it's not only the corporate folk. Over the years, I have attended scores of meetings held at dozens of companies during which compensation experts presented an extremely thorough description of each compensation element used across the industry, along with their recommendations for how to fit in with the pack. But rarely did they mention how their recommendations would motivate the desired behaviors—or even what those behaviors *are*. Sadly, executive compensation processes seem to have quite a bit in common with high schoolers: They are highly susceptible to peer pressure and are designed to promote conformity with the industry…"because Jimmy is doing it." What a distraction this whole process has become!

As discussed throughout this book, managers and, particularly, board members often care more about how they are perceived than about results. It sounds dreadful, but in the case of a typical board member, this is actually quite rational, since they are disproportionally exposed to bad outcomes in terms of reputational risk, and they usually don't partake significantly (monetarily) in the fruits of good outcomes. If a company blazes a new trail with a compensation package full of seemingly logical, but untested, features, and if the outcome proves to be an excessively large payday for executives relative to performance, the head of the compensation committee may be publicly criticized. Such criticism can make it difficult for directors to renew their positions or land new ones. And the looks they get at conferences and cocktail parties can be borderline ruthless, too. After all, what's the upside if the groundbreaking compensation plan does succeed in motivating exceptional performance? It varies by director and company, but usually a relatively small percentage of their total personal wealth is invested in the stock of the company. So, they typically play it safe.

The beaten path, with its lack of PR risk, can look attractive to executives, as well. As with directors, they are less likely to attract negative attention if they're just following industry standards. In addition to this pressure to conform, for any compensation plan to be implemented, it must be endorsed and championed by the CEO, the CFO, and the head of human resources. Ultimately, the board's compensation committee must approve the plan, though the process should be led by management if it's to motivate owner-like behaviors and reinforce an ownership culture. Executives must understand the current adverse incentives, embrace a path to reinforce better behavior, and adopt the principles discussed below.

To illustrate the range of obstacles to motivating the right behavior, let's consider two identical companies. Company A is led by a founder who, despite her company's having gone public eight years ago, still owns 25% of the outstanding shares, which makes up over 90% of her wealth. She participates in all the executive compensation plans that her executive team participates in, but her salary and her long- and short-term incentive opportunities are all roughly 10% below median for comparable CEOs. She simply hasn't made it a priority to push for salary increases, because she would prefer that the money be spent on her team.

The CEO of Company B has been in his position for eight years and receives an annual salary that is at the 80th percentile relative to the rest of the industry; due to the wide dispersion of CEO salaries in his industry, it is 25% higher than the median. His target annual bonus is 125% of salary, as compared to a norm of 100%, and in addition he receives grants of restricted stock and stock options every year that are each valued equal to his salary (to keep it simple, we won't use performance share units that have performance tests in this example, though these are discussed below). One-third of the restricted stock vests on the first, second, and third anniversaries of the date of grant; he normally sells all the shares that aren't needed to comply with the company's executive stock-ownership guidelines. The options, which vest after one year, have a 10-year life. He has been told it doesn't usually make economic sense to exercise stock options early in their life; but to diversify his personal wealth, he has usually held options between one and two years before cashing them out. Of course, this varies as he tries to sell more when the stock seems high, which is tough, given the blackout periods when executives cannot transact in the company's stock.

On the surface, it seems that both CEOs should be motivated to do what is best for the long-term good of their shareholders—but in reality their motivations are quite different. What will drive the change in their personal wealth over the next five years? Clearly, our Company A CEO will benefit financially only if there is strong five-year TSR from dividends and share-price appreciation. To accomplish this requires improvements in her company's results while it makes substantial, effective investments in the future to maintain or drive the future growth rate and, therefore, the valuation multiple.

For Company B's CEO, however, the single-most-important determinant of his personal wealth over the next five years is whether he is still CEO in five years. So, he will be extremely careful to avoid any risk exposures that may cost him his job, which is fine if it means prudent risk aversion for the company; but unfortunately that attitude will often lead to an overly conservative strategy and business culture, along with less investment and less growth. That's OK by him, though, since his annual bonuses can still remain high as long as the slower growth is budgeted. The second-most-important influence on his wealth is his ability to consistently sandbag the compensation committee with endless stories of how the sky is falling in order to explain each year why growth and profitability are going to be extra tough that year. He laments, "I know I said the same thing last year, and we did well, but this year is really going to be tough because of x, y, and z." It doesn't matter in most companies whether performance improves, just that it beats the budget. So, a low budget is every bit as valuable for management as a good performance—and it's often easier. Thus, this CEO sets aside any thought of setting stretch-goals to fire up the troops and get them thinking outside the box, lest his actions give the compensation committee the crazy idea that they should raise the performance targets.

The third-most-important influence on Company B's CEO compensation is to maintain and increase his already-above-market salary. Of course, the high salary means extra money in his pocket, but it's even more important that it be kept high since the target bonus is 125% of salary, and since the restricted stock and stock options are each granted at 100% of salary. So, each dollar of salary translates to $4.25 of total target compensation. For many CEOs, the total compensation multiplier is even higher. One of the important factors in benchmarking CEO salaries is company size, whether viewed in terms of revenue, assets, market capitalization, number of employees, or other metrics. This causes an incentive to grow that may be tough to accomplish when a conservative management style has caused underinvestment. This roundabout inducement to enlarge the business can motivate a megamerger even when the economics are marginal. Earlier in this book, we noted that acquisitions tend to be associated, on average, with better long-term TSR, but only when adequate cash flow is generated over time. Acquisitions "to grow for growth's sake," or really for CEO compensation's sake, rarely end well—except, of course, for the CEOs.

It's unlikely that Company A's CEO would be excessively risk-averse. She should be expected to manage risks, but not be afraid to pursue worthwhile investments and projects. She probably wouldn't obsess over her salary, though she would want it to be fair, and we shouldn't expect her to launch any megamergers that just make the company bigger. The typical CEO package, alas, does a poor job of encouraging Company B's CEO to act like A's.

Most complaints about executive compensation by journalists and investors focus on how much a CEO makes, not how she or he makes it. This tendency was articulated well in 1990 by Professors Michael Jensen and Kevin Murphy in their *Harvard Business Review* article titled "CEO Incentives: It's Not How Much You Pay, but How."[1] There they wrote:

> There are serious problems with CEO compensation, but excessive pay is not the biggest issue. The relentless focus on how much CEOs are paid diverts public attention from the real problem—how CEOs are paid. In most publicly held companies, the compensation of top executives is virtually independent of performance. On average, corporate America pays its most important leaders like bureaucrats. Is it any wonder then that so many CEOs act like bureaucrats rather than the value-maximizing entrepreneurs companies need to enhance their standing in world markets?

Thank you, Professors Jensen and Murphy—almost 30 years later, these thoughts ring every bit as true as the day they were written.

In certain situations, executives are not paid enough for outstanding performance; in many companies this is as big a problem as overpaying underperformers is in other companies. Consider, for example, Transocean, the leading offshore driller, which delivered 480% TSR over the five years from the end of 2002 through the end of 2007. In three of those five years its annual incentive plan for senior executives paid *nothing*, and in the other two years it paid an average of target annual incentives. But the company's TSR was 5.9 times that of the S&P 500, so it is clear that management was underpaid. Sure, they made money on their long-term incentives, but why have an annual plan if it doesn't reward outstanding value creation? Beyond the risk of managers' making suboptimal decisions, companies in these situations are likely to have a hard time recruiting and then retaining executive talent.

The executive compensation industry is huge and replete with many thousands of experts, pundits, and advisors. Hundreds of journals, conferences, academic studies, and all sorts of governance experts are at the beck and call of interested compensation committees and managements. Somehow, though, despite all this effort, and undoubtedly the best of intentions, executive compensation is a mess—full of terrible compensation strategies, structures, and execution. One telling example of good intentions gone awry is the widespread use of relative TSR by U.S. companies.

The Relative TSR Conundrum

In the 1990s, few people had ever heard of "relative TSR,"[2] but it was up-and-coming. Over 50% of S&P 500 companies now use some form of relative total shareholder return to determine executive compensation, and many believe it's a highly effective measure. To some, relative TSR rewards success while limiting the risk that large payouts might accumulate and attract media attention simply because of an upward-drifting stock market or industry. To the rest of us, relative TSR just weakens the alignment between shareholders and executives while amplifying compensation volatility and uncertainty.

To determine relative TSR, companies typically calculate the percentile ranking of a company's TSR over a period against the TSR of a list of public companies; these can include the constituents of a stock index, the members of an industry, or a customized set of comparable publicly traded companies. The performance cycle, or period for measurement, is often three years; to dampen market volatility, share prices are often averaged over 30 to 90 days at the start and end of the cycle. The stock with the top TSR in the comparison group is labeled as being in the 100th percentile; the stock at the bottom is labeled zero; and the rest are distributed in between, using the standard percentile method.

The conceptual idea behind relative TSR is to recognize skill, without being distracted by luck and randomness, so as to deliver compensation that's "fair." The intent is to deliver more shares to an executive team that leads a tough industry and fewer to an executive group that trails in a high-performing industry. Energy and utility companies first adopted relative TSR because they and their peers face many industry-wide market influences, such as exposure to cyclical and volatile energy prices. Nowadays, relative TSR is used across all industries.

Management is typically granted a number of performance share units (PSUs), which are conditional company shares. An alternative is to grant performance share options (PSOs). The number of shares or options that vest at the end of the cycle is determined by using the relative TSR performance test. For example, it could be that if a company's relative TSR is 75th percentile or higher, the executives are granted twice as many shares as indicated by the number of PSUs. From the 50th percentile up to the 75th percentile, they may receive between 100% and 200%. Between the 25th and 50th percentile, they could get between 50% and 100% of the shares; and if they perform at less than the 25th percentile, they forfeit their PSUs altogether. Many alternative vesting profiles are in use, but this is the approach used in the testing that is discussed below.

When a company delivers a top relative-TSR result, it gives its managers a double benefit, since the relative-TSR ranking can deliver up to twice the shares. And, of course, the share price has typically risen, so each share is worth more. But if the only reason the stock did well was that their market or industry itself did well, the shares may each be worth more; however, depending on how the company's relative TSR ranks, it may forfeit all or some of the potential maximum number of PSUs. In principle, this emphasis on both absolute and relative performance seems ideal; but as we will see below, it doesn't work as well in practice.

Our first capital market research project on relative TSR used 2016 data for an article that we published on CFO.com; then we updated and improved the analysis through 2017 for an article in *Workspan*. In the latter project, we conducted two studies on the relative TSR of the companies in the Russell 1000 that were public for the full period of each study; in every case, the starting and ending share prices were averaged over 60 days to reflect the 30- to 90-day conventions that companies typically use. The first study also showed weak pay-for-performance linkage.

We studied the 712 Russell 1000 companies that were public throughout the entire period from the end of 2005 through the end of 2017. Ten cycles were studied, with the first being from the end of 2005 to the end of 2008, and so on through the end of 2017. Each company's TSR was compared with that of the whole group, and each was assigned a percentile rank in each cycle. We ran the results for each company for each cycle through the typical PSU-vesting logic, described above, and then we averaged the vesting for each company over the 10 cycles. When we compared this average of those 10 cycles to what the vesting percentage *would* have been if based on cumulative relative-TSR performance over the full period, we found a large gap between the average rewards to management and the cumulative returns for shareholders.

Consider the semiconductor company NVIDIA. Over the full 12-year cycle, NVIDIA's cumulative TSR was 1,712%. This was 98th percentile, an enormously high TSR that should have generated an equally fantastic reward. Indeed, if it were cumulative relative TSR over the long term that had mattered, this level of performance would have generated the maximum 200% vesting. However, due to the pattern of the cycle-by-cycle relative TSR, NVIDIA's average relative-TSR ranking was only 44th percentile. And if it had used exactly the above-described version of the relative TSR test, its executives would have averaged only 79% vesting. This appears rather far out of alignment with the shareholders' return, with management seeming to be vastly underpaid. Across the whole sample, management teams would have either over-vested or under-vested, on average, by 45% of their total original number of PSUs. This is such a large average deviation from the intended outcome that it completely dismisses any notion that relative TSR is useful for aligning management with owners over time.

With pay schemes based on relative TSR, then, many managers end up feeling underpaid relative to shareholders. In other cases, many shareholders wish they'd earned a higher TSR to reflect the high level of executive pay. When managers feel underpaid it can be demotivating for management; and when management appears overpaid, it can face a public relations crisis, which in turn fosters attention from activist investors.

Also, within each relative-TSR cycle the awards earned can vary considerably, depending on which day the cycle ends. To demonstrate this, we examined the relative-TSR percentile ranking for each company during 52 three-year cycles ending as of each week in 2017. For example, at the start of 2017, Celgene would have vested in 148% of its PSUs. This vesting dropped to 122% for the cycle ending at the conclusion of one month. Then over the following weeks, the vesting percentage would have increased until it reached the cap of 200% by mid-April, where it stayed for two months. But as the middle of the year approached, a substantial deterioration occurred in relative TSR; for December its relative TSR was bottom-quartile, so no PSU vesting would have been triggered. With only a few months of movement in the vesting date, the value of this allegedly long-term incentive would have reached either the cap or the floor. Again, either the managers or the owners are likely to feel shortchanged.

Although, in principle, relative TSR appears attractive, in reality it does not align managers and owners over long periods and, within a given cycle, the executives will vest in vastly different numbers of shares, depending on the day the three-year cycle ends. Many executives already discount the value of stock awards, and using relative TSR only exacerbates this, which is not at all helpful for attracting or retaining talent.

After our research, we began to advise clients to reduce their reliance on relative TSR and, in pursuit of that goal, we implement performance tests based on fundamental growth, margin, and return metrics. The main point of this discussion of relative TSR, though, is to illustrate how easy it is to design compensation frameworks that seem to make logical sense but that in reality do a poor job of instilling an appropriate ownership mentality.

The Main Compensation Goals and Tradeoffs

Our main compensation goal is to simulate ownership that encourages managers to think and act like long-term, committed owners. Admittedly, it's hard to design these types of incentives.

To illustrate some of the difficulties, consider an owner of a mom-and-pop hardware store. It has been quite profitable for years, but then a Lowe's big-box store opens across the street. Reality sets in fast. Can the owner beat Lowe's? Probably not…they have a larger store, more variety, and lower consumer prices because they buy at scale. If the owner can beat them, perhaps with great service, and can continue to thrive—great. But if they realize they can't, they close their shop fast to preserve capital—much more quickly than a corporate-owned branch that could spend months or years justifying why performance is down, presenting corrective measures, and lingering as a weak competitor that bleeds cash every darn day. It's OK with the corporate manager that profits are down, as long as it's explainable. Of course, he has the hidden motivation of protecting his own job, and perhaps those of his subordinates. After all, he may feel a greater allegiance to them than to a group of anonymous shareholders. The owner of the small store, though, feels frustrated by the turn of events but doesn't need to justify himself to anybody else. It's hard, but not impossible, to design incentives that emulate this owner-like thinking in these types of circumstances.

When designing a compensation plan, three overriding decisions must be made: Which measures will be used? How will targets be set? And how leveraged or sensitive will the incentive payments be if performance is above- or below-target? Naturally, many other important considerations will crop up that need to be taken into account, yet these three are the ones we will now focus on.

I am, of course, partial to the Fortuna Advisors performance measure, RCE, but any measure or combination of measures can be used that accomplishes the following:

- Balances the desire to drive cost efficiency and capital productivity, or, in other words, to achieve high returns on capital, while investing in future growth
- Emphasizes long-term value creation while at the same time motivating outstanding current performance
- Encourages P&L investments, such as R&D and marketing (if important to the business), on a consistent basis relative to any capital expenditures and acquisitions that appear on the balance sheet
- Relates well to company TSR, on average, over time (for private companies, it should relate well to TSR for public peers)

When these criteria are met by a single measure, such as RCE, that solution is vastly preferred to asking management to balance two measures, which would create a potentially confusing optimization challenge. One multi-measure approach that works is to set up a grid with growth on one axis and return or margin on the other axis. My colleagues and I have designed such an approach for PSU tests, to replace relative TSR, but care must be taken in defining the measures and calibrating the performance requirements to ensure that higher payouts generally occur when higher TSR is expected based on past experience. When management, and especially CFOs, determine such grids based on gut feel alone, they often overemphasize margins and returns while underemphasizing growth and investment.

The table in figure 66 comes from the Varian Medical Systems proxy issued in 2018.[3] It illustrates the vesting of performance share units, depending on revenue growth and margin improvement. As it clearly states in the proxy, "the targets for Three Year Revenue Compound Annual Growth Rate and Three-Year Change in EBIT as a Percentage of Revenue in the payout matrix were set based on the median results of our Business Model Peers." By calibrating the table against what delivered strong TSR for the company and its business model peers in the past, the company has confidence that if management achieves a high PSU vesting, it will have delivered the type of performance that usually leads to strong TSR. The linkage to value creation is undoubtedly clearer to management than it would be with relative TSR, and at the same time the company would avoid stock market volatility problems.

		Three-Year Sales Growth CAGR				
		≥0.0%	3.5%	7.0%	10.5%	14.0+%
Three-Year ΔEBIT Margin	4.0%	100%	133%	167%	200%	200%
	2.0%	67%	100%	133%	167%	200%
	0.0%	33%	67%	100%	133%	167%
	-2.0%	0%	33%	67%	100%	133%
	≥-4.0%	0%	0%	33%	67%	100%

Figure 66—Performance Test for Varian Medical Systems Performance Share Units

Note that the table is not based on budgeted EBIT margin or some absolute level, but rather on improvement over the three years. This feature dramatically improves the relationship to TSR. A similar table can be used to calibrate annual bonuses, as well.

As discussed extensively in chapter 6 and throughout the book, targets should always be defined as an improvement over the prior year, rather than based on budgets or plans. Due to the way RCE is defined, for about half the companies out there, investors have priced the company's stock at or below the level that reflects future flat RCE. For these companies, and even for those where the market has priced in modest RCE improvement, it is sufficient to simply set the target RCE at the actual RCE achieved the prior year. Compensation committee members often seem surprised that we recommend a target improvement of zero—but that's because they haven't yet fully internalized what RCE actually *is*.

National Oilwell Varco, often referred to as NOV, is a large oilfield services and equipment company. The customized version of RCE that it implemented is known as NOV Value Added, or NVA. As it states in the company's proxy statement issued in 2018, "Achieving NVA results flat to the year prior's actual performance requires management to earn the cost of capital on new investments and to sustain the performance of existing activities."[4] Some companies are so successful and their share prices so high that investors already have "baked in" the present value of significant future RCE improvements. If, however, a company's stock has been up and down, and if this premium valuation is likely to be temporary, it is generally best to revert to measuring performance against the prior year's RCE. If this premium valuation has been persistent for three to five years, it would not be fair to shareholders to provide management with full target incentive payouts merely for reaching the prior year's actual RCE. Instead, the plan should have a preset Expected Improvement in RCE that is either a fixed number or a fixed percentage of Gross Operating Assets at the start of the year.

To ensure that managers know the deal as thoroughly as owners do, it's best to establish the approach to target-setting and then set it in stone for multiple years. Therefore, for companies requiring an Expected Improvement in RCE, it is best to evaluate the amount of RCE baked in the share price on an annual or quarterly basis over the prior three to five years, and then commit to use the average as the target for the next three to five years.

After we define the measure and establish the framework for target setting, we then need to determine how leveraged or sensitive the plan will be when performance goes above or below the targeted performance. A long time ago in a faraway land—well, actually in New York City—my good friend Steve O'Byrne taught me that there are three primary objectives in designing and calibrating incentives and, unfortunately, you can't optimize them all simultaneously. But before going down that path, it's important to know that Steve is one of the very few compensation experts, out of the scores I have met, who truly understands the importance of simulating ownership in incentives.

Among Steve's many innovations is what he calls wealth leverage,[5] which in simple terms reveals how linked the executive's personal wealth is to changes in the wealth, or market value, of the company. If, when the share price rises 1%, the executive's wealth also rises 1%, wealth leverage is considered 100%. This would pretty much be the case for the CEO of Company *A* above, since her company ownership constitutes nearly all her personal wealth. But in the case of Company *B*, a considerable portion of its CEO's income is driven by salary, payouts set as a multiple of salary, plus annual incentives that reward sandbagging as much as performance. And that CEO can sell any shares he wishes to, so as to diversify his investments. His wealth leverage would be decidedly less than 100%, so he has far less motivation to drive the company value higher. Steve O'Byrne has developed an uncanny ability to use information published in financial statements and in corporate proxies to rank executives based on their wealth leverage to show who is willing to truly expose their pay to performance—and who, by contrast, is just trying to hedge and secure more compensation regardless of performance. He has also demonstrated that companies with higher wealth leverage tend to deliver higher TSR, which is consistent with the notion that incentives are truly an investment that can generate a return if designed and calibrated correctly.

Steve has used his wealth leverage approach to determine what an executive should have been paid, given his or her performance; by comparing these figures to actual total compensation, he identifies what he calls "excess pay."[6] In other words, Steve's approach doesn't only examine whether pay was "high" or "low"; he goes further, to identify what *should* have been paid as the benchmark, given the company's performance and also the compensation package's wealth leverage. If a management team has low-wealth leverage, which protects their pay when performance declines, and yet their pay skyrockets when performance turns up, Steve would fairly describe that as "excess pay." The guy is a true innovator whose methodology is much better than simply branding anyone making a lot of money as a "fat cat" and then walking away.

For me, though, the best lesson from Steve was the first he taught me about 25 years ago, which follows. The three main goals of executive compensation are: (1) to attract and retain executive talent, (2) to motivate executives to create more value, and (3) to do so at a reasonable total cost. You simply cannot optimize these three goals simultaneously; tradeoffs are needed.

To illustrate the tradeoffs, consider figure 67. Let's imagine that a company initially sets its pay-for-performance curve for its annual incentive plan at line *A*.

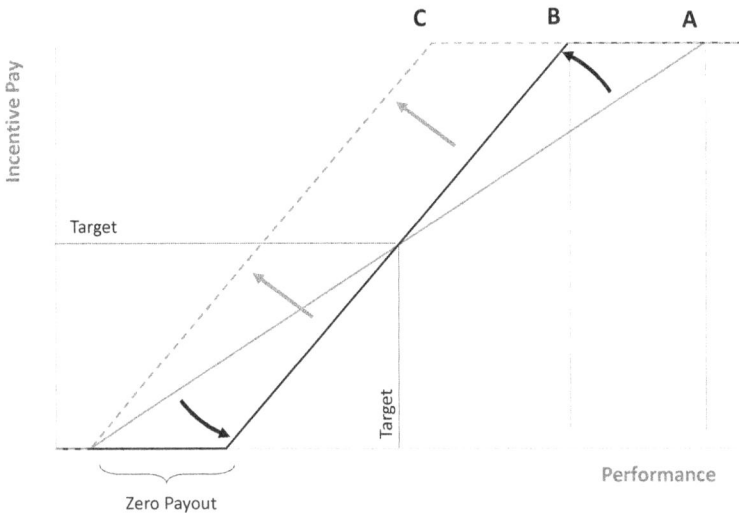

Figure 67—Tradeoffs between Motivation, Retention, and Cost

If target performance is achieved, executives receive a target annual incentive payment. If they perform higher than target performance, then they receive a higher annual incentive payment until performance increases enough to reach the cap. If performance is below target, so is pay until it reaches zero. Some executives ask to remove the cap, but the quid pro quo is to remove the floor, and as a general rule they don't want to write checks to the company if performance declines too much.

To help client executives understand these implications, I believe it's always important to prepare simulations of payouts based both on management's projections and on historical performance trends for their company *and* their peers. Sometimes this review leads management to believe there is not enough of a payout when performance is strong, so they say motivation will be weak and therefore they must seek to increase the incentive leverage. That is, they want each increment of performance improvement to lead to a greater pay increase.

To add leverage, we can rotate the pay-for-performance curve around the point where target performance provides target pay until we land on line *B*, which is steeper. This new incentive will be more motivating since the incremental payouts rise and fall faster; and management will be hungrier to improve performance since they get a bigger share themselves. Other levels of performance would have had a payout on line *A,* but would deliver zero payout on line *B.* This creates a higher probability of zero payout, which can make it harder to attract and retain executive talent.

This too we can fix by sliding line *B* to the left until it aligns with line *C*, which has the same slope as *B* (that is, it is equally steep) but also has the same potential for zero payout as *A*. This new plan is very good at motivating, attracting, and retaining executives, yet it does so at a much higher average cost. The three main goals of motivation, attraction/retention, and cost cannot be simultaneously optimized—again, tradeoffs are required to design an optimal plan for any given company.

The financial performance of certain companies, in some industries, is more volatile or cyclical. So, as a general rule such companies should flatten their pay-for-performance curves so that their larger swings in performance are dampened, resulting in similar pay volatility. In figure 67, this would be line *A*.

Another important factor that affects the bonus sensitivity tradeoff is company culture. A corporation's culture consists of a great many important elements, but the aspect that's important here is how aggressive or conservative that culture is. When executives are encouraged to reach for the stars, take more risks, and drive success, without feeling afraid of manageable failures, a somewhat steeper incentive curve is in order. In such a culture, it's fine that pay jumps up or down and is more differentiated across various business units, since this reinforces the culture. But in more conservatively managed companies, a flatter curve may be better. Again, the best way to test this is through simulations of forecasted and historical performance using the track record of the company and its peers.

Compensation Package Design

Before we design a compensation package, we should establish our compensation goals and some key criteria. How aggressive do we want to be in motivating success? In other words, how much leverage do we want? What is the time horizon for decision-making? This will dictate the nature of, and balance across, a number of elements of the compensation package, some of which would necessarily reinforce longer- or shorter-term thinking. As we roll incentives down to business-unit management, how much do we want to emphasize local accountability and success versus motivating teamwork and sharing best practices? These and other considerations must be discussed before designing a compensation plan so that there is a frame of reference.

As there is no truly *typical* situation for setting compensation, there is no one-size-fits-all solution. The main elements I will discuss are the split of salary, target bonus, and long-term incentive, followed by strategies and alternatives for each of the three main elements of a compensation package.

When it comes to salary, that's one of those peculiar situations in life when less is more. If we are trying to motivate owner-like behavior, why would we want the big, dead anchor of a high fixed salary in the mix? The reason many executives are given high salaries is not that they need some minimum income, at least not CEOs. It's that everything else in compensation is granted as a percentage or multiple of salary. So, let's stop that right away and separate the two.

For now, let's consider cash compensation only. Since salary requires solely that the executive keep the job, it is of lower risk than other variable elements of compensation. Annual incentives, for example, vary year to year and therefore carry more risk. Sure, they may be higher, but they could be lower, too. In finance, we discount cash flows for risk, and we can do the same with compensation. If a dollar of salary is worth one dollar, then a dollar of target annual incentive plan payment, which can end up being worth more or less, must be worth *less* than one dollar. This follows the basic principle that stable cash flows are worth more than variable cash flows, so for variable cash flows to have the same value, they must be targeted at a higher level.

One of the great things consulting firms do well regarding executive compensation is gather, sort, and apply data. Let's say that in a given industry the median CEO salary is $500,000 and the median target bonus is 100% of this, or another $500,000. Let's further assume that the bonus can rise to 200% or drop to zero, based on performance. So, in a great year the bonus will be two times $500,000, or $1,000,000, and total cash compensation will be $1,500,000. Sounds great, but of course the pendulum can swing both ways and the bonus can be zero.

We all like to think people are perfectly rational, but they're not (of course). In 1979, the psychologists Daniel Kahneman and Amos Tversky created their famous "prospect theory" that asserts that decision-making is typically based on the potential value of losses and gains rather than the final expected outcome, and finds that people evaluate these results using heuristics (a fancy word for the decision-making rules). When people are offered a choice formulated in one way, they may be risk-averse, but when offered the same choice formulated differently, they may display risk-seeking behavior. For example, as Kahneman says, people may drive across town to save $5 on a $15 calculator but not to save $5 on a $125 coat.

One very important result of the work of Kahneman and Tversky is demonstrating that people's attitudes toward risks concerning gains may be quite different from their attitudes toward risks when losses are involved. For example, when given a choice between receiving $1,000 with certainty versus having a 50% chance of $2,500, many may well choose the certain $1,000 in preference to the uncertain chance of getting $2,500, even though the mathematical expectation of the uncertain option is $1,250. This is a perfectly reasonable attitude that is described as risk aversion. But Kahneman and Tversky found that the same people, when confronted with a certain loss of $1,000 versus a 50% chance of no loss or a $2,500 loss, often do choose the risky alternative. This is called risk-seeking behavior. This behavior is not necessarily irrational, though it *is* important for compensation designers to recognize the asymmetry of human preferences.

So, if we evaluate the value of the target bonus, we might say $1 of target bonus is worth only $0.80 of salary, though of course this would vary based on the characteristics of each incentive plan. The $0.80 is where managers would be indifferent. In other words, the variable (risky) target bonus of $500,000 is really viewed by the executive as being worth the same as about $400,000 of stable (low-risk) salary. If we set each component of total expected cash compensation at the benchmarked industry medians for salary and target bonus, this point is somewhat academic. It is what it is....

But if we want to consider changing the mix, it's a critical point. If we take away some salary and offer a higher target bonus, we need to replace each $1 of salary reduction with $1.25 of target bonus, if the relationship in the prior paragraph holds (remember that in different situations this $1.25 will be higher or lower). If we don't follow this and treat $1 of target bonus as the same as $1 of salary, given a shift to less salary and more bonus to improve the alignment of executives with owners, the executives may view the change in package as a pay cut. Oh, sure, in a great year the new package will pay more, but there is an equal and opposite downside exposure, and managers would rightfully want something to make up for the extra risk.

Keeping the 1.25:1 ratio, the three packages would be valued similarly by the executive, as detailed in figure 68.

Of course, executives would like to experience both the conservative downside *and* the aggressive upside, but to provide the appropriate risk-reward relationship we should always strive for symmetry whether the plan is conservative, market median, or aggressive. The question of which one is best comes down to the culture and strategic objectives of the organization.

If a company sticks to its culture, what its management finds is that it has many "good employees" who may not actually fit with the culture. For example, a company may decide to be conservative in business strategy, organizational culture, and compensation strategy. To do this, it will be extra careful about risk-taking, which means management will turn down some investments that others may accept, because the value creation is not adequate for them to feel comfortable taking on the risk.

	Conservative	Market Median	Aggressive
Salary	$600,000	$500,000	$400,000
Target Bonus	$375,000	$500,000	$625,000
Target Total Compensation	$975,000	$1,000,000	$1,025,000

The following shows what happens, in both good and bad times, to these different mixes of salary and target annual incentives:

	Conservative	Market Median	Aggressive
Good Times (Upside Scenario)			
Salary	$600,000	$500,000	$400,000
Max. Bonus (2x)	$750,000	$1,000,000	$1,250,000
Max. Total Compensation	$1,350,000	$1,500,000	$1,650,000
Bad Times (Downside Scenario)			
Salary	$600,000	$500,000	$400,000
Min. Bonus (0x)	$0	$0	$0
Min. Total Compensation	$600,000	$500,000	$400,000

Figure 68—Compensation Mix and Payout Variation

From a cultural perspective, a premium will be placed on being careful in a risk-averse company when developing plans and approving decisions. Such a company would be more likely to hedge its bets than to take on a "Big Hairy Audacious Goal," or BHAG, a term that James Collins and Jerry Porras coined in their 1994 book, *Built to Last: Successful Habits of Visionary Companies.*[7] A BHAG encourages companies to define visionary goals that are strategic and emotionally compelling. These goals may encourage reaching for the stars, but they can also involve betting the company on the outcome. A conservative culture would shun such ideas and prefer instead to pursue a series of smaller, more-predictable, and less-risky goals.

This conservative company would be best served by an incentive plan that reinforces the low-risk culture by emphasizing salary and less-leveraged incentive components. That is, it would take larger swings in performance to achieve high or low payouts.

Such a company would likely have many employees, perhaps even some with solid skills and strong motivation, who would feel frustrated by the conservative strategy, culture, and compensation package. They would buck the culture, try to change it, and seek to instill an entrepreneurial spirit—but would be constantly met with resistance and outright objections. Some executives might recognize their skills and fear losing such employees, but they usually wouldn't realize that trying to retain them would be unlikely to succeed in the longer term and that doing so would likely weaken the company culture.

The same is true, in reverse, for a company with an aggressive business strategy, culture, and compensation package. It will have skilled and effective employees who, by nature or circumstance, feel uncomfortable in the environment and seem unhappy with the volatility of their pay. For them, the idea of launching a new BHAG that could prove highly lucrative but risk years of bonus pay may not be tolerable.

Unfortunately, there is no perfect answer to how aggressive or conservative a company's strategy should be, but *the culture and compensation package should be aligned*. If it has employees who don't fit the culture and seek to resign or, worse, threaten to quit unless demands are met, it's better to let them leave. Even if they are skilled, it's advisable not to dilute the desired strategy and culture by keeping them.

Better Annual Incentives

Once a company has established its business strategy, desired culture, and compensation strategy, the next question is how to design an annual incentive plan that reinforces an ownership culture. In reality, well-designed long-term incentives will do more to cement the partnership between executives and shareholders, though an annual plan to reinforce the ownership culture is also valuable.

An annual incentive plan requires four elements. We would need to define the measures, the methodology for setting targets, the sensitivity if the performance is above- or below-target, and the system of caps and floors that limits payouts in extreme circumstances. Although we would need considerable expertise to customize an appropriate performance measure and then to calibrate the targets and sensitivities, the principles required are straightforward.

As discussed throughout this book, the most reliable measure to link to compensation is RCE, which should always be tailored to the business dynamics and accounting conventions of both the company and its industry. More than any other measure, RCE rises when "good" things happen and declines when "bad" things happen; using RCE improves the incentive to invest in the future and eliminates the incentive to milk old assets long after they should have been replaced.

Most companies are priced to maintain their current RCE with small increments of improvement or decline, as mentioned earlier. For these companies, the best target-setting mechanism is to establish the target RCE each year equal to the actual RCE performance in the prior year. This improves on more commonly used methods in three ways. First, it breaks the cycle of setting targets off a budget or plan, which encourages sandbagging and underperformance. Second, it removes the potential for year-end gaming of the system, such as offering discounts to pull January sales into December, temporarily driving down accounts receivable, and having other cascading effects. Third, and most important, it encourages managers to treat the capital as if it were their own. If they invest capital that doesn't cover the required return, and then the RCE declines, they are paid less, and vice versa, of course.

As discussed above, we should set targets with a built-in expected improvement for companies that already have an expectation of higher RCE in the future baked into their stock price. But unfortunately, it is hard to do the reverse for companies that are valued low enough that investors have baked in an expectation that the current level of RCE is not sustainable. In principle, the target RCE each year should be set at the prior-year RCE less an expected decline. In practice, however, prevailing compensation and investor-relations practices are such that setting targets as a systematic decline from actuals each year is hard for compensation committees to agree to. In these cases, targets are generally set equal to the prior-year actual, and management must accept this if they want to accrue the behavioral benefits that come along with the rest of the compensation improvements. With any luck, success will affect expectations and investors will drive share prices higher, to reflect new expectations of more-sustained or even improving performance after a few years; and management will then benefit through their long-term incentives that are tied to the share price.

Though there is some room for making the pay-for-performance curve a bit steeper or flatter, the range of acceptable bonus sensitivities should be based on the volatility of RCE. Some businesses are highly volatile or cyclical, and their median year-to-year change in RCE can be 3%, 4%, or even 6%–8% of gross operating assets. In other more-stable businesses, these variations are generally 1% or less. This is illustrated in figure 69.

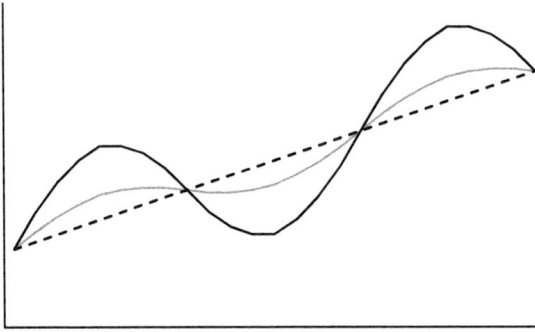

Figure 69—Stable vs. Volatile RCE

If we used the same bonus sensitivity for the two businesses whose RCE is shown in the figure, the bonuses for the volatile business would be bouncing between the bonus cap and floor, while the stable business would get almost the same bonus each year, as shown in figure 70.

Using the same bonus sensitivity for both businesses also leads to extremes for the volatile business. The stable business has the opposite problem. Note that both businesses earn payouts that average above 1x because both businesses create value and improve RCE over time. By varying the bonus sensitivity based on historical and expected RCE volatility, we can provide similar compensation volatility in both businesses. Consider the two incentive-payout relationships shown in figure 71.

By flattening the pay-for-performance curve for the volatile business, we make the bonus sensitivity more suitable for that business. Again, management has some flexibility if it wishes to be more conservative or aggressive, but if you were in their shoes you wouldn't want to move one curve toward the other too much. Note that, when we change the slope, we solve the volatility problem; another benefit is that we wind up rewarding the stable business managers who have achieved cumulative improvement with a bit higher average payout, because the underlying upward trend is being rewarded against a steeper curve. This makes sense, because generating cumulative long-term improvements in a very stable business is harder but more valuable.

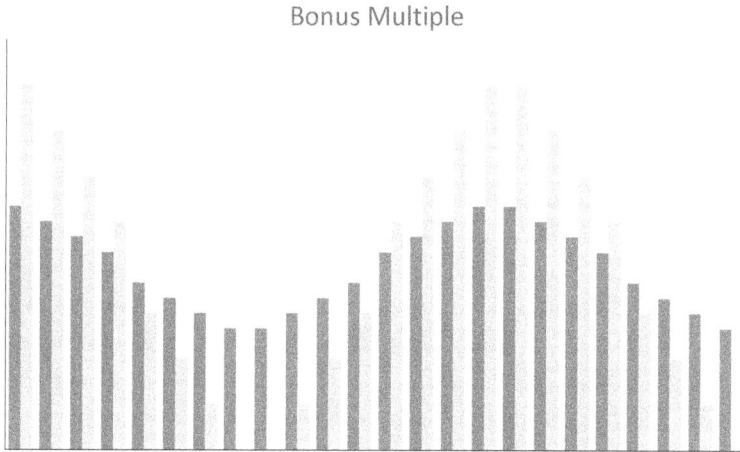

Bonus Multiple

Figure 70—Stable vs. Volatile Bonus Multiple

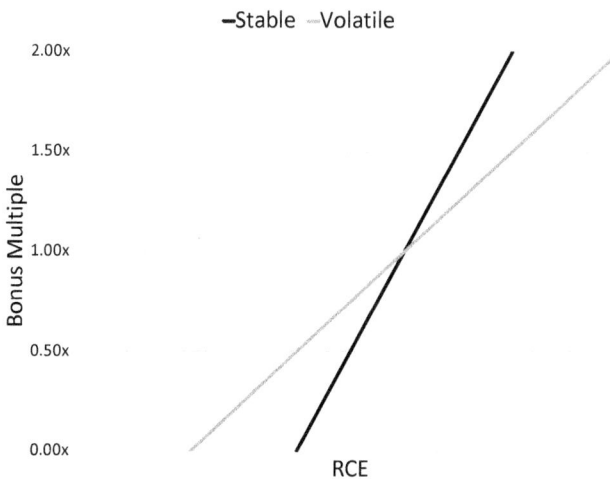

Figure 71—Pay for Performance Bonus Sensitivity

Annual incentive plans generally have caps and floors, as do many features of long-term incentive plans. Some years ago, I realized that companies need to modify the target-setting formula in years after performance surpasses a cap or a floor. In order to avoid discouraging improvement after the cap is reached, and to discourage our writing off the kitchen sink after the floor is reached, we set the target for the following year at the point where the floor or cap was reached. This allows the company to limit the payout in any given year while ensuring that the cumulative payout over time directly relates to cumulative RCE improvement. So, the cap isn't really a cap per se on what can be earned over time; it's more a cap on what can be paid in any given year. The excess performance above the cap (or below the floor) is rolled into the next year, in the form of a target RCE that is below (or above) the prior year's actual result.

It's fundamental to everything covered in this entire book that readers clearly understand the beneficial, owner-like behaviors motivated by this annual incentive plan. To illustrate how this simple and highly effective compensation model works, consider the baseline case shown in figure 72.

Baseline		Year 1	Year 2	Year 3	Year 4	Year 5	Total
A	RCE	$100.0	$105.0	$110.0	$115.0	$120.0	$125.0	
B	ΔRCE		$5.0	$5.0	$5.0	$5.0	$5.0	$25.0
C	Bonus Sensitivity		$20.0	$20.0	$20.0	$20.0	$20.0	
D=B/C	Performance Multiple		0.25x	0.25x	0.25x	0.25x	0.25x	
E	Target Multiple		1.00x	1.00x	1.00x	1.00x	1.00x	
F=D+E	Overall Incentive Multiple		1.25x	1.25x	1.25x	1.25x	1.25x	
	Target Annual Incentive		$100,000	$100,000	$100,000	$100,000	$100,000	
	Annual Incentive Payout		$125,000	$125,000	$125,000	$125,000	$125,000	$625,000

Figure 72—Baseline RCE Incentive Simulation

Rows *A* and *B* show that this baseline business forecasts strong RCE, at $100 million, and improving by $5 million per year. Row *C* shows that the bonus sensitivity is $20 million, which is the amount RCE would need to increase in a year to double the bonus, or to decline in a year to zero it out. In this case, since RCE improves by

$5 million, the performance multiple is 0.25x, or simply 5 divided by 20. This is added to the target multiple of 1.0x, which is earned when the change in RCE is zero, to determine the overall incentive multiple of 1.25x. The executive's target incentive payout of $100,000 is multiplied by the 1.25x multiple, and the actual payout is determined to be $125,000.

Basically, if RCE rises you are paid more, and if it declines you get less. That's it—there's no negotiation of budgets and targets. So, stop spending time and effort on anything that doesn't help improve the business over time! As this forecast is based on smoothly improving RCE, the payouts are the same each year. Yet, as we will see, generally this is not the case.

What if a one-off bad performance happens one year? Maybe it's a temporary labor strike or a raw material shortage that leads to elevated costs and choked production. But perhaps, after it happens, performance is expected to normalize the following year. In most bonus plans, executives get "whacked," which is a technical compensation term. Their bonus suffers in the year of the one-off hit, and often the budgeted target is raised for the following year when the one-off problem is expected to be resolved. But the bonus is lost forever. In the recommended incentive plan, RCE declines so the payout also declines in the year of the one-off; but as long as it really *is* one-off and if performance recovers the following year, RCE improves and the money is earned back. The executive loses only the time value of (the) money. This is demonstrated in figure 73.

One-Off Decline		Year 1	Year 2	Year 3	Year 4	Year 5	Total
A	RCE	$100.0	$90.0	$110.0	$115.0	$120.0	$125.0	
B	ΔRCE		-$10.0	$20.0	$5.0	$5.0	$5.0	$25.0
C	Bonus Sensitivity		$20.0	$20.0	$20.0	$20.0	$20.0	
D=B/C	Performance Multiple		-0.50x	1.00x	0.25x	0.25x	0.25x	
E	Target Multiple		1.00x	1.00x	1.00x	1.00x	1.00x	
F=D+E	Overall Incentive Multiple		0.50x	2.00x	1.25x	1.25x	1.25x	
	Target Annual Incentive		$100,000	$100,000	$100,000	$100,000	$100,000	
	Annual Incentive Payout		$50,000	$200,000	$125,000	$125,000	$125,000	$625,000
	Incremental Payout		-$75,000	$75,000	$0	$0	$0	

Figure 73—RCE Incentive Simulation with One-Off Bad Year

The difference in performance from the baseline case is caused by a raw material shortage in year one that causes RCE to decline by $10 million instead of rising by $5 million (as in the baseline case). The overall incentive multiple declines to 0.50x and the payout is only $50,000, which is $75,000 less than in year one of the baseline simulation. By the end of the year, luckily the industry recovers from the raw material shortage, and the RCE in year two is the very same $110 million as in the baseline case. The one-off problem in year one does not recur, and performance is back on track by year two. Just as the ΔRCE in year one was $15 million below the baseline case, the ΔRCE in year two is $15 million above baseline, so the $75,000 forfeited in year one is earned back dollar-for-dollar in year two (again, less the time value of money). Once managers understand this, they behave differently! Sure, they still try to mitigate the impact of the raw material shortage in year one, because they would prefer to earn, say, $55,000 or $60,000 instead of just $50,000. But they will spend far less time worrying about these temporary setbacks so they can devote more time to overcoming persistent strategic obstacles, like reacting to a revolutionary product that a competitor is developing. To belabor the point, they act more like owners.

Permanent Decline			Year 1	Year 2	Year 3	Year 4	Year 5	Total
A	RCE	$100.0	$90.0	$95.0	$100.0	$105.0	$110.0	
B	ΔRCE		-$10.0	$5.0	$5.0	$5.0	$5.0	$10.0
C	Bonus Sensitivity		$20.0	$20.0	$20.0	$20.0	$20.0	
D=B/C	Performance Multiple		-0.50x	0.25x	0.25x	0.25x	0.25x	
E	Target Multiple		1.00x	1.00x	1.00x	1.00x	1.00x	
F=D+E	Overall Incentive Multiple		0.50x	1.25x	1.25x	1.25x	1.25x	
	Target Annual Incentive		$100,000	$100,000	$100,000	$100,000	$100,000	
	Annual Incentive Payout		$50,000	$125,000	$125,000	$125,000	$125,000	$550,000
	Incremental Payout		-$75,000	$0	$0	$0	$0	

Figure 74—RCE Incentive Simulation with Permanent Decline

Now, let's consider figure 74. Perhaps in this case a new product was launched by a competitor that immediately steals some of our market share, which then stabilizes at a lower level. Like the one-off example, RCE declines to $90 million in year one, yet this time no full recovery occurs the next year. Instead, RCE rises at the same $5 million per year as the baseline case, but from this new, lower level. The lost annual incentive payout of $75,000 in year one is never recovered, because all the years that follow have the same payout as the baseline. The accountability for this more-permanent performance decline is immediate and absolute, but, happily, the incentive system immediately resets at this new level, providing an opportunity to start earning above-target bonuses again as soon as RCE improves from the new base. It's almost like giving managers one-year exposure to stock and stock options, where the RCE is the stock price.

Although it's a little complex, an interesting and constructive relationship can be noted between the impact of the one-off decline and the permanent decline on both shareholder wealth and the executive's incentive. First, let's consider the investors: In the one-off case they lose $15 million of RCE, which has a present value of $15 million. If we simply assume that their required return is 10% in the permanent decline case, then the permanent decline of $15 million causes a net-present-value loss of $150 million, or $15 million divided by 10% (the present value formula for a perpetuity). So, the permanent decline is worth 10 times as much to the investor. The executive has to wait a year to get the $75,000 that is forfeited in year one of the one-off case. Like investors, executives place a premium on certain money now versus potential money later. Who knows if performance will really improve with certainty? Since the manager's annual incentive is exposed to risks similar to those of the shareholders, let's assume the manager's personal discount rate is also 10%. So, the cost of waiting a year for the $75,000 is simply 10% multiplied by $75,000, or $7,500 in lost time value of money. The executive's loss in the permanent decline case is $75,000. Notice that the ratio of $15 million to $150 million for the investor is the same ratio as the $7,500 to $75,000 for the executive, so that the relative importance of one-off and permanent RCE changes is perfectly aligned.

Indeed, this is perhaps more important for the upside, since executives earn 10 times as much for sustainable improvements as they do for one-off improvements; achieving the former has a significant impact on both strategy and execution priorities. Sustainable improvements are therefore much more valuable to both the investor and the executive who is motivated to improve RCE.

Perhaps the most powerful attribute of the RCE incentive plan is what happens to annual incentives if management makes an investment that causes a short-term decline in RCE but is expected to drive significant RCE over time. Just like an owner, the manager is exposed to the cost and the benefit, and can decide if the size of the benefit and the confidence or likelihood that it will occur is enough to justify the risk. Consider figure 75, which shows the baseline case modified by management's pursuit of an investment that takes time to pay off.

	Baseline + Investment		Year 1	Year 2	Year 3	Year 4	Year 5	Total
A	RCE	$100.0	$90.0	$107.0	$122.0	$135.0	$145.0	
B	ΔRCE		-$10.0	$17.0	$15.0	$13.0	$10.0	$45.0
C	Bonus Sensitivity		$20.0	$20.0	$20.0	$20.0	$20.0	
D=B/C	Performance Multiple		-0.50x	0.85x	0.75x	0.65x	0.50x	
E	Target Multiple		1.00x	1.00x	1.00x	1.00x	1.00x	
F=D+E	Overall Incentive Multiple		0.50x	1.85x	1.75x	1.65x	1.50x	
	Target Annual Incentive		$100,000	$100,000	$100,000	$100,000	$100,000	
	Annual Incentive Payout		$50,000	$185,000	$175,000	$165,000	$150,000	$725,000
	Incremental payout		-$75,000	$60,000	$50,000	$40,000	$25,000	
	IRR		55%					

Figure 75—RCE Incentive Simulation with Good Investment

Perhaps the new investment is the launch of a new brand extension into an adjacent product. The project kicks off in year one with some capital investment to build the capacity, followed by heavy marketing to position the new product with consumers. Sales begin in the second half of year one but only become significant in year two, so year one is an investment year with RCE declining by $15 million. Management nevertheless expects sales to pick up in year two and to continue growing at a declining rate in years three through five. By year five, RCE is fully $20 million higher than the base case. The executive takes a hit to the annual incentive of $75,000 in year one but earns an extra $175,000 over the next four years.

Is this enough to motivate the investment? The cash flows to the executive represent an annualized internal rate of return of 55%, which is significantly higher than the executive's 10% required return established above. Another important element of the decision must be noted, and it's one of the most important behavioral aspects of this entire incentive program: *How confident is the executive that the forecast is achievable?* Do they fear the capital and marketing investments may actually be higher? Are they convinced of the sales forecasts? Is pricing reasonable? Cost estimates? Will there be any cannibalization of sales on existing products and, if so, what will that cost them? Have they adequately considered their competitors' reactions? After the executive considers *all* this and more, the ultimate question is whether the executive is willing to risk $75,000 of his or her own money, in the form of forgone incentive in year one, in exchange for the $175,000 later.

This presents a nearly perfect simulation of ownership. Investment proposals in such a corporate environment are no longer mere marketing documents aimed at convincing executives or directors that an investment is worthwhile. Before trying to convince anyone else of the value of the investment, executives must consider for themselves whether that is a good investment. Who says an annual incentive can't motivate short- and long-term thinking at the same time?

We could run many more simulations that prove the value of these incentive designs, and their consistency and reliability, when facing the various cultures and industries in which companies partake. But these scenarios as presented demonstrate how the RCE incentive approach can reinforce the ownership culture discussed throughout this book.

Better Long-Term Incentives

My former partner Bennett Stewart advocated a stock-option approach in which options would be somewhat in the money when granted, though the exercise price would rise over time.[8] His intention was to simulate a leveraged management buyout without putting the company at risk. It's as if the management would be buying shares, where the exercise price represents debt and where the difference between the exercise price and the stock price at the time of grant would represent the equity owned by management. The rising exercise price was intended to simulate interest on the debt, so management would only make money when the stock price rose faster than the exercise price. It was a superb idea, but unfortunately it was fraught with tax and accounting problems. Alas, the accountants, tax practitioners, and regulatory professionals of the world simply weren't ready for Bennett's innovative solution.

Long-term executive compensation practices have become more and more complex over the years. Where restricted stock and stock options were once the predominant tools, we now have stock-appreciation rights, performance cash, deferred stock units, performance share units, performance options...and countless other alternatives and features. What's more, the quest for better and more effective mousetraps has led to incentive methods that often do a *worse* job of motivating management to think and act like long-term owners.

Perhaps, along the lines of Bennett's thinking, today's compensation committees should look to how private equity motivates executives. Management wins if private equity investors win and vice versa. Managements typically earn a "promote," which is an equity participation that increases depending on how high the IRR is for the investors. They tend not to worry as much about whether the success was skill or luck; they simply reward success. And perhaps that helps them achieve more success.

Often investors get a minimum return before management actually participates. This can be anywhere from 5% to 10% and is often described as an internal rate of return, or IRR. Note that, in this situation, IRR and TSR are indistinguishable. Any value created above this is shared between management and investors, according to a chosen formula. For example, management may get 15%, 20%, or 25% of any value created above the minimum IRR. Generally, the larger the company, the smaller the share that goes to management, because executive human capital is essentially smaller in relation to the financial capital; there are, of course, additional possible drivers of the percentage, such as the experience and negotiating power of the executive team.

Often another, higher IRR threshold looms, above which management will receive an even higher percentage of the value created. This is designed to step up the motivation after substantial success is already achieved, since improvement opportunities become scarcer as more and more are realized. Though the specifics vary, it is usually the case that the more money investors make, the more management earns, which forges a strong alignment of interests.

Public company compensation committees could reach outside their normal comfort zone and implement long-term compensation structures that work more like those in private equity. This could directly copy the private equity arrangements or could be a simplified stock and stock-option structure designed to accomplish similar objectives.

To emulate the typical private equity deal, a company could establish a subsidiary for the purpose of holding treasury stock that management can earn going forward. The subsidiary could be financed with, say, 10% in equity from management, via either paid-in capital or a time-vested grant. The remainder could be financed with debt or preferred stock along with a pay-in-kind feature, so that the amount of financing builds every month to a minimum threshold before management participates.

The value of management's stake would increase if the value of the company grows faster than the pay-in-kind financing. This would replace the typical annual equity grants over, say, five years with a single front-loaded opportunity, requiring the size of the equity pool to be calibrated so as to deliver an appropriate midpoint payoff relative to standard practice. Admittedly, though more feasible than Bennett Stewart's rising exercise price options, implementing this subsidiary structure is also fraught with all sorts of legal, accounting, and tax complications; ultimately, it may prove too complicated or tendentious for investors and proxy advisory firms.

However, a simplified stock-option structure *can* be used to mimic the private equity approach in a manner that is more consistent with normal public company practices. In place of the next five years of LTIP (Long-Term Incentive Plan) grants, management could instead be granted one front-loaded package of stock options that would come in five tranches, each with different vesting dates and exercise prices.

The first tranche could vest in one year and have an exercise price 8% above a benchmark share price of, say, the three-month trailing average price. The second tranche might vest in two years and have an exercise price 16% above the benchmark share price, and so on. Each tranche would be exercisable over one to three years after it vests.

This structure is extremely well aligned with the annual RCE-incentive structure discussed above, and it would reinforce all the same behaviors. Results matter more than variances, and the long-term trend matters more than the year-to-year path. As opposed to making annual grants, where a share price decline is almost rewarded by granting new stock and options at lower prices, the inevitable short-term share price fluctuations don't matter much to the executive. This package would provide a huge potential payoff if management is very successful but precious little if they fail to create value. Though this sort of plan carries a greater potential for retention risk if the share price permanently declines, that must be weighed against the prospect of much stronger motivation to succeed.

Even if such an approach doesn't replace all other long-term incentives, many companies will find that weaving some elements of this into their normal compensation approach can be beneficial, even if they choose not to embrace it completely. But whether such an approach to long-term incentives is even contemplated, company management and the compensation committee should be sure to consider the behavior being encouraged as the primary determinant of long-term incentive design.

Notes

1   Michael C. Jensen, "CEO Incentives: It's Not How Much You Pay, But How," *Harvard Business Review*, no. 3 (May-June 1990).

2   Adapted from Gregory V. Milano, "A Theory of Relativity Misses the Mark," CFO.com, November 13, 2017, accessed January 15, 2019, http://ww2.cfo.com/compensation/2017/11/theory-relativity-misses-mark/; *see also* Gregory V. Milano, "The Relative TSR Conundrum," *Workspan* magazine by WorldatWork, May 2018.

3   Schedule 14A (Proxy Statement), filed by Varian Medical Systems, Inc., December 21, 2018.

4   Schedule 14A (Proxy Statement), filed by National Oilwell Varco, Inc., March 30, 2018.

5   Stephen F. O'Byrne, "Total Compensation Strategy," *Journal of Applied Corporate Finance* 8, no. 2 (1995).

6   Stephen F. O'Byrne, "Measuring and Improving Pay for Performance," in *The Handbook of Board Governance* (Hoboken, NJ: John Wiley & Sons, 2016), 536–54.

7   James Collins and Jerry Porras, *Built to Last: Successful Habits of Visionary Companies* (Harper Business, 2011 edition).

8   Bennett Stewart, "Remaking the Public Corporation from Within," *Harvard Business Review*, July-August 1990.

FIFTEEN

Getting Managers and Employees to Act Like Owners

THEY SAY YOU can lead a horse to water but you can't make it drink. I don't know much about horses, but I *do* know that you can implement new performance metrics and business processes, and then you can back them up with supportive incentive programs. However, it's very hard to get managers and executives to change their long-standing habits and behaviors. Implementing the ideas presented in this book is not about metrics, models, or processes; it's about *changing human behavior*. It's change management and it is successful only about half the time, according to researchers in the field.

By far the most important first step in creating an ownership culture is to get senior executives to buy in and commit to a new way of thinking and behaving. It would be so easy to "talk the talk" and expect people to do things differently because they've been told to, yet it doesn't work that way. Even after a full day of training, people tend to go back to their desks and do what they've done before. It takes constant reinforcement to overcome the natural human tendency to maintain familiar habits and behaviors.

It is also critical that a company's executives establish a "protocol" to reinforce the behaviors they seek, accompanied by constant reminders and reinforcements. For example, in many companies, managers fear operating reviews when their numbers are short of plan. That fear can contribute to an incentive to sandbag, even after the incentive targets are no longer derived from the plan. Executives must learn how to act in this new world by always emphasizing that, when it comes to value, more is always good and less is always bad. And they must realize that creating value is not easy, especially given the intensity of competition in most industries. So, it can be helpful to maintain a set of brief statements that convey a clear and simple message, such as "I'd rather plan for $10 million of profit and achieve $8 million than plan for $5 million and achieve $6 million. In other words, I'd rather make $8 million than $6 million." When managers fall back into old negotiating behaviors, even these simple mantras can help reset their perspective.

When a superior asks a business or department head if they can improve performance in their plan or budget, it can be good to remind them that this higher performance will make *both* of them richer. "We are both on the same side of the table," you can say, "so it's worth trying to figure out a better plan and then aim to achieve it."

Or, when a subordinate presents a forecast and asks a senior executive to approve a major investment, it's important to remind them that the forecast is useful only for making decisions, and in the end it's the results that matter. If the new investment beats the minimum required return, then RCE will rise, value will be created, and bonuses will also rise. With that being said, the crucial question to ask subordinates is: "Do you have enough confidence in your forecasted RCE improvements that you are willing to put your own money on the line?"

It is vital to have the right spending authorities at each level of the organization. If managers must ask permission for even trivial expenditures, they will have a harder time embracing an ownership culture. But senior executives shouldn't feel any pressure to increase authorities too quickly. By always asking whether subordinates have enough confidence in their forecasted RCE improvements before approving investments, managers cultivate the feeling of ownership. Over time, as the ownership culture takes hold and is clearly embraced by most of the organization (it will never be adopted by all), it may be reasonable to increase local autonomy for decision-making, but only after the intended RCE accountability has been established and is clearly embraced.

Many years ago, when I was collaborating on an EVA implementation with Sir Roderick Deane, then the CEO of New Zealand Telecom, the rollout plan was driven by a cascading leadership structure. When I trained the direct reports to the CEO, he kicked off the session with a pretty meaningful 20- to 30-minute introduction on why we were doing this and what it meant to him. Just before he turned it over to me, he advised his leadership team that the next step was for me to train their direct reports, and that they would be responsible for the session kick-off comments. Knowing they would need to speak about EVA in front of their team, in their own words, Deane wisely knew they were sure to pay attention to my training. And his words conveyed no doubts at all about his commitment to our effort. As the EVA training percolated throughout the organization, each group received an initial introduction from their leader at the start of training, which encouraged them to pay attention.

One of the major obstacles to change is the aloofness people feel in organizations that seem to be in a constant state of culture change. They wonder, "What will they be teaching us *next* week?" And they whisper, "Maybe if we ignore it, it will go away and be replaced by some new fad next week." This attitude can be a major obstacle that makes the effort much harder—but it's important to avoid throwing in the towel and to recognize that strong, decisive leadership will be needed to reinforce the new behaviors for some time before the changes stick. It will be worth it.

Though the entire company leadership needs to be the face of the change, it's important that this leadership be supported by teams with the knowledge and skills to establish a training and support network for the larger organization. When these ownership principles and methodologies are new, there is simply too high a risk that strategic situations and financial figures will be misinterpreted, so having experts is essential. For example, when I was a partner at Stern Stewart, I met numerous times with a large oil and gas services company about implementing EVA; in the end, they didn't engage us but instead entrusted their finance department with the implementation. I felt frustrated at the time, but years later I learned that the decision was much worse for them than for me. They did a poor job of designing the approach, and an even poorer job of getting the organization to understand and embrace it.

Over a decade later, another company brought us in to work on an implementation, and several executives had been at the company mentioned in the prior paragraph. We took the time to discuss what happened with the previous failed implementation. Most of these managers expressed their frustration by telling me outright: "EVA doesn't work." But then I found out that their former employer had emphasized the absolute level of EVA in bonus plans, *not* the improvement. So those lucky enough to run the highest-return businesses earned huge rewards, even if the EVA improvement was subpar, and the leaders of the weakest businesses could do nothing to earn much bonus at all. The poor-performing businesses drastically needed top talent to execute a turnaround, yet nobody wanted to work there.

Also, as the company used the typical EVA approach of measuring net profits against a capital charge on net capital, the milking of old assets became an art form while the prospect of investing in the future wasn't a priority at all. I learned of this when one of the managers attended my training session at the new company, and he remarked, "I know how to beat this EVA game! You go get the oldest [that is, most depreciated] piece-of-crap asset you can find, and you shine it up so it looks new." I explained that in fact the new metric— a customized version of RCE—uses a capital charge based on gross assets, so no matter how old and depreciated an asset becomes, the capital charge stays the same. After resisting the idea at first, he told me a few days later, "You're geniuses!" I then said I estimated that the original company had underperformed by so much, and for so long, that they had potentially left "a billion dollars" of market capitalization on the table—and then I joked that we wouldn't have charged them even half that much to help them get it right.

Communication, Training, and Coaching

Internal leadership and the external implementation teams need to identify every potential obstacle to success before the rollout. They must involve people at different levels, in different regions, and in different functions to be sure they understand the potential roadblocks and identify workarounds. For example, managers across many companies have become so used to negotiating budgets that you can explain a hundred times that budgets are no longer used as incentive targets; and yet, when the first budget comes in, managers will still sandbag it. It may seem nonsensical—and it is—but this just shows the inertia of conditioned human behaviors.

To combat this tendency, the start of the budget process can include a refresher on the new framework and offer some examples of how to stretch the thinking and to plan more aggressively. One way to identify such obstacles is to accompany the initial internal communication of the new management approach with an electronic questionnaire that encourages people to answer the question, "this may not work because _____." The findings can serve as a checklist when developing communications and training materials.

When writing an article or making a presentation, experts say you need to first tell your audience what you are going to tell them, then you tell them, and finally you tell them again—this time in fewer words. An overall communications, training, and coaching program works the same way—through repetition. Initial communications set the stage by notifying the audience that changes are coming, with some indication of what the changes will be. It's best at this point to refrain from any level of detail that will sidetrack the message, but instead to keep it high-level and clear. Often you will place more emphasis on the goals of the new management paradigm and less on how it will be accomplished. One client included the following message:

VA Is Everyone's Business

Our business requires a lot of capital. We renew our fleet and facilities, purchase equipment and parts. We expand into markets where our clients go. Growing our business, gaining market share, buying new equipment, and opening new locations all require capital—which is either borrowed, directly invested by, or retained on behalf of our shareholders. We attract capital by promising to deliver an adequate return to shareholders.

If we don't, they will invest elsewhere.

It can be very helpful to have additional information available on demand when the initial communications are made. As much as we want to keep the messages simple so that they are well understood, some employees will be curious and want to learn more. Some of them may well turn out to be "culture leaders," so giving them access to more information, perhaps through a company portal or intranet site, can help get them on board. But even if this can't be achieved simultaneously with the launch, instructions should be provided for those who want more information, perhaps an email address or a phone number to call.

In addition to providing more in-depth training, as will be discussed below, communication should continue regularly. Sometimes it can be part of other normally scheduled communications, such as an internal newsletter, and can gradually share more about the new program, offering examples of things that have changed and the resulting benefits. One company explained it to employees with examples like this:

> **Identifying Operating Inefficiencies:** Can you find ways to reduce waste, trim inventories, control expenses, or operate equipment more efficiently? If you can, you're improving performance.
>
> **Generating Revenues:** Are there things you can do to increase sales by better serving customers, further improving the quality of our products, or gaining a competitive advantage?

Sometimes it helps to quote a great leader. Here's an example (used by a company that was *not* Coca-Cola):

> Here's what the chairman of Coca-Cola Company, Roberto Goizueta, says about the beneficial effect that charging for capital has on inventories: "I learned that when you start charging people for their capital, all sorts of things happen. All of a sudden, inventories get under control. You don't have three months' [supply] sitting around for an emergency."

It can be helpful to pose questions to get people thinking about how they can contribute. One client posed the following questions to their employees:

> **BUILD:** *Commit fresh resources to endeavors that will more than cover the cost of the new capital employed.*
> - What new equipment should we buy to provide new or better products to our customers?
> - What equipment should be upgraded to lower costs or improve quality?
> - What training activities will make people more effective?

- What marketing efforts will improve customer and end-user satisfaction and will result in increased sales and profits?
- Can we spend less capital and achieve the same or better-quality result?

OPERATE: *Increase profits without tying up any more capital.*
- How can we provide better service to our customers or sell more products without spending more?
- How can we cut defects or increase yield?
- What vendors can supply the same or better materials at lower prices?
- How can we manage internal budgets more prudently?
- How can we reduce working capital?
- How can we decrease cycle time?
- How can we increase productivity of existing assets?

HARVEST: Withdraw capital from activities that produce an inadequate return compared to other uses for that capital.
- What products or customers aren't as profitable as we want?
- What operating expenses aren't getting us enough value?
- What assets should be sold or shut down?

As the basic practical ideas and activities behind an ownership mindset begin to sink in, a comprehensive training program should take it to the next level. Many types of training will be needed for people in various roles. The most in-depth training will be given to financial experts who need to understand the application of RCE inside out and also to help others. At the other end of the spectrum is the training of lower-level managers and supervisors who may need to know the basic concepts but will never really have to do any calculations using the new financial metrics. A good initial training program can consist of a brief video or computer-based training that goes beyond the scope of the initial communications, but stays at a high enough level to avoid losing most people's interest or buy-in. The emphasis in this case is always on principles and guidelines.

Rather than focus on either of these extremes, the following will describe an effective training approach for a fairly senior operating team of managers. For example, a business-unit management team may consist of a dozen or so managers representing a range of disciplines, including operations, marketing, sales, administration, and finance. The financial leader, in all likelihood, would have already participated in financial experts training, but often joins his or her colleagues for their training to help make sure they all understand it and also to establish a partner-like bond while conveying the feeling that "we are in this together."

The training of financial experts should aim to provide them with an in-depth understanding of "why" the new management processes work the way they do, perhaps offering them capital market research findings showing how companies that have improved these metrics have, on average, delivered much better results for shareholders. But the training of an operating team should focus more on "what" the new management processes are and "how" they are to be used. As much as possible, we want managers to be using the new metrics and analytics during the training in much the same way we expect them to be used in real situations.

One recent training program my colleagues and I conducted began with a high-level discussion of the nature of ownership and what it means to act like an owner. Examples were used that all began with words like, "Let's imagine you started your own business..." or, "Consider a situation where your neighbor starts a business and you agree to invest in it...." Of course, we are getting them accustomed to the new mindset before we have even explained what it is! This helps them develop an emotional connection with the principles, so that we can come back to them at any point in the training to reinforce more-specific points. It is far more important that everyone understands the nature of the cultural change than that they're able to do the math. (That's why we have a finance department.)

With that said, we do want everybody to go through the fundamental math at least once. But if we did this by handing them the company's financial statements, we would lose them right away. So, we need to build simple cases that are each designed to illustrate and elucidate the principles behind RCE. The client sometimes competes with small competitors, known colloquially as "mom and pops," so we built the cases around this scenario. The company provides services to oil companies, and the initial case was based on a $1 million investment needed to buy a set of assets to support a work team. This investment entailed cash operating costs of $350,000; a total of $550,000 in annual revenue received from the customers; income taxes simply set at 13% of EBITDA; and a required rate of return on capital of 12%. The trainees were separated into groups of three, given the information, and asked to calculate RCE for this small business. Lo and behold, the RCE is positive, as shown in figure 76.

First, you need customers who want to consume your services - - - ▸	**Revenue**	**$550,000**
Then you're going to incur costs - - - ▸ (salaries, utilities, insurance)	Operating Expenses	($350,000)
	EBITDA	$200,000
Then you've got to pay the gov't - - - ▸	Taxes (13% on EBITDA)	($26,000)
	Gross Cash Earnings	**$174,000**
	Gross Operating Assets	$1,000,000
But remember the folks who - - - ▸ provided capital	Required Return	12%
	Capital Charge	**($120,000)**
Only after "paying them" back - - - ▸ have you created any value	**RCE (Value Creation)**	**$54,000**

Figure 76—Baseline Training Case

If this was indeed your business, you'd be quite happy—since you've earned more than the required return on investment!

The second case, shown in figure 77, was designed to build on this situation by contemplating a growth investment. To establish a new team to provide similar services, we need to invest another $1 million in assets. But this time we struggle to secure a customer, so the assets sit idle. Fortunately, we didn't fully staff up, since we saw it was going to be hard to put the assets to work, but the investment still had an incremental cost of $50,000.

Adding an idle asset is rarely good, and in this case it drives RCE down from a positive $54,000 to a negative $109,500. Notice that Gross Cash Earnings only declines $43,500, or just over a quarter of the total RCE decline. From this example, the trainees learn that the P&L is in fact an incomplete indicator of the cost of idle capacity.

	Baseline	*Case 2*
Revenue	$550,000	$550,000
Operating Expenses	($350,000)	($400,000)
EBITDA	$200,000	$150,000
Taxes (13% on EBITDA)	($26,000)	($19,500)
Gross Cash Earnings	$174,000	$130,500
Gross Operating Assets	$1,000,000	$2,000,000
Required Return	12%	12%
Capital Charge	($120,000)	($240,000)
RCE (Value Creation)	$54,000	($109,500)

Figure 77—New Idle Assets

The training went on from there to consider a deal with the customer to engage both service teams for a 10% discount, which would lead to much better RCE, though still not as high as the initial single work team. The lesson here is that making bad investments can have lingering negative implications. We then added working capital, including poor receivables collection, and it became clear how much capital can be consumed in poor cash-conversion-cycle times. Finally, we tightened up accounts receivable collection, and our RCE improved, demonstrating that improved capital efficiency is interchangeable with cost reduction.

The cases went on—15 of them in total. The attendees had fun working out the simple math and gibing back and forth as each team stood up to take their turn explaining their answers. Since they were working in groups, nobody faced any embarrassment if they struggled with the math. Each case taught another aspect of what they need to know, and the participants all left the session with a better sense of how to improve performance than any sort of lecturing could have done.

As a bonus, even the facilitators learned a lot in the process, which helps to improve each of their successive training sessions. Moreover, the interactive experience helped unearth needs and opportunities that can be elevated to the senior team. All of it amounts to an important part of the "soak time" necessary to bring the framework to life.

If we stopped there, they would have had an enjoyable day, and then gone back to work and done what they have always done—since, as you know, changing behavior is tough. We can't risk the most-senior managers' not using RCE, as that would rub off on everyone else. So, the next step is to coach them. The training involves simple examples of real-world decisions, but our aim during the coaching process is to get the senior execs to talk about actual decisions they are now dealing with, or have faced in the past. By encouraging such a discussion of a series of real decisions faced by the managers, we get the chance to work out the answers together. This could include the evaluation of new capital investments, brainstorming the pricing of a product or a major proposal bid, or just about anything else the manager wants to know how to answer by using RCE.

Closing the Deal

It's always good to help managers see how the new decision processes in which we train them will drive cost efficiency, capital productivity, and overall value creation, which will all be beneficial for the company and—if the company is a major employer and taxpayer—for the greater community, as well. But managers also need to know what's in it for them, so, by all means, explain to them the new incentive calculations. In fact, if the bonus calculations are explained early in the training day, each of the illustrative cases can close with a determination of the bonus implications. Managers will internalize the need for prioritization when decision *A* increases their bonus by $195 and decision *B* adds $25,000. We *want* the managers to see a direct connection between what's good for the company and what's good for *them*. This will strongly reinforce the ownership culture we seek.

Once they have adopted and implemented RCE, companies should identify and celebrate real-world decisions that have succeeded in increasing RCE. This will communicate to everyone in the organization that improving RCE is both valuable and worthwhile. It's strongly advisable to document special cases in company newsletters and other internal communications. Some companies have gone so far as to set up a knowledge management system to keep track of all the RCE wins, and then they use it to share best practices across the organization. Even if an RCE improvement that works in one business unit can't be directly replicated in another, it may stimulate the thinking to come up with improvement ideas that are achievable.

One company even set up an RCE task force that received intensive training designed to step up its expertise to the point where it could then support local teams seeking RCE improvement solutions to particularly tough historical problems. It rotated junior managers from all sorts of backgrounds through the task force, and those participants became RCE champions when they went back to their day jobs.

Every team leader has to "walk the walk" every chance they get. The principles of owner-like behavior need to be discussed regularly as the basis for decisions and tactics until they become second nature, which could take years. Some executives think the organization should change faster, "because we said so." But change management doesn't work that way. Constant reinforcement is needed.

It's important to recognize, going in, that an ownership culture is different from the typical bureaucratic culture, so some managers may not feel comfortable in this new environment. Many will welcome the mindset, while others may need some leadership and coaching to get them on board, like that shown in the prologue of this book. But there very well may be 10% or more of managers who resist change, usually in subtle ways. Some may opt out and seek employment elsewhere in organizations that better fit their needs. Others may even need to be "managed out" to signal the company's commitment to fostering a deliberate culture. But instituting and supporting an ownership culture will also help attract more-entrepreneurial managers who would not have even considered joining a bureaucratic organization. These shifts in human capital can be necessary to effect cultural change, so they must be handled directly and carefully.

Once, when conversing with an Amazon executive, I was impressed not just with the quality of the company's leadership principles, which she shared with me and are shown in figure 78, but also with how the executive emphasized that these are not platitudes to frame and mount in the conference rooms. Rather, they are business commandments by which one does one's job. Frequently, one or more of the leadership principles are raised in meetings to guide the way toward the right decision. Every company should embrace such an approach by establishing its own set of such principles, perhaps called "Owner-Manager Principles," and then actually using them day in and day out to guide decisions. This can truly close the loop on reinforcing the effective behaviors we seek.

Amazon Leadership Principles

We use our Leadership Principles every day, whether we're discussing ideas for new projects or deciding on the best approach to solving a problem. It is just one of the things that makes Amazon peculiar.

Customer Obsession: Leaders start with the customer and work backwards. They work vigorously to earn and keep customer trust. Although leaders pay attention to competitors, they obsess over customers.

Ownership: Leaders are owners. They think long term and don't sacrifice long-term value for short-term results. They act on behalf of the entire company, beyond just their own team. They never say "that's not my job."

Invent and Simplify: Leaders expect and require innovation and invention from their teams and always find ways to simplify. They are externally aware, look for new ideas from everywhere, and are not limited by "not invented here." As we do new things, we accept that we may be misunderstood for long periods of time.

Are Right, a Lot: Leaders are right a lot. They have strong judgment and good instincts. They seek diverse perspectives and work to disconfirm their beliefs.

Learn and Be Curious: Leaders are never done learning and always seek to improve themselves. They are curious about new possibilities and act to explore them.

Hire and Develop the Best: Leaders raise the performance bar with every hire and promotion. They recognize exceptional talent and willingly move them throughout the organization. Leaders develop leaders and take seriously their role in coaching others. We work on behalf of our people to invent mechanisms for development like Career Choice.

Insist on the Highest Standards: Leaders have relentlessly high standards — many people may think these standards are unreasonably high. Leaders are continually raising the bar and drive their teams to deliver high quality products, services and processes. Leaders ensure that defects do not get sent down the line and that problems are fixed so they stay fixed.

Think Big: Thinking small is a self-fulfilling prophecy. Leaders create and communicate a bold direction that inspires results. They think differently and look around corners for ways to serve customers.

Bias for Action: Speed matters in business. Many decisions and actions are reversible and do not need extensive study. We value calculated risk-taking.

Frugality: Accomplish more with less. Constraints breed resourcefulness, self-sufficiency and invention. There are no extra points for growing headcount, budget size or fixed expense.

Earn Trust: Leaders listen attentively, speak candidly, and treat others respectfully. They are vocally self-critical, even when doing so is awkward or embarrassing. Leaders do not believe their or their team's body odor smells of perfume. They benchmark themselves and their teams against the best.

Dive Deep: Leaders operate at all levels, stay connected to the details, audit frequently, and are skeptical when metrics and anecdote differ. No task is beneath them.

Have Backbone: Disagree and Commit: Leaders are obligated to respectfully challenge decisions when they disagree, even when doing so is uncomfortable or exhausting. Leaders have conviction and are tenacious. They do not compromise for the sake of social cohesion. Once a decision is determined, they commit wholly.

Deliver Results: Leaders focus on the key inputs for their business and deliver them with the right quality and in a timely fashion. Despite setbacks, they rise to the occasion and never settle.

Figure 78—Amazon Leadership Principles

The Value of a Long-Term Outlook

According to research by the McKinsey Global Institute, long-term companies[1] exhibit significantly better performance than others. Revenue for these companies cumulatively grew 47% more, on average, from 2001 to 2014, and with far less volatility. What's more, long-term companies also showed higher earnings growth and hit more-stable earnings throughout the financial crisis. And as the McKinsey study also notes, the difference in value creation becomes even clearer when measured through economic profit, which I believe I have demonstrated throughout the book to be a much more suitable measure of performance. From 2001 to 2014, long-term companies generated a whopping 81% more economic profit than all other companies.[2]

So, it should be clear that companies that embrace a long-term outlook consistently create greater value—therefore, we can trust that the misnomer of "long-termism" used to refer to poorly evaluated investments can be summarily rejected with the dissemination of this research. But, as we have also mentioned throughout the book, it's not that easy to change a company's culture and investment outlook. This is where this prescription for an ownership culture can be of tremendous value to corporate organizations.

Companies that embrace an ownership culture to promote a balanced, long-term outlook will make more good investments, will be more accountable for delivering desirable returns on those investments, and will create more value. They will go by what investors do, rather than what they say, and they will generate more cash flow, deliver higher returns, and see their share price rise faster than at their peer companies. Most important, they will feel less concerned with what their share price is next week or next month, and more concerned about what their share price will be in the long run.

At this point, a reread of the Prologue might tie together many of the messages of this book.

Note

1 The determination of what constitutes a "long-term" company was made by using a Corporate Horizon Index that factors investment, earnings quality, margin growth, quarterly management, and earnings-per-share growth. For more on this, refer to the methodology section of the study. Dominic Barton, James Manyika, Timothy Koller, Robert Palter, and Jonathan Godsall, "Measuring the Economic Impact of Short-Termism," Discussion paper, McKinsey Global Institute, February 2017.

2 Ibid.

Acknowledgments

I AM ALMOST ashamed to admit there have been several times in my life when I felt I had "figured it all out." But each time I sank into this complacency, something happened—or, more often, some*one* happened—and I realized there was more to learn. In this context I must confess that even now there is still more to learn, so look out for new articles by me over time as new ideas and developments material-ize. As for my learning thus far, I must give credit to those who have influenced my thinking and helped test my ideas and hypotheses. Much credit must be given—but of course any mistakes or errors are mine alone.

It is customary in business books to first acknowledge professional contributions and then to turn to the support of family and friends. But I feel compelled to start with my wife and business partner, Michelle (Burnett) Milano. For it is not just a cliché for me to say, "I couldn't have done it without her," it's also true. She shares my conviction about the importance of motivating and getting the best out of human behavior, though she approaches it slightly differently, and she has helped me be better at what I do in many important ways. She never once has let me get away with an incomplete or confusing explanation in something that I've written or presented. On many occasions, her prodding for clarity led to new revelations that would have remained undiscovered without her. And when I first began writing after we founded Fortuna Advisors, she read everything I wrote and provided more input than anyone else.

While on the subject of my family, I'd also like to recognize my father, Vincent, for being a great mentor who read many of my early articles and, as a result, helped me improve my writing. And over the years my now-grown kids, Liz, Joe, JP, and Nick, have been very supportive as well, even when my work kept me away from home more than it should have.

Perhaps the most important professional influence on my work has been John Ballow, who hired me out of engineering and into business analysis at the Grumman Corporation. His most memorable advice was that, if we worked hard, we could someday get "real" jobs, pay increases, and promotions. At a holiday party years later at another company, John noted, laconically, "Well, we got pay increases and promotions." When I joined his group, he said McKinsey & Company was handing out its new book on valuation[1] and nobody was reading it, so he wanted me to absorb it and sum it up in a presentation. I presented the material scores of times to train people across Grumman. In so doing, a fire ignited inside me that burned with a curiosity to figure out better ways to measure shareholder value and then to use it to unlock better managerial behavior. As with Michelle, I don't think I could have done much of what I have accomplished without John.

Through my work with John, I met Joel Stern and Bennett Stewart, who had popularized Economic Value Added, a version of economic profit; they greatly influenced my thinking. I fondly remember going to South Africa and New Zealand with Joel, and to Australia with Bennett. Countless other colleagues at Stern Stewart positively influenced my thinking, including Mich Bergesen, Don Chew, Mack Ferguson, David Glassman, Steve O'Byrne, Marcus Pertl, Justin Pettit, Mark Shinder, Dennis Soter, and Erik Stern. I also wish to acknowledge many client executives for expanding my views and helping me stay focused on managerial behavior, including Dr. Karl-Hermann Bauman at Siemens, Sir Roderick Deane at Telecom New Zealand, Jan Leschly at SmithKline Beecham, Bob Shapiro at Monsanto, and Herb Sklenar at Vulcan Materials, to name a few.

When I left Stern Stewart, I was one of the world's foremost experts in implementing EVA, but talking to me then would have been like walking into an ice cream store that only sells one flavor: no fun at all.

My next career stop was inspired by a very good friend, Jim McTaggart. Jim cofounded and led the very successful consulting firm Marakon and is currently a highly valued senior advisor to Fortuna Advisors. Jim elevated my sense of business strategy and fostered my ability to link strategic and financial thinking in ways that have benefited my clients, as well as surely the preceding chapters. He introduced me to the team at BERA Brand Management, and together we have collaborated on the linkage between brands, financial performance, and valuation multiples, which is important for optimally allocating resources and maximizing value. Jim also reviewed an early manuscript of this book and provided extensive advice that has immeasurably improved these pages.

Jim introduced me to Ramesh Karnani, a former Marakon partner who, along with Glenn Welling (who now leads Engaged Capital), was co-head of the Buyside Insights Group that used the HOLT valuation framework within the investment banking division at Credit Suisse. Ramesh is one of the smartest people I have ever met, and he channeled my work in more-strategic ways that I never would have considered without him. And beyond his actual input, Ramesh's Socratic style of asking questions to steer my thoughts, rather than simply providing answers, was nothing short of magical.

As discussed in the book, it was learning the HOLT framework that opened my eyes to the fact that there were more flavors of ice cream. I have long believed HOLT is too complex to use internally at most companies (though it is great for investors), yet the nature of its Cash Flow Return on Investment (CFROI) measure inspired many ideas we tested when creating our Residual Cash Earnings framework. I am forever grateful to Ramesh and Glenn, and to others in our group, including Steve Treadwell, who joined and contributed in the early days of Fortuna Advisors, as well as Kevin Bravo-Ferrer, Eric Gregg, Shant Madjarian, John Pierce, and, most importantly, John Cryan, who cofounded Fortuna Advisors with me.

If these acknowledgments were ordered by influence, and not chronologically, John Cryan's name would have appeared near the top. I have worked with many people who think more or less like me, but John is that rare person who understands corporate finance and business economics, but thinks quite differently. John is an avid reader and walks into every client situation knowing nearly everything about their strategies and tactics, and having scoped out *why* their financial results and valuation are what they are. He fluidly pulls all this together by "putting the story behind the numbers" to provide insights and advice at a very high level. For sure, John and I have disagreed on solutions at times, but because of this our clients were ultimately better served than if either of us had simply been yes-men.

My current partners, Frank Hopson and Marwaan Karame, have contributed immensely to the content of this book, as well. Frank was there as a senior associate when we founded the firm, and in addition to leading all our original research, he built almost all the standard models we use in the majority of our client projects. Our firm has been able to produce more cutting-edge market research and insightful analysis for our clients because of the time Frank took to build advanced, but practical, models. And clients appreciate Frank's pragmatic, no-nonsense approach to developing fact-based answers to tough questions.

Marwaan came in with a quite different and valuable set of experiences and insights when he joined us in 2014, and helped reinvigorate our creative thinking on how to solve client problems. When the energy industry collapsed, we needed to diversify, and Marwaan has led our healthcare research and client work in the years that followed and up to the present. To Marwaan's credit, he has also taken the time to provide me a good deal of feedback on how I relate to clients and prospects, and I am very thankful for that, too.

We have had many wonderful employees at Fortuna Advisors, and all have contributed to our research and many of the important points made in this book. Immense thanks to Allison Cavasino, Arshia Chatterjee, Michael Chew, Dave Fedigan, Jason Gould, JinBae Kim, Luke Kim, Jeff Routh, Logan Sharp, Joe Theriault, Jack Vander Aarde, and Riley Whately. Although all these colleagues have expanded and reinforced my understanding of the topics presented herein, four deserve special recognition.

First comes Jeff, who was there when we opened our doors and who worked with Frank on all our original research and early client work. Jeff became so close with one CFO that he frequently received calls directly with questions and analysis requests, which isn't bad for a guy a few years out of school. Next comes Riley, who only joined us in 2019, but who has already started filling the gap left by John Cryan, as he brings a more-strategic mindset to our work. Third is JinBae, who worked at both Fortuna Advisors and Fortuna Investors, and who contributed immensely to our client work as well as our research, including conducting the research behind "Companies That Do Well Also Do Good."[2]

Joe Theriault was a part of Fortuna Advisors and Fortuna Investors for over seven and a half years and was our third-longest-running employee or partner after Frank and me. He made extremely important contributions to our client work, to our research, and to this book— particularly as the first person to review the initial draft and provide critical feedback. Joe and I probably see eye to eye better than almost anyone I have every worked with, and I look forward to seeing Joe continue to accomplish great things.

I must also recognize a few of our Fortuna clients for their support and thoughtful collaboration in developing our thinking. First up is Bill Chiles, former CEO of Bristow Group, the first company to hire us. When Bill initially saw a simulation of our incentive design, he asked, "Where have you *been* my whole life?" I thank Bill for his practical understanding of our framework as well as his guidance on how to make it come to life for his managers. After a few small projects, Jonathan Baliff joined Bristow as CFO, and we grew into a more-comprehensive business analysis advisor to the company. I cherish the memories of, and lessons learned from, my numerous conversations with Jonathan about plans, investments, strategy, and organizational dynamics, both while he was CFO and later on as CEO. On the client side, Jonathan has probably been the most important influence on the development and refinement of our Fortuna Advisors approach.

Great thanks are also due to Claus Aagaard and Ben Almanzar Perez at Mars Inc., Gary Bischoping at Varian Medical Systems, Clay Williams at National Oilwell Varco, Todd Simmons at Simmons Group, Jeremy Thigpen at both Transocean and National Oilwell Varco, Paul Clancy at Biogen and Alexion, Carl Lukach at DuPont and Univar, and, last but not least, John Briscoe at Transocean, Weatherford, and Bristow. These and many other important executives pushed us to make all that we do more and more practical and accessible to their employees, and in so doing helped shape many of the insights detailed in this book.

When I completed my first draft of the book, it contained most of my ideas, but it never would have been as clear or readable without the helpful wording and content editing of Michael Chew, which he did before joining us at Fortuna Advisors in 2019. Michael did a terrific job of proof-testing my ideas and challenging the completeness of my arguments, and then improved the flow and structure. I am forever thankful to him.

Finally, my thanks to Holly Brady for her wonderful management of the production process, to Mark Woodworth for his insightful final copyediting, and to Diana Russell for her creative cover and interior design work.

There are hundreds more I could mention—many thanks to them all.

Notes

1   McKinsey & Company, Inc., Tim Koller, Marc Goedhart, and David Wessels, *Valuation: Measuring and Managing the Value of Companies* (Hoboken, NJ: John Wiley & Sons, 1990).

2   Gregory V. Milano, Michael Chew, and JinBae Kim, "Companies That Do Well Also Do Good," CFO.com, May 15, 2019, http://fortuna-advisors.com/2019/05/15/companies-that-do-well-also-do-good/.

GLOSSARY

ABC: activity-based costing

BDVA: Blue Dynamics Value Added

BERA: Brand Equity Relationship Assessment

CAGR: compound annual growth rates

CEO: Chief Executive Officer

CFROI: cash flow return on investment

DCF: discounted cash flow

DSO: days of sales outstanding

EBIT: Earnings Before Interest and Taxes

EBITDA: earnings before interest, taxes, depreciation, and amortization

EBITDAR: earnings before interest, taxes, depreciation, amortization, and rent

EPS: earnings per share

EVA: economic value added

FCF: free cash flow

GAAP: generally accepted accounting principles

GCE: gross cash earnings

GCM: GCE margin, or gross cash margin

GOA: gross operating assets

IRR: internal rate of return

LBO: leveraged buyoutL

LTIP: long-term incentive plan

NOPAT: net operating profit after tax

NPV: net present value

PE Multiple: price-to-earnings ratio

PSU: performance share unit

R&D: research and development

RCE: Residual Cash Earnings

RCM: residual cash margin

ROE: return on earnings

ROE: return on equity

ROIC: return on invested capital

RONA: return on net assets

RPI: RCE profitability index

SRA: Strategic Resource Allocation

TSR: total shareholder return

WACC: weighted average cost of capital

Index

Gregory V. Milano is the founder and chief executive officer of Fortuna Advisors LLC, a shareholder value advisory firm that specializes in owner-like incentive compensation design, strategic resource allocation, and implementing long-term value-based business management principles. A significant focus of his capital markets research has been on measuring the tradeoffs between growth and capital efficiency decisions and weighing capital deployment alternatives. He is a leading expert in behavioral finance and capital allocation. Before founding Fortuna Advisors, Greg was a partner at Stern Stewart and a Managing Director at Credit Suisse. He began his career as a flight systems design engineer with the Grumman Corporation. He has nearly 30 years' experience in management consulting, is a regular commentator on Bloomberg TV and has appeared on CNBC and Sky Business News, and has had his work featured in *Fortune*, *The Wall Street Journal*, the *Financial Times*, *WorldatWork*, *The Sunday Times*, *Sunday Business*, and *Financial Director*. He is a regular contributor to the *Journal of Applied Corporate Finance* (and also serves on its advisory board), to CFO.com, and to *FEI Daily*, and he has published over 100 articles and studies in the last 10 years.

gregory.milano@fortuna-advisors.com

www.ingramcontent.com/pod-product-compliance
Lightning Source LLC
Chambersburg PA
CBHW071538210326
41597CB00019B/3044